The Role of Contradictions in Spinoza's Philosophy

Spinoza is commonly perceived as the great metaphysician of coherence. The Euclidean manner in which he presented his philosophy in the *Ethics* has led readers to assume they are facing a strict and consistent philosophical system that necessarily follows from itself.

As opposed to the prevailing understanding of Spinoza and his work, *The Role of Contradictions in Spinoza's Philosophy* explores an array of profound and pervasive contradictions in Spinoza's system and argues they are deliberate and constitutive of his philosophical thinking and the notion of God at its heart. Relying on a meticulous and careful reading of the *Theological-Political Treatise* and the *Ethics*, this book reconstructs Spinoza's philosophy of contradictions as a key to the ascending three degrees of knowledge leading to the *Amor intellectualis Dei*.

Offering an exciting and clearly-argued interpretation of Spinoza's philosophy, this book will interest students and scholars of modern philosophy and philosophy of religion, as well as Jewish studies.

Yuval Jobani is Assistant Professor at the Department of Hebrew Culture Studies and the School of Education at Tel-Aviv University.

Routledge Jewish Studies Series
Series Editor: Oliver Leaman
University of Kentucky

Studies, which are interpreted to cover the disciplines of history, sociology, anthropology, culture, politics, philosophy, theology, religion, as they relate to Jewish affairs. The remit includes texts which have as their primary focus issues, ideas, personalities and events of relevance to Jews, Jewish life and the concepts which have characterized Jewish culture both in the past and today. The series is interested in receiving appropriate scripts or proposals.

Medieval Jewish Philosophy
An Introduction
Dan Cohn-Sherbok

Facing the Other
The Ethics of Emmanuel Levinas
Edited by Seán Hand

Moses Maimonides
Oliver Leaman

A User's Guide to Franz Rosenzweig's Star Of Redemption
Norbert M. Samuelson

On Liberty
Jewish Philosophical Perspectives
Edited by Daniel H. Frank

Referring to God
Jewish and Christian Philosophical and Theological Perspectives
Edited by Paul Helm

Judaism, Philosophy, Culture
Selected Studies by E.I.J. Rosenthal
Erwin Rosenthal

Philosophy of the Talmud
Hyam Maccoby

From Synagogue to Church: The Traditional Design
Its Beginning, Its Definition, Its End
John Wilkinson

Hidden Philosophy of Hannah Arendt
Margaret Betz Hull

Deconstructing the Bible
Abraham ibn Ezra's Introduction to the Torah
Irene Lancaster

Image of the Black in Jewish Culture
A History of the Other
Abraham Melamed

From Falashas to Ethiopian Jews
Daniel Summerfield

Philosophy in a Time of Crisis
Don Isaac Abravanel: Defender of the Faith
Seymour Feldman

Jews, Muslims and Mass Media
Mediating the 'Other'
Edited by Tudor Parfitt with Yulia Egorova

Jews of Ethiopia
The Birth of an Elite
Edited by Emanuela Trevisan Semi and Tudor Parfitt

Art in Zion
The Genesis of National Art in Jewish Palestine
Dalia Manor

Hebrew Language and Jewish Thought
David Patterson

Contemporary Jewish Philosophy
An Introduction
Irene Kajon

Antisemitism and Modernity
Innovation and Continuity
Hyam Maccoby

Jews and India
History, Image, Perceptions
Yulia Egorova

Jewish Mysticism and Magic
An Anthropological Perspective
Maureen Bloom

Maimonides' *Guide for the Perplexed*
Silence and Salvation
Donald McCallum

Muscular Judaism
The Jewish Body and the Politics of Regeneration
Todd Samuel Presner

Jewish Cultural Nationalism
David Aberbach

The Jewish–Chinese Nexus
A Meeting of Civilizations
Edited by M. Avrum Ehrlich

German-Jewish Popular Culture Before the Holocaust
Kafka's Kitsch
David Brenner

The Jews as a Chosen People
Tradition and Transformation
S. Leyla Gürkan

Philosophy and Rabbinic Culture
Jewish Interpretation and Controversy in Medieval Languedoc
Gregg Stern

Jewish Blood
Reality and Metaphor in History, Religion and Culture
Edited by Mitchell B. Hart

Jewish Education and History
Continuity, Crisis and Change
Moshe Aberbach; edited and translated by David Aberbach

Jews and Judaism in Modern China
M. Avrum Ehrlich

Political Theologies in the Holy Land
Israeli Messianism and its Critics
David Ohana

Collaboration with the Nazis
The Holocaust and After
Edited by Roni Stauber

The Global Impact of the Protocols of the Elders of Zion
A Century-Old Myth
Edited by Esther Webman

The Holocaust and Representations of the Jews
History and Identity in the Museum
K. Hannah Holtschneider

War and Peace in Jewish Tradition
From the Biblical World to the Present
Edited by Yigal Levin and Amnon Shapira

Jesus Among the Jews
Representation and Thought
Edited by Neta Stahl

God, Jews and the Media
Religion and Israel's Media
Yoel Cohen

Rabbinic Theology and Jewish Intellectual History
The Great Rabbi Loew of Prague
Meir Seidler

Israeli Holocaust Research
Birth and Evolution
Boaz Cohen

Modern Gnosis and Zionism
The Crisis of Culture, Life Philosophy and Jewish National Thought
Yotam Hotam

The European Jews, Patriotism and the Liberal State 1789–1939
A Study of Literature and Social Psychology
David Aberbach

Jewish Women's Torah Study
Orthodox Religious Education and Modernity
Ilan Fuchs

Emmanuel Levinas and the Limits to Ethics
A Critique and a Re-Appropriation
Aryeh Botwinick

Judaism in Contemporary Thought
Traces and Influence
Agata Bielik-Robson and Adam Lipszyc

Jewish Cryptotheologies of Late Modernity
Philosophical Marranos
Agata Bielik-Robson

The Ugliness of Moses Mendelssohn
Aesthetics, Religion and Morality in the Eighteenth Century
Leah Hochman

A History of Czechs and Jews
A Slavic Jerusalem
Martin Wein

Boundaries, Identity and Belonging in Modern Judaism
Edited by Maria Diemling and Larry Ray

The Name of God in Jewish Thought
A Philosophical Analysis of Mystical Traditions from Apocalyptic to Kabbalah
Michael T Miller

Rabbis of Our Time
Authorities of Judaism in the Religious and Political Ferment of Modern Times
Marek Čejka and Roman Kořan

Rabbinic Judaism
Space and Place
David Kraemer

The Role of Contradictions in Spinoza's Philosophy
The God-intoxicated Heretic
Yuval Jobani

The Role of Contradictions in Spinoza's Philosophy
The God-intoxicated heretic

Yuval Jobani

Translated by Aviv Ben-Or

LONDON AND NEW YORK

First published 2017 by Routledge

2 Park Square, Milton Park, Abingdon, Oxfordshire OX14 4RN
711 Third Avenue, New York, NY 10017

Routledge is an imprint of the Taylor & Francis Group, an informa business

First issued in paperback 2018

Copyright © 2016 Yuval Jobani

The right of Yuval Jobani to be identified as author of this work has been asserted by him in accordance with sections 77 and 78 of the Copyright, Designs and Patents Act 1988.

All rights reserved. No part of this book may be reprinted or reproduced or utilised in any form or by any electronic, mechanical, or other means, now known or hereafter invented, including photocopying and recording, or in any information storage or retrieval system, without permission in writing from the publishers.

Notice:
Product or corporate names may be trademarks or
registered trademarks, and are used only for identification and explanation without intent to infringe.

British Library Cataloguing-in-Publication Data
A catalogue record for this book is available from the British Library

Library of Congress Cataloging-in-Publication Data
A catalog record for this book has been requested.

ISBN: 978-1-138-12353-3 (hbk)
ISBN: 978-0-367-02684-4 (pbk)

Typeset in Times New Roman
by Wearset Ltd, Boldon, Tyne and Wear

To my parents, Moshe and Miryam, for their unconditional love and abiding support; *mine is theirs* ...

Contents

Acknowledgments   xiii

Introduction   1

PART I
Revised religion: on the contradiction in the concept of God in the first kind of knowledge   13

1   Moral *or* political religion? On the contradiction between the two models of revised religion in the TTP   15

PART II
The contradictions in the concept of God in the second kind of knowledge   45

2   Spinoza's conception of causality and the first two contradictions in the system: (1) infiniteness *or* finiteness; (2) immanence *or* transcendence   51

3   The contradictions regarding the essence and perfection of the things that follow from God   63

4   The contradiction between static unity and dynamic multiplicity in existence   83

5   The conatus of God and the five contradictions embedded within it: (1) static – dynamic; (2) efficient causality – final causality; (3) substance – mode; (4) finiteness – infiniteness; (5) the contradiction between good and evil in God   98

6   Eternity and time: the contradiction and the circularity   119

PART III
The contradiction in the concept of God in the third kind of knowledge   143

7   The philosopher and the grain merchant: on contradiction and its concealment in the Spinoza–Blijenbergh letters   145

8   The intellectual love of God and the contradiction between the internal and external causes in God   161

Afterword   187
Index of names and subjects   192
Index of references   197

Acknowledgments

This book reflects a long journey into Spinoza's writings. It developed out of joint studies, long conversations, and spirited debates on Spinoza's philosophy that I held with teachers, friends, and students throughout the years. Prof. Menachem Lorberbaum first introduced me to the gripping complexities of the theo-political problem in Spinoza's philosophy, and for several years we studied the Ethics in chevruta, as if it were one of the tractates of the Babylonian Talmud. Dr. Ran Sigad revealed to me the secrets of Spinoza's metaphysics and did so with his characteristic noble generosity in long conversations and silences that carried on deep into the night. I had the great privilege of being Dr. Sigad's student and his influence is woven into the fabric of this book, which would never have been written without him.

Prof. Michael Walzer invited me to be his research assistant at the Institute for Advanced Study in Princeton, and helped me frame Spinoza's thinking in the wider context of the ongoing Jewish political tradition. The conversations we had on Spinoza and other heretics around the institute's famous pond still reverberate in me. In the years I was in Princeton I had the privilege of engaging in stimulating and enlightening dialogues with some of the most important contemporary Spinoza scholars, who helped me formulate the ideas in this book. Prof. Jonathan Israel read and responded to various parts of the book, and made a critical contribution to its consolidation. I also learned much from Prof. Edwin Curley who regularly participated in the research seminar on Modern Philosophy in Princeton, and also organized a research workshop at the University of Leiden which spurred me to reorganize my arguments about the Theologico-Political Treatise. Furthermore, during my stay at Princeton, Prof. David Biale from the University of California, Davis, Prof. Julie Cooper from Chicago University, Prof. Aurelian Craiutu from Indiana University, Prof. Carlos Fraenkel from Oxford University, Prof. Gideon Katz from Ben Gurion University, Prof. Ron Margolin from Tel Aviv University, Prof. Eric Schlisser from Leiden University, and Prof. Richard Shweder from Chicago University very much assisted me in writing the manuscript. I am deeply grateful to all of them.

Student friends very much helped me in preparing the book and bringing it to publication. Aviv Ben-Or from Brandeis University in Boston, where I had the privilege of teaching a seminar on Spinoza, took upon himself the challenging translation of the book into English and Jeremy Fogel meticulously edited the translation with an impressive philosophical sensitivity. Hanit Benglas helped with various technical issues. I thank them all for their dedication.

While writing I was fortunate to receive the support of various institutions and foundations: The Institute for Advanced Study at Princeton, the Schusterman Center at Brandeis, the School of Philosophy, the School of Education, and the Kelman Center for Jewish Education at Tel Aviv University, the Fulbright foundation, the Posen foundation, the Dan David foundation, the Alexander von Humboldt foundation, and the European Union Marie Curie Reintegration Grant.

My parents, Moshe and Myriam, and my brother Itamar, have been an unwavering source of support throughout the years. Finally, I am especially grateful to my beloved Keren and our amazing children Yonatan, Tom and Uriah for a little noise, and a lot of happiness and true love.

He [Spinoza] has a strange metaphysics, full of paradoxes.

(Leibniz, Winter 1676, after a series of meetings with Spinoza in the Hague)

Introduction

The main argument

Twentieth and twenty-first century philosophy has brought about the need to rethink metaphysics. Onto-theological and theological-political structures that have dominated the philosophical tradition well into modernity have undergone far reaching reevaluations. Spinoza's thought has often been perceived as the moment in which these structures congealed. Yet, much as Emmanuel Levinas taught us that a rethinking of metaphysics necessitates a reassessment of Descartes as its point of departure, indeed as a thrilling moment of considering the relation between totality and infinity, so too a reassessment of the towering figure of Spinoza at the advent of modernity can bring us to a threshold of renewed metaphysical thought. For no one better than Spinoza articulated the meaning of the advent of a new world while deeply understanding the faded promise of the old. It is in this spirit that I turn to reassess Spinoza's philosophy in this book.

Spinoza's revision of religion ranks among the most comprehensive and thorough projects of modern philosophy. At the core of this project is Spinoza's attempt to revise the theological concept of God through philosophical criticism. Despite his bold and outright attack on theology's concept of God, Spinoza did not come to the conclusion that the concept of God is in itself a false concept that should be abolished. On the contrary, Spinoza concludes that the concept of God is indeed true and of the highest importance, but one that had hitherto been imbued with an incorrect and distorted meaning. Therefore, in order to revise the traditional concept of God, Spinoza endeavors to refine it, removing all the dross of superstition, and to cast it in the mold of reason.

Spinoza himself, and subsequently his most prominent interpreters, point out the presence of logical contradictions in the theological concept of God, and the absence of those contradictions in the philosophical concept of God, as the decisive difference between the two. It is due to this difference, though not solely because of it, that the relation between the theological concept of God and the philosophical concept of God is considered to correspond to that between falsehood and truth.

Contrarily, my main argument in the present book will be that Spinoza's philosophical alternative to the theological concept of God also contains logical contradictions. These contradictions in the concept of God are found not only in its multitude-oriented version in the first kind of knowledge, but also in its rational and redemptive versions in the second and third kinds of knowledge, respectively. However – and this is the main point – while the theological concept of God is destroyed by the logical contradictions prevalent in it, Spinoza's concept of God is constructed from the logical contradictions contained within it and is founded upon them in each one of the three kinds of knowledge.

On the surface this argument seems untenable, not only because "the truth does not contradict the truth," (Letter 21, IV/126) but also because it is "absurd" to claim, as Spinoza explicitly asserts in the *Ethics*, that "a Being absolutely infinite and supremely perfect," namely, God, "would involve a contradiction" (I.P11 Alt. Dem. II/53).[1] Moreover, this claim is outrageous; for if it were indeed correct, the status of contradiction in Spinoza's philosophy has been misunderstood for over 300 years.[2]

Nevertheless, my central argument in this book will be that a careful and meticulous reading of the *Theological-Political Treatise* (TTP from here on) on the one hand, and the *Ethics* on the other, necessarily leads to the conclusion that Spinoza's concept of God is based on logical contradictions in each of the three kinds of knowledge. This conclusion will rely on a reading of Spinoza's writings according to the following methodology.

Methodology

Adhering to the law of contradiction is the basic instinct in reading a philosophical text. This instinct is particularly strong when approaching Spinoza's works, especially the *Ethics*. This is not only because Spinoza gained a reputation as a pure rationalist, but mainly because his choice to present his philosophy by means of the Euclidean model gives the reader the impression that they are facing a strict, consistent philosophical system that necessarily follows from itself.

But truth is indifferent to our instincts in general, and to our instinct of reading in particular. Therefore, my point of departure will challenge the assumption that, because of its form, Spinoza's philosophy is Euclidean. As long as this assumption is not grounded in the text itself, it is the same as a prejudice; this is why I will be considering content over form in Spinoza's philosophy. Consequently, definitions, axioms, propositions, proofs, and even scholia that don't fall in line with adherence to the law of contradiction, will be presented as such. Thus, I will avoid the natural tendency to place the responsibility for the flaws found in canonical texts on the reader; instead, the author – in this case Spinoza – will be held accountable.[3]

Moreover, the tendency to attribute consistency to Spinoza's philosophy is prevalent not only among readers of the *Ethics* but also among readers of the TTP. In this work, Spinoza adopts a writing method of concealment in which he contradicts himself intentionally while making numerous statements as lip service to his different audiences. Consequently, the tendency to attribute consistency to his philosophical system is reinforced, though from an entirely different angle. Given the intended textual obscurity that is prevalent in the TTP, the reader's natural tendency is to attribute the contradictions encountered in the text to Spinoza's writing method of concealment, which was intended to protect him and the society in which he lived.

Following Strauss, the prevalent assumption is that all of the contradictions in the TTP are ascribed to rhetorical flourish, which serves Spinoza in concealing his consistent, contradiction-free alternative to the theological concept of God.[4] However, this assumption is also unacceptable as long as it is not grounded in the text itself. Even if Spinoza uses intentional contradiction as a method of concealment, we cannot assume *a priori* that the position Spinoza is concealing does not itself contain contradictions. Therefore, my reading method will not adopt the assumption of any classification or categorization of the contradictions that arise from the TTP.[5] Here, as well, I will prefer content over form, even if this preference leads to troubling conclusions regarding the consistency of the arguments in the TTP.

Therefore, both in the TTP and in the *Ethics*, despite how perplexed we might become from contradictions that arise in our study, we should not attribute them to our own lack of understanding of these canonical texts. Were we to do this, we would be consecrating Spinoza's texts while subjugating, like the very theologians of whom Spinoza disapproves, "reason, the greatest gift and the divine light, to the dead letters [*mortuis literis*]" (TTP, XV, p. 188 [182], slightly rephrased).[6] Indeed, no philosopher in the history of Western philosophy has surpassed Spinoza in his opposition to the consecration of texts, canonical though they may be.

Spinoza's philosophy is conducted below the surface as much as it is above. Therefore, despite its impressive monumental architecture, its proper understanding requires a fundamental and meticulous textual excavation. Although it is not the only motive to conceal his views, Spinoza's theological-political cautiousness forces him to adopt a double-layered mode of writing whenever dipping his quill in ink. As Strauss claims in his classic *Persecution and the Art of Writing*:

> [O]ne cannot leave it at the impression that while the TTP is, of course, exoteric, the *Ethics* is Spinoza's esoteric work simply, and that therefore the solution to all the riddles of the TTP is presented explicitly and clearly in the *Ethics*. For Spinoza cannot have been ignorant of the obvious truth which, in addition, had been pointed out to him if not by Plato, at any rate by Maimonides, that every book is accessible to all who can read the language in which it is written; and that therefore, if there is any need at all for hiding the truth from the vulgar, no written exposition can be strictly speaking esoteric.[7]

According to Strauss, the Euclidean presentation in the *Ethics*, just like the Scriptural presentation in the TTP, serves Spinoza as a veil behind which he conceals his true views regarding God. Indeed, as I will aim to demonstrate, just as Spinoza's concept of God is not biblical, it is also not Euclidean, despite that it is embedded with elements and fundamental insights from Athens on the one hand and Jerusalem on the other.

Accordingly, Strauss rightfully demands that the reading of the *Ethics* should be conducted with the same wariness and extreme caution used when reading the TTP. Meeting this requirement makes reading the *Ethics* even more exhausting than the TTP;[8] not only do the readers of the *Ethics* constantly feel as though they are about to drown in the thousands of references in the textual ocean that Spinoza left behind, but they are also forced to be on guard throughout the length of the text. Every definition, axiom, proposition, demonstration, and even scholium must be double-checked in search of Spinoza's true position concealed in a possible alternative subtext.[9]

Indeed, Strauss focused exclusively on the TTP in his pioneering study of concealment via contradiction in Spinoza's philosophy, while leaving it to others to investigate the status of contradiction in the *Ethics*. Moreover, in his study of the TTP, Strauss argues that concealment via contradiction stems from the philosopher's obligation to protect himself and the society in which he lives; he posits that the need to speak in a manner intelligible to the multitude (*ad captum vulgi loqui*) was the only consideration that led Spinoza to conceal his true philosophy behind numerous contradictions.[10]

In the following, I aim to complete Strauss' study on concealment through contradiction in Spinoza's philosophy in two ways: first, I will extend the framework of analysis by including *both* the TTP as well as the *Ethics*, the latter of which has still not been studied in the context of contradiction and concealment; and, second, I will expose additional considerations, aside from theological-political caution, which justify the contradictions not only in Spinoza's concept of God in the first kind of knowledge, but also in his concept of God in the second and third kinds of knowledge. The linkage between the three kinds of knowledge and the three corresponding concepts of God arises from Spinoza's definition of religion, upon which the structure of this book is based.

Spinoza's definition of religion, the structure of the book and its central arguments

In the fourth part of the *Ethics*, during the course of the exposition of his moral philosophy, Spinoza defines religion as follows:

> whatever we desire and do of which we are the cause insofar as we have the idea of God, *or* insofar as we know God, I relate to religion [*religio*].
> (IV.P37, Schol 1, II/236)[11]

Methodologically, Spinoza deviates here from a formal Euclidean system when he frames the definition as a proposition's scholium, rather than include it where it belongs in one of the other five lexicons found in the *Ethics*.[12] However, the location of the definition of religion is not exceptional; as we will soon see, in the *Ethics* Spinoza presents numerous definitions outside of where one would expect to find them in a Euclidean system.[13]

In terms of content, however, this definition of religion *is* exceptional. Spinoza defines religion as action derived from knowledge of God;[14] note: knowledge of God, not necessarily *true* knowledge of God. In other words, for Spinoza religion signifies the entire range of activities that is derived from the idea of God that we possess, whether that idea of God is the result of true knowledge or whether it is the result of false knowledge.

And so, if we link Spinoza's definition of religion (IV.37, Schol 1, II/236) to the three kinds of knowledge in his philosophical system (II.40, Schol 2, II/122), we can distinguish between three levels of religion accordingly: religion in the first kind of knowledge; religion of the second kind knowledge; and religion of the third kind of knowledge.

Already, at our point of departure, Spinoza's definition of religion stands out as deviating from a formal Euclidean system in that it underscores divergent and contradictory content. Religion, according to Spinoza's definition, marks the falsehood of the first kind of knowledge and the truth of the second and third kinds of knowledge (II.41, II/172).

The core of the structure of this book, which will focus on Spinoza's revision of religion, is the correlation between religion and knowledge. Each of the three parts of the book explores the way in which Spinoza revises the concept of God, the organizing concept of religion, in each of the three kinds of knowledge respectively. Structurally, the first part of the book primarily analyzes the TTP, while the following two parts focus mainly on the *Ethics*. Indeed, these two works constitute the most developed and comprehensive iteration of Spinoza's revised religion; the TTP focuses on religion in the first kind of knowledge, and the *Ethics* focuses on religion in the second and third kinds of knowledge. In the first kind of knowledge, Spinoza aims to revise the superstitious concept of God among the multitude. As such, his project in the TTP is dedicated to refashioning the religious imagination.[15] On the other hand, in the second and third kinds of knowledge Spinoza seeks to revise the concept of God through reason grounded in strict logical consistency. Therefore, the ascent from the first to the second and third kinds of knowledge completely changes the nature of Spinoza's revised religion in that it transforms it from a theological-political project to a metaphysical-existential one.

Synopsis

The following is a brief synopsis of the structure of the book and its main arguments.

The central argument in Part I of the book is that Spinoza presents in the TTP, if not explicitly but implicitly, two contradictory models of revised religion whose goal is to ensure the stability of society.

In the first part of the TTP (Chapters 1–15), Spinoza presents a revised religion that is founded on a reduction of the religious to the moral, wherein obedience to God is reduced to obedience to the laws of morality. In the second part of the TTP (Chapters 16–20), however, Spinoza presents a revised religion that is founded on a reduction of the religious to the political, wherein obedience to God is reduced to obedience to the laws of political authority. The concept of God in the first kind of knowledge contradicts itself because it functions distinctly as a morally oriented concept in the first part of the TTP, but distinctly as a politically oriented concept in the second part.

Furthermore, a careful reading of the TTP reveals five interconnected contradictions which lead to the conclusion that Spinoza puts forth two wholly opposed models of revised religion:

1 In the first part of the TTP the biblical prophet is presented as the ethical hero of the revised religion, while in the second part he is presented as a dangerous political rebel.
2 In the first part of the TTP, Spinoza chooses Jesus to serve as the role model of revised religion since the latter advances ethical excellence. Contrarily, in the second part, Spinoza chooses the Roman military leader Manlius Torquatus (fourth century BCE) – who had his son killed for violating military command – to serve as the role model of revised religion, because Torquatus promotes blind obedience to the political authority.
3 In the first part of the TTP, the ecclesiastics of the revised religion are intended to be teachers of morals who aren't subordinate to the political authority. In the second part of the TTP, however, the ecclesiastics are made out to be agents of the state who deal in propaganda.
4 In the first part of the TTP the right to interpret the foundations of faith is granted to everyone. In the second part, however, this right is granted to the political authority alone.
5 In the first part of the TTP, *justice* is defined as "a constant and perpetual will to assign each man his due" (TTP, IV, p. 59 [59]), while in the second part *justice* is defined as "a fixed intention to assign to each person what belongs to them in accordance with civil law" (TTP, XVI, p. 203 [196]). It is impossible to ignore the blatant grafting of the phrase "accordance with civil law" onto the second definition of *justice*. Whereas in the first part of the TTP justice is defined strictly according to *moral* standards, in the second part it is defined strictly according to *political* standards.

I will then turn to demonstrate, through a careful reading of Spinoza's analysis of the ancient Hebrew state, that the contradiction between the reduction of the religious to the moral on the one hand, and the reduction of the religious to the political on the other, does not destroy the concept of God in the first kind of knowledge but rather constructs it. Indeed, this theoretical contradiction creates a balance between the obligation of citizens to the moral law and their obligation to the laws of the state; and in this way, the concept of God in the first kind of knowledge fulfills its goal as a concept intended to ensure the stability of society.

In Part II, which is the crux of the book, my central argument is that the concept of God in the second kind of knowledge contains numerous logical contradictions. However, these contradictions do not destroy the concept of God but rather construct it. As an absolute concept God must contain all, every thing and its opposite; moreover, as *wholly other* and completely different in essence God must have His own logic in whose framework contradiction constructs its object instead of destroying it.

Just as in the first kind of knowledge contradiction does not destroy but constructs the concept of God from the point of view of social stability (the only point of view of religion in the first kind of knowledge), in the second kind of knowledge contradiction does not destroy but constructs the concept of God from the point of view of reason (the only point of view of religion in the second kind of knowledge). Just as in the first kind of knowledge the concept of God was constructed by tensions and contradictions in order to ensure social stability, in the second kind of knowledge the concept of God is constructed from the opposite binaries and contradictions embedded within it in order to reflect God *or* existence in its entirety; indeed, for Spinoza God and existence are one and the same.

During the course of Part II, nine crucial contradictions, which I refer to as "contradictions of depth," will be revealed in the concept of the God of reason. Each of these contradictions individually, and even more so collectively, support the claim that Spinoza intentionally chose the principle of contradiction as the organizing principle of the concept of God in the second kind of knowledge.[16]

In the opening discussion of this part, a critical examination of Spinoza's definition of God (I, D.6, II/45) will serve as a point of departure for revealing the non-Euclidean character of Spinoza's entire philosophical system.

The second chapter will explore the first two contradictions that arise from Spinoza's neglecting and contradicting his own axiom of causality (I, A.4, II/46): (1) the contradiction between the finite and the infinite and (2) the contradiction between immanence and transcendence in Spinoza's concept of God.[17]

In the third chapter two additional consequences of Spinoza neglecting and contradicting his axiom of causality will be presented: (3) the contradiction regarding the essence of things that follow from God – Spinoza presents the essence of things that follow from God as one that both involves existence and as an essence that does not involve existence; and (4) the contradiction regarding the perfection of those things that follow from God is presented at once as both absolute and only partial.

In the fourth chapter an additional contradiction will be examined: (5) the contradiction between viewing reality as a static unity on the one hand and viewing it as a dynamic multiplicity on the other. Alongside the strict Parmenidean portrait of existence in the *Ethics* that presents it distinctly as a barren wasteland of uniform and unchanging infinite existence, Spinoza also offers a Heraclidean portrait of existence that presents it as an entity with infinite parts, caught in an endless stream, not only in the domain of logic, but also in the domains of space and time.

The fifth chapter explores the *conatus*, a principle situated at the heart of Spinoza's metaphysical system, and reveals five contradictions embedded in it. Two of these contradictions have already been presented (and therefore will be noted here according to their original numbering): (1) the contradiction between the finite and infinite and (5) the contradiction between the static and dynamic. The three additional contradictions are: (6) the contradiction between the efficient cause and the final cause; (7) the contradiction between the definition of substance (I, "General Definition of the Affects," II/45, p. 3) and the definition of mode (I, "General Definition of the Affects," II/45, p. 5); and (8) the contradiction between the good and the evil in God.

The sixth and final chapter of Part II will be dedicated to presenting (9) the contradiction between eternity and time and the circularity between the two; even though Spinoza claims explicitly that eternity and time contradict one another, he also claims that they derive from one another. In the same vein, Spinoza considers existence solely as eternal, and he *also* considers existence as both eternal and temporal, while positing equivalence between them.

The main claim in Part III is that the contradiction that arises from God's intellectual love of himself does not destroy the concept of God in the third kind of knowledge, but constructs it in that it ensures God's salvation, which is none other than the salvation of man, who loves God by means of his intellect.

This claim opposes the common position in scholarship on the *Ethics* that considers the contradiction caused by the intellectual love of God in Spinoza's system as the most destructive among all the other contradictions present in it; the love of God turns him into an effect of an external cause, thus completely negating his true knowledge, his infiniteness, and his freedom; additionally, in this framework God is rendered subject to distinct human affect.

By contrast, I will argue that while, on the one hand, all things that follow from God are contradicted and destroyed by an external cause (III.4, II/145), God is, on the other hand, constructed by an external cause (V.35, II/302). God constructs, on the basis of an external cause, his love for himself, which enables him to break his own boundaries and increase his existence or his perfection (according to the definition of love, joy, and perfection; III, DefAff 6, II/192, DefAff 2, II/192, and II, Def 6, II/85, respectively). Transforming the most evidently destructive contradiction for all things following from God into a constructive and redemptive contradiction for God, presents the apex of the uniqueness of God's existence as *sui generis*.

This interpretation of the issue of the intellectual love of God will be supported by an analysis of the correspondence between Spinoza and Blijenbergh. Although Spinoza does not break his silence in this exchange of letters regarding the meaning of contradiction in his system (he even explicitly denies its existence), during the course of the correspondence he repeatedly conflates the contradiction in the concept of God with the intellectual love of God. He thus leads us between the lines to the insight that only through proper understanding of the intellectual love of God – one of the more complex and enigmatic issues in Spinoza's thought – can we grasp the ultimate and complete meaning of contradiction in the concept of God within his system.

A final note: Spinoza takes care to conceal the different contradictions in his system behind a fortified wall of heavy silence. Therefore, not only is he not willing to reveal the meaning of the contradictions embedded in his system, he does not even *admit* to their existence. Despite this, Spinoza intentionally left behind narrow fissures in this heavy wall of silence through which it is possible to glance at the inner heart of the system. However, as someone who was devoted to the craft of esoteric writing, Spinoza took care that these fissures too would be concealed. Consequently, only those who do not despair from the logical contradictions cast upon them during the course of studying the system are capable of recognizing these fissures; and in order to reveal the hidden secrets of Spinoza's system, they encircle its wall out of intellectual love for God.

Notes

1 Citations from the *Ethics* will be formatted according to the abbreviations in Benedictus De Spinoza, *The Collected Works of Spinoza: Volume I*. Edited and translated by Edwin Curley, Princeton: Princeton University Press 1988, p. xix.
2 It is important to note that even Strauss, who in *Persecution and the Art of Writing* focused specifically on the contradictions and their status in the TTP, saw them only as a means by which Spinoza conceals his consistent, contradiction-free concept of God. See Leo Strauss, *Persecution and the Art of Writing*. Chicago: Chicago University Press, 1988, pp. 142–202. Sigad, in presenting his own original philosophy, which he does through an analysis of the *Ethics* (among other philosophical works), does consider the contradictions in Spinoza's concept of God as contradictions that construct this concept; however, he applies this claim to the second kind of knowledge alone. He does not treat the contradictions in the first kind of knowledge, and thinks that in the third kind of knowledge the contradictions destroy Spinoza's concept of God, thus bringing his philosophical system to the point of total collapse. See Ran Sigad, "God as Final Cause in Spinoza," *Iyyun: The Jerusalem Philosophical Quarterly* 43, pp. 375–398 [Heb.], and the references there on page 398.
3 The instinctive tendency to attribute consistency to Spinoza's philosophical system was already prevalent among those with whom he corresponded. Even Blijenbergh, who locates a logical contradiction in Spinoza's philosophical position, writes to him "I fear here that I must not properly understand your meaning, for your conceptions seem to me too penetrating for you to commit such a grave error" (*The Collected Works of Spinoza*, Letter 20, IV/109). In a similar vein, Oldenburg writes to Spinoza: "I approve very much of your geometric style of proof, but at the same time I blame my own obtuseness that I do not follow so easily the things you teach so exactly" (ibid., Letter 3, IV/10). For an extended discussion of the Spinoza-Blijenbergh correspondence see the third part of this book, chapter one. See also the discussion of Spinoza's letters to de Vries and Hudde in Part III, Chapter 7.
4 Strauss passed down this convention, among others, to Shlomo Pines, "Spinoza's *Tractatus Theological-Politicus*, Maimonides, and Kant," in Segal (ed.), *Further Studies in Philosophy, Scripta Hierosolymitana, XX*, Jerusalem: Magnes Press, 1968, pp. 3–54; Steven B. Smith, *Spinoza, Liberalism, and the Question of Jewish Identity*. New Haven: Yale University Press, 1997; and Aviezer Ravitzky, *Religion and State in Twentieth Century Jewish Thought*. Jerusalem: The Israel Democracy Institute, 2002.
5 As Akkerman claims in the introduction to the Latin-French edition of the TTP, even if Spinoza compiled the text from excerpts written during different periods and contexts, it is clear that his purpose was to arrange a new and consistent work. See

Traité Théologico-Politique, Oeuvres III. Texte établi par F. Akkerman. Traductions et note par J. Lagrée et P.-F. Moreau. Paris: Presses Universitaires de France, 1999, p. 8. See too Fokke Akkerman, "Studies in the Posthumous Works of Spinoza, On Style, Earliest Translation and Reception, and Modern Editions of Some Texts" (Doctoral dissertation). Groningen: Krips Repro Meppel 1980. Biderman and Kasher suggest that the earliest text embedded within the TTP is the apologia that Spinoza composed close to the date of his excommunication. See Shlomo Biderman and Asa Kasher, "Why Was Baruch de Spinoza Excommunicated?" in David S. Katz and Jonathan I. Israel (eds), *Skeptics, Millenarians, and Jews*. Leiden: E.J. Brill, 1990, pp. 98–141.

6 All quotations from the TTP are taken from Benedict De Spinoza, *Theological-Political Treatise*. Translated by Michael Silverthorne and Jonathan Israel, Cambridge: Cambridge University Press, 2007. This is the language used by Spinoza in opposing Rabbi Jehudah Al-Fakhar, who states that reason "should be subordinate to Scripture and indeed wholly subjected to it" (TTP, XV, p. 187 [181]). The expression "dead letters" (*mortuis literis*) is explicitly Pauline, and represents Judaism as being subject to the "letter that kills" (*littera enim occidit*; II Corinthians 3:6). Moreover, in my opinion, by using the expression "dead letters" Spinoza relates to the fact that the Jewish Torah scrolls are written without vocalization. In his Latin book of Hebrew grammar, after explaining to his readers that in the Hebrew language vowels are indicated not by means of letters but by means of diacritical markings, Spinoza notes: "Among the Hebrews vowels are called 'souls of letters,' and letters without vowels are 'bodies without souls' [*corpora sine anima*]" (*Hebrew Grammar*, in *Benedict Spinoza. Spinoza: Complete Works*. Translated by S. Shirley, Indianapolis and Cambridge: Hackett, 2002, p. 588). For a discussion of possible kabbalistic sources for Spinoza's statement in this context, see Menachem Lorberbaum, "The Republic in Hebrew: On the Hebrew Translation of the Political Terminology of Spinoza," *Iyyun: The Jerusalem Philosophical Quarterly* 53 (2004), pp. 185–208 [Heb.].

7 Strauss, *Persecution and the Art of Writing*, p. 187. In a footnote, Strauss adds here a reference to Maimonides's introduction to the *Guide for the Perplexed*; to Plato's *Seventh Letter* (341 d4-e3 and 344 c3-d5); and to *Phaedrus* (275c). For discussion on whether Strauss himself adopted the concealing method of writing see Hayyim Rechnitzer, *Leo Strauss and the Theological-Political Problem*, PhD diss., Hebrew University, 2002 [Heb.], pp. 223–235.

8 Spinoza himself, in a rare moment of non-geometric reasoning, relates to his geometric method as "cumbersome" (*prolixo*) (IV.P18, Schol, II/222).

9 This point has been dealt with in different ways and contexts by several of Spinoza's commentators, including: Jonathan Bennett, *A Study of Spinoza's Ethics*. Cambridge: Cambridge University Press, 1984, p. 65; Richard Mason, *The God of Spinoza: A Philosophical Study*. Cambridge: Cambridge University Press, 1999, p. 35; and Yermiyahu Yovel in the introduction to his Hebrew translation of the *Ethics* (Baruch Spinoza, *Ethics*. Translated by Yermiyahu Yovel, Tel Aviv: HeKibbutz HeMeuhad, 2003 [Heb.], p. 44). For a survey of projects dedicated to a critical analysis of the Euclidean nature of the *Ethics*, including efforts to formalize it, see Shaul Rosenfeld, "The Possibility of a Philosophical System," PhD. Diss., Tel Aviv University 2006 [Heb.], pp. 317–321.

10 See Strauss, *Persecution and the Art of Writing*, pp. 176–186.

11 *Porrò quicquid cupimus, et agimus, cujus causa sumus, quatenus Dei habemus ideam, sive quatenus Deum cognoscimus, ad Religionem refero*. Neither Yovel nor Guttmann maintain the correspondence between Spinoza's hierarchization of religion and his precise, systematic hierarchization of knowledge. See Yermiyahu Yovel, *Spinoza and Other Heretics: The Marrano of Reason*. Princeton, NJ: Princeton University Press, 1992, pp. 254–256; and Julius Guttmann, *Religion and Science: Essays and Lectures*. Translated by Shaul Aish. Jerusalem: Magnes Press, 1955, [Heb.], pp. 204–205.

12 Four lexicons appear at the opening of each of the first four parts of the *Ethics*, and an additional lexicon concludes the third part.
13 From the plethora of examples regarding this issue it will suffice to mention four: "Morality" (*pietas*) and "Being Honorable" (*honestas*) are defined in the same scholium in which the definition of religion also appears (IV.37, Schol 1, II/236); "veneration" (*veneratio*) and "dread" (*horror*) are defined in III.52, Schol, II/180.
14 From a systematic standpoint, "desire" for Spinoza qualifies an action. Indeed, desire (*cupiditas*) is defined as "appetite [*appetitus*] together with consciousness of the appetite" (III.9, Schol, II/148). Desire is *conatus*, the principle denoting the striving of every thing to preserve its independent action, when relating "to the Mind and Body together" (ibid. II/147).
15 See Lorberbaum, "Spinoza's Theological-Politcal Problem," *Hebraic Political Studies*, Vol. 1, No. 2 (Winter 2006), pp. 203–223.
16 From here on I will deploy the term "contradiction of depth" in order to denote a logical contradiction in a fundamental metaphysical issue, such as the relation between the finite and the infinite, time and eternity, static and dynamic existence, etc.
17 The enumeration of contradictions here refers to the order of their presentation in the second part of the present book.

Part I
Revised religion

On the contradiction in the concept of God
in the first kind of knowledge

1 Moral *or* political religion?
On the contradiction between the two models of revised religion in the TTP[1]

In the fall of 1665, having already sent the first drafts of the *Ethics* to his philosopher friends in Amsterdam, Spinoza decided to interrupt the writing of his magnum opus in order to deal with a grave problem. This was not a metaphysical problem but an existential one in the most basic sense: how can a philosopher (in this case Spinoza himself, who witnessed the collapse of the liberal regime of Johannes de Witt) ensure his personal security and freedom to philosophize in a society in which religion plays a central role?[2]

Spinoza's problem has plagued Western philosophy since its origins.[3] In the second half of the fifth century BCE Anaxagoras and Protagoras were exiled from Athens on the charge of heresy, the same reason for which Socrates was executed, along with the accusation of corrupting the youth. Plato approached writing *The Republic* while grappling with a similar issue: how to establish a state that will not put its philosophers to death the way that Athens did to Socrates? The solution Plato suggested was radical: for the state not to harm the lives and freedom of thought and expression of the philosophers, the latter must become the rulers and sovereigns of the state. However, the solution of the philosopher-king was met with the scorn of a realist on the part of Spinoza, who suggested a new solution to the old problem.[4]

For Spinoza the stability of the state is a necessary condition for the philosopher's personal security and freedom of thought and expression. However, this stability would not be achieved as long as the conflict between the institutions of religion and state remains unsolved. As a result, he deemed it necessary first and foremost to unravel the theological-political problem.[5] For this reason, Spinoza dedicated an entire philosophical work, *The Theological-Political Treatise*, to deal with the ancient conflict between religion and politics that had cast a shadow on philosophers and philosophy from time immemorial.[6]

The clash between religion and politics is the result of a firm, mutual demand for supremacy. Religion proclaims its supremacy from the absolute nature of the source of its authority – God – and is therefore not prepared to bow down to the authority of the state. By contrast, political authority perceives its supremacy to be a factual-conceptual matter; in the same way that an item cannot be considered a chair if it was not intended to be used for sitting, no social institution can be considered a political authority if it does not demand for itself supremacy and if it is not capable of realizing that supremacy.[7]

Indeed, the clash between religion and politics is not only a conceptual matter, but also – and predominantly – a result of the long, complicated relationship between the two. Therefore, the solution to the conflict between religion and politics must be based not only on a conceptual analysis but also on an investigation of the actual roots of the conflict; such an investigation is presented in the TTP in the framework of Spinoza's genealogy of religion.

Spinoza's genealogy of religion

Spinoza opens the introduction to the TTP with an examination of the psycho-philosophical roots of the religious phenomena (TTP, Preface, pp. 3–8 [5–9]). At the focus of this study, which might be called Spinoza's genealogy of religion, Spinoza examines man's attempt to achieve existential stability in both the psychological and social spheres.

I. The sense of instability facing nature

In the first stage of the genealogy Spinoza considers the existential implications of man's ignorance regarding the laws of nature. Not only does this ignorance prevent man from controlling nature and exploiting it for his uses, but also, and principally, it induces a sense of instability and fear that increases as man's expectations and demands of nature become more and more exaggerated. Spinoza does not clarify whether the first stage of the genealogy connotes a historical condition, or merely a psychological one that hurls whomever encounters it to the next stage of the genealogy in which they oscillate between superstitions.[8] Moreover, it is entirely clear that the first stage of the genealogy connotes the essence of man as a creature oscillating between fear and hope;[9] as we will see shortly, all of man's attempts to attenuate this existential oscillation end in its intensification.

II. The oscillation between superstitions

The existential oscillation described above engenders, preserves, and cultivates superstition, which is none other than a chain of fictitious causality that man imposes upon nature. He does so in order to come to know the rules controlling nature, thereby abating his fears and obtaining for himself a sense of security and stability. Since, according to Spinoza "everyone is prone to superstition," (TTP, Preface, p. 4 [5])[10] it is not possible to understand human nature without understanding the nature of superstition. Consequently, in the TTP Spinoza outlines a philosophy of superstition in whose framework he attempts to understand superstition through reason. Whoever is not a philosopher is not capable of living without superstition. Indeed, superstition expresses man's status in existence as a limited creature trying to break free of his boundaries. As long as humans fail to achieve their goals, their fear overcomes them; and the greater the fear, the greater the irrationality of their superstitions. Neglecting reason creates myriad superstitions that assume the existence of a god whose relations with humans are anchored in rigid and fixed laws of reward and punishment. According to the TTP, superstition is none other than a fabrication of the concept of God that is meant to provide humans with the sense of stability they long for.[11]

The sense of stability that superstition imbues in man is the result of the knowledge it supposedly grants him regarding the laws that organize his relationship with God. This knowledge seemingly grants man the ability to maneuver (for example, in order to achieve a or to escape from b, one must do c) and teaches him to recognize his boundaries (for example, it is not possible to achieve c and d simultaneously). Man feels more secure and protected in a world in which "the rules and bounds of the game" are known to him, even if only apparently. As such, one who seeks refuge in the shadow of superstition is rewarded at first with a sense of stability. Nonetheless, because superstition is a false faith, a product of the illusions of man's mind, the result can only be that it will disappoint those who adhere to it. This disappointment leads man to adopt a new superstition that will again imbue him with a sense of stability, only to later disappoint again, and so forth. In this way the existential oscillation returns to haunt man; however, now the fear of nature is replaced by the fear of falsehood that man imposes upon nature. Therefore, he who flees from the fear cast upon him by nature to the bosom of superstition will, in the end, be filled with an even greater fear.

III. The foundation of religion

Spinoza presents the foundation and establishment of religion as an expression of man's attempt to break free of the oscillation between superstitions described here. In the following passage Spinoza presents the heart of his concept of religion in the TTP:

> [I]t is easy for people to be captivated by a superstition [*superstitio*], but difficult to ensure that they remain loyal to it.... Such instability of mind has been the cause of many riots and ferocious wars ... "nothing governs the multitude as effectively as superstition"; Hence people are easily led, under the pretense of religion, sometimes to adore their kings as gods and at other times to curse them and detest them as the universal scourge of mankind. To cope with this difficulty, a great deal of effort has been devoted to adorning religion [*religio*], whether true or false, with pomp and ceremony, so that everyone would find it more impressive than anything else and observe it zealously with the highest degree of fidelity.
>
> (TTP, Preface, pp. 4–5 [6–7])

The oscillation between superstitions spills over from the psychological sphere to the political; due to this oscillation, the multitude, filled with fear and incited by corrupt manipulators, build political entities and destroy them. In order to prevent the damage from this oscillation, set rituals and ceremonies were established for superstition that were intended to ensure the stability of the psychological and social lives of the multitude. Consequently, superstition became religion. It is important to note that in this passage and beyond in the TTP, Spinoza maintains a fundamental separation between superstition (*superstitio*) and religion (*religio*); the former undermines the stability of society, while the latter maintains and protects it.

IV. The deterioration of religion into superstition

In the final stage of the genealogy, Spinoza describes the deterioration of religion back to superstition as a result of the loss of the former's ability to ensure the stability of society. This depiction does not pretend to be historical.[12] Spinoza does not attempt to teach us a chapter from the annals of the development of human religion,[13] but seeks to advance his concept of religion through its presentation as the original concept of religion. For this reason Spinoza weaves the motive of deterioration (which is a distinctly medieval one) into his genealogy of religion and presents religion's current condition as damaged and in need of repair.[14]

According to Spinoza, the religious entity is by definition subordinate to the political entity. Therefore, the moment in which religion is instituted as an independent entity that is not dependent on the political entity is the moment in which religion returns to being superstition.[15] Without any external supervision, the religious institution becomes corrupt and dangerous to the stability of society. As an independent entity, religion comes into friction and conflict with the other branches of culture, particularly with politics and philosophy, Spinoza's focus in the TTP. In addition, the struggles between different factions that vie to appropriate the vast sources of power of the religious institution turn religion into a continuous source of social instability.

The definition of religion in the TTP and distinguishing between "existing religion" and "revised religion"

In the TTP Spinoza does not offer a definition of religion in the first kind of knowledge; however, from his genealogy of religion it is possible to extract the following definition: religion is but a superstition that distorts the concept of God in order to stabilize society.[16] Religion does not supersede superstition because of the truth of its concept of God, but only by virtue of its ability to stabilize society. The advantage of religion is social; religion regulates the relations between human beings, and not the relations between human beings and God. Moreover, a political project without religion is doomed to failure. Indeed, without religion, politics is not capable of overcoming the danger the volatility of the multitude poses to the stability of society.

However, Spinoza's definition of religion relates to what is desirable, not to what exists. From this definition it follows that what we generally perceive to be religion is none other than superstition that damages the stability of society. Therefore, in discussing Spinoza's criticism of religion in the TTP, I suggest distinguishing between the following two terms: "existing religion" and "revised religion." By "existing religion" I mean the religion that undermines the stability of society by standing in opposition to the authorities of the state. This term does not connote a specific historical religion, neither that which existed in seventeenth century Holland nor that which exists today. The qualifier "existing" expresses the fact that Spinoza's departure point in the TTP is that the existing religion undermines the stability of society and should therefore be revised. By the term "revised religion" I mean the religion that promotes the stability of society and overcomes the conflict between religion and the state. Despite the fact that Spinoza himself uses the term "universal religion" (*religio catholica*),[17] I prefer the term "revised religion" because the term "revised" connotes a thing that was repaired after it had been damaged, as well as something re-vised to be made proper. These meanings unite in Spinoza's project of revising religion in the TTP.

As a realist who scorned political utopias, Spinoza was obliged to prove that he related to human beings as they were, and not as he wanted them to be;[18] because he felt personally threatened by the theological-political problem, he was obliged to present a fundamental, detailed, and full portrait of revised religion, not merely a brief and general description. But does Spinoza fulfill this obligation? The answer to this question will be discussed in the following section.

The problem of revised religion in the TTP

On the one hand, Spinoza claims in the TTP that existing religion is defective because it undermines the stability of society; on the other hand, he argues that it is impossible for society to exist without religion. It follows that it is not possible to solve the theological-political conflict by means of removing religion from society, since society without religion is not a possibility.[19] The solution to the theological-political conflict must be carried out through a revision of the existing religion or through establishing a revised religion that will ensure the stability of society.

"What is revised religion?" is the core question of the TTP; despite this, it is not at all clear how it is resolved within the framework of the TTP. This vagueness is the result of two main causes: the first is that the esoteric character of the TTP, which involves intentional contradictions and numerous statements made as lip service to different audiences, makes it difficult for the reader, no matter how critical, to follow Spinoza's solution to the theological-political problem;[20] the second cause is that in the TTP Spinoza does not conduct an organized and thematic discussion of revised religion. Excluding Chapter 14, which deals with the foundations of faith of the revised religion, Spinoza does not directly clarify how to establish a revised religion, the ways in which it justifies itself before the multitude, the character of its role models, the excellence (*virtus*) that it attempts to cultivate, as well as other subjects that should stand at the center of any initiative seeking to replace the existing religion with a revised one. Instead of suggesting a systematic and organized solution to the theological-political problem that subverts the stability of society and threatens the lives of philosophers and their freedom of thought and expression, Spinoza dedicates the bulk of the TTP to critiquing revealed religion in general, and Judaism in particular.[21] The focus on existing religion as defective – valid though it may be – raises a piercing question: beyond pointing out the problem, does Spinoza present a solution? In addition to his denunciation of existing religion, does Spinoza suggest an alternative model of revised religion?

Since, according to Spinoza, it is not possible for society to exist without religion, answering the last question in the negative would have grave consequences. It would mean that in the TTP, a work that Spinoza completed and published, a serious problem arises with decisive implications for Spinoza's personal safety as well as for his freedom of thought and expression, and this without him even attempting to put forth a solution. If pointing out this absurd conclusion is not enough to reject the last possibility, the following argument can be made: the danger to which Spinoza, whose signature was "caution!" (*caute*), exposed himself with the publication of the TTP in the theological-political climate of late seventeenth century Holland, proves that he was convinced that the TTP was not an "abstract study, that is to say of the kind of studies that were never meant to be of use,"[22] but in fact a book containing a practical and effective solution to the problem of existing religion.[23]

As such, the problem of revised religion in the TTP is created by the clash between the two claims presented above: on the one hand it is clear that Spinoza considered the TTP to be a philosophical work that includes a solution to the defects of existing religion, namely, the establishment of a revised religion; on the other hand, it is not at all clear what that revised religion actually is, i.e., what is Spinoza's actual solution to the theological-political problem. And why, if at all, is it important to Spinoza to conceal his solution to the theological-political problem in the TTP?

The contradiction between the reduction of the moral to the religious and the reduction of the religious to the political in the TTP

It is possible to partially diminish the vagueness that characterizes Spinoza's treatment of the defects of existing religion if we take into account that substantial parts of his solution are embedded within discussions pertaining to the abolition of the authority of the revealed religions.[24] Therefore, we should read Spinoza's criticism of the existing religion carefully and extract from it, like photographs from negatives, the outlines of the revised religion. In other words, because the critical process that Spinoza directs towards existing religion is interwoven with the alternative, positive process of establishing a revised religion, a close study of the first process should circumvent the problem of the ambiguity in the presentation of the second process.

Adopting this interpretive method – i.e., reading the TTP from the point of view of the project of revising religion – leads to conclusion the TTP can be divided into two parts in which two different and contradictory models of revised religion are presented.

In the first 15 chapters of the TTP, Spinoza presents a revised religion based on the reduction of the religious to the moral in whose framework obedience to God is reduced to obedience to moral law (Chapters 1–15, hereafter: the first part of the TTP). Contrarily, in the five final chapters, Spinoza presents a revised religion based on the reduction of the religious to the political in whose framework obedience to God is reduced to obedience to the law of the authorities of the state (Chapters 16–20, hereafter: the second part of the TTP).

By positing two models of revised religion in the TTP – though not always explicitly – Spinoza is thrown into several grave contradictions within his project of revising religion. The main contradiction between the two parts of the TTP (the other contradictions, as we shall see, derive from it) is in the definition of the key concept of the revised religion: obedience to God. In the first part of the TTP, Spinoza argues firmly that the only point of convergence between man and God, upon which obedience to God is based, is moral action. Indeed, only on this point does man (every man, even if he is not a philosopher) stand alone, without an intermediary, facing God.[25] Spinoza's basic assumption in the first part is that as opposed to metaphysical knowledge, which is limited to a small number of philosophers, knowledge of the moral law is the shared gift of all men (TTP, XIII, p. 173 [168]). The moral laws are the word of God inscribed in the heart of every man in that they are based on basic human intuitions; as such, moral laws enable direct obedience to God without the mediation of other individuals or social institutions (TTP, XII, p. 167 [162]).

The unmediated nature of obedience to God, which characterizes Spinoza's stance in the first part of the TTP, is completely negated in the second part; there Spinoza locates political authority between the individual and God, explicitly stating that "no one can rightly obey God ... if, as a consequence, they do not obey all the decrees of the sovereign power" (TTP, XIX, p. 243 [232]). The obedience to God in the first part of the TTP is identified with "love of [one's] neighbor" (TTP, XIV, p. 181 [176]) while in the second part it is identified with blind obedience to political authority.[26] Indeed, in the second part of the TTP, Spinoza instructs unambiguously to obey political authority without question even when its commands are unethical (TTP, XVI, pp. 200–201 [194]); he also blames whoever does not unconditionally obey the authorities of the state of being "impious" (*impium*) (TTP, XX, p. 253 [242]). The stark contradiction between the two definitions of obedience to God, a core concept of Spinoza's revised religion, leads to five additional contradictions. Each one of these five additional contradictions, and all the more so the five of them together, demonstrate that in the TTP Spinoza suggests two different models of revised religion that negate one another.

1 *The contradiction in the figure of the biblical prophet.* The figure of the biblical prophet in the revised religion is presented in a wholly positive way in

the first part of the TTP, and in a completely negative light in the second. In the first part of the TTP, during the course of his reduction of the religious to the moral, Spinoza indeed negates the medieval identification of the prophet with the philosopher. Yet he chooses the biblical prophet as the role model of his revised religion by presenting him as an ethical ideal.[27] Contrarily, in the framework of the reduction of the religious to the political, where Spinoza is interested in ensuring complete obedience to the authorities of the state, he speaks ill of the biblical prophets who "had more success, it should be noted, in antagonizing than reforming people by means of the liberty which they usurped to admonish, scold, and rebuke" (TTP, XVIII, p. 232 [223]). Additionally, when discussing the opposition of the biblical prophet to the king as such, that is, as one who holds political power, Spinoza denigrates the position of the prophet and prefers to adopt the point of view of the king. The same prophets that are presented in the first part of the TTP as representatives of the spirit of kindness, integrity, and good, are presented in the second part of the TTP as a collection of capricious, troublesome, and rebellious individuals who damaged religion and the state more than they did them benefit.[28]

2   *The contradiction in the characteristics of the role models and the kind of excellence that revised religion seeks to cultivate.* In the first part of the TTP, Spinoza positions Jesus as the central role model of his revised religion, while at the same time he seeks to cultivate moral excellence among the believers.[29] On the other hand, in the second part of the TTP, Spinoza prefers citizens who blindly obey those who occupy the seat of power, his example being none other than the Roman military leader Torquatus, who had his own son beheaded for violating military orders.[30] In this context, there is obvious (and perhaps intended) symbolism referring to the fact that Jesus' crucifiers were soldiers of the Roman Empire.

3   *The contradiction in the role designated to ecclesiastics.* If in the course of the reduction of the religious to the moral Spinoza intended that the ecclesiastics take on the role of teachers of morals who glean a moral lesson for the masses from Scripture,[31] during the course of the reduction of the religious to the political he turns them into agents of the state "who teach the people piety by the authority of the sovereign powers and adapt it by their rulings to the public interest" (TTP, XIX, p. 247 [236]). It is entirely clear that the addition "by the authority of the sovereign powers ... by their rulings" completely changes the designation of the ecclesiastics; indeed, it changes them from independent critics of political authority to its agents and emissaries.

4   *The contradiction regarding the right of interpretation of the foundations of faith.* In the first part of the TTP Spinoza argues that each and every person is permitted to interpret the foundations of faith as he wishes.[32] Contrarily, in the second part of the TTP, Spinoza argues that the right to interpret the foundations of faith is strictly that of the political authorities.[33] Spinoza is consistent in the two parts of the TTP only in his claim that the right of interpretation of the foundations of faith should be expropriated from the control of the ecclesiastics.[34]

5   *The contradiction in the definition of justice.* While reducing the religious to the moral, Spinoza defines justice as "a constant and perpetual will to assign each man his due."[35] By contrast, when reducing the religious to the political Spinoza defines justice as "a fixed intention to assign to each person what belongs to them in accordance with civil law."[36] It is impossible to ignore the blatant grafting of the ending "in accordance with civil law" that places the definition of justice in the second part of the TTP in direct contradiction with the definition of justice in the first part. While in the first part of the TTP justice is determined according to moral standards only, in the second part it is determined according to standards that are entirely political.

Spinoza's esoteric writing demands careful reading. However, a careful reading of the TTP does not remove the contradiction between the two models of revised religion, but rather it worsens it, as can be seen from the five by-products of this contradiction that have been presented here. Furthermore, not only does Spinoza refrain from suggesting an explicit, clear solution to this contradiction in the TTP, he does not even acknowledge its existence. Thus it is not conceivable that he who wrote the TTP in such a stratified way and knew from considerations of esotericism how to plant intentional contradictions in the text, would not have paid attention to the main contradiction between the two parts of the TTP. And assuming that Spinoza was indeed aware of this contradiction, it is not reasonable to think this testifies to his oscillating between two different models of revised religion without the ability to decide between them.

Indeed the TTP, as has already been noted, is a book that Spinoza completed and published despite the dangers of doing so. From here it follows that first, Spinoza was aware of the contradiction between the first and second parts of the TTP; second, that Spinoza chose not to reveal the meaning and intent of this contradiction; and, third, that Spinoza believed that the TTP, along with the contradiction between its two parts, contains an effective and practical solution to the theological-political problem. We will now turn to Spinoza's analysis of the ancient Hebrew state, from which it is possible to extract the idea of the "constructive contradiction" which, as we will see, enables an understanding of the meaning of the contradiction between the two models of revised religion in the TTP, as well as the reason for concealing this contradiction.

The "constructive contradiction" in the concept of God and the role of religion in the ancient Hebrew state

Spinoza understood that basing the religious solely on the moral, or solely on the political, would prevent the revised religion from obtaining its final goal, namely ensuring the stability of society. Basing revised religion on morals alone is liable to arouse rebellions and uprisings on the part of the believers who are not prepared to obey laws of the state that are not in line with the moral laws. On the other hand, basing revised religion on obedience to the political sovereign alone is also liable to undermine the stability of society, from the following consideration: in the framework of the reduction of the religious to the political, the obedience of the citizens to the sovereign is unconditional. Therefore, in order to stabilize the political sphere the sovereign is obliged to choose – without any external compulsion – to conduct moral policies that are in line with the ultimate conclusions of reason.[37] However, according to Spinoza, the Platonic ideal of the philosopher-king is an invalid one, and another king will not be obligated to morals.[38]

Therefore, only by choosing both of the ways Spinoza suggests in the two parts of the TTP, neither of which manages to revise religion on its own, can the stability of society be ensured. What appears at first as a contradiction that destroys religion's ability to stabilize society is in fact a *constructive contradiction* that strengthens and fortifies this stability. While the existing religion tends to serve as an opposition to the moral and/or the political, the revised religion combines support of the political authority with placing moral limitations on its conduct. This balance between a moral focus and a political one existed, according to Spinoza, in the way that religion functioned in the framework of the ancient Hebrew state.

Spinoza turns to the ancient Hebrew state in order to extract from it a means of creating, guarding, and cultivating social stability; these are means that will enable "to organize everything in such a way that each person, of whatever character, prefers public right to private advantage" (TTP, XVII, p. 211 [203]).[39] Even though an in-depth study of the ancient Hebrew state brings Spinoza to the conclusion that it is impossible as well as unwanted to imitate the Hebrew state in every way, "it [the Hebrew state][40] nevertheless has numerous features that are at least well worth noticing, and which it would perhaps be very wise to imitate" (TTP, XVIII, p. 230 [221]).[41] Spinoza makes note to praise the establishment of a civilian military in the ancient Hebrew state, supporting the decentralization of rule that existed after the death of Moses (TTP, XVII, pp. 214–223 [207–215]), and even extracting from a discussion of the history of the state a conservative political conclusion opposing fundamental changes in the existing government, even if the goal of such changes would be to convert a tyrannical monarchy to a civilized democracy (TTP, XVIII, pp. 234–237 [226–228]).[42]

According to Spinoza, the religion of the ancient Hebrew state fulfilled the original role of religion as a mechanism that aims to ensure the stability of society. In order to serve this role, Spinoza claims, religion in the ancient Hebrew state was not only a servant of the authorities, but also a critic who limited the misconduct and arbitrariness of the political authority. The double role of religion found expression in its significance within the framework of the civilian military that Moses established as the founder of the ancient Hebrew state.

> [H]e [Moses] ordered all men from the age of twenty to sixty to take up arms for military service, and to make up their expeditionary forces from the people alone. They were to swear allegiance not to their commander or

Moral or *political religion?* 25

the high priest but to religion and God. They were therefore called the forces or armies of God, and among the Hebrews God for his part [was called] the God of armies. For this reason, in great battles, on whose outcome depended either victory or disaster for the whole people, the ark of the covenant went in the midst of the army, so that the people seeing their king virtually present should fight with all their strength.

(TTP, XVII, p. 217 [209])

On the one hand, at the end of this paragraph religion is presented as the servant of political authority; religion is presented as an auxiliary tool to war, which only the top commander of the army, the representative of the political authorities, can declare (ibid.). In order to achieve supreme sacrifice of the soldiers in war, the concept of God is presented by the state as "the God of armies." On the other hand, at the start of the paragraph religion is presented as beyond the scope of political authority. The soldiers are not sworn followers of the commander, the representative of the political authority, and not of the high priest – the head ecclesiastic – but rather they exclusively swear allegiance to "religion and God" (ibid.); and because in the ancient Hebrew state religion was reduced to morals, the first loyalty of the soldiers in the military was to morals (TTP, XVII, p. 224 [216]). However, the separatist character of the ancient Hebrew state reduced charity towards one's fellow man to charity towards the fellow citizen alone (ibid.).

The independence of religion from the political authority instilled the former with an important critical strength. Indeed, in order to realize its essence as a tool for stabilizing society, religion must not only train the hearts of the citizens to obey the political authority, but it must also force the political authority to conduct a moral policy. In this way revised religion creates a type of parallelogram of powers that ensures the stability of society.[43] In order not to upset this balance, Spinoza is not ready to justify the implementation of any direct means, certainly not rebellion against the political authority, regardless of whatever moral deterioration might come to pass.[44] Religious rebellion is a stark contradiction in the concept of religion; in such an uprising religion would harm the stability of the society it is supposed to protect. Alternatively, religion must express its independence from political authority in a less radical but more effective way. It must act towards the creation of a moral social sphere that will force the political authority interested in the support of its citizens to conduct a moral policy that will be accepted by them. Any deviation from the moral policy approved by the citizens will gravely endanger the political authority. Indeed, the danger exposed to the state by its citizens, in the event that they should choose to revolt against it, is greater than the danger exposed to the state by its enemies.[45] Thus the existence of a moral social sphere is meant to force the political authority, which seeks its own benefit, to conduct a moral policy.

In order to create a moral social climate, revised religion must assimilate the moral laws into the hearts of the multitude; and because assimilation as the result of philosophical understanding is not appropriate for the multitude, all that is left is a set and ordered repetition of the moral laws.[46] This issue found its expression in the ancient Hebrew state in the following way:

> [T]he whole people was ordered to congregate in a certain place once every seven years to learn the Laws from the priests, and, in addition, that everyone had an obligation to read and reread the book of the Law by himself continually and attentively.... The leaders therefore had to take very good care, if only for their own sakes, to govern entirely according to the prescribed laws, which were quite clearly understood by all, if they wanted to be held in the highest honor by the people who at that time revered them as ministers of God's government and as having the place of God. Otherwise they could not escape the most intense kind of hatred, among their subjects, as intense as theological hatred tends to be.
> (TTP, XVII, p. 220 [212])

The theological emotions that were presented in the preface to the TTP as the gravest danger to the stability of society (TTP, p. 5 [6])), are employed in the framework of revised religion for the defense of the stability of society. The fear of "theological hatred" obligates those holding positions of power to conduct a moral policy. Revised religion cultivates stability and exhibits a hostile attitude towards any attempt of change or innovation. The ecclesiastics in the ancient Hebrew state are understood by Spinoza as guardians of the existing law (the right to legislate is denied from the political authorities) and as exclusively possessing the right to deliver to the political authorities God's answers to their questions (the ecclesiastics themselves were forbidden from initiating questions directed towards God). The ecclesiastics served as yes-men to those holding seats of power, except that they were obliged to be the representatives of the accepted morals that limited the freedom of action of the political authorities.[47] Regarding the ecclesiastics in the ancient Hebrew state prior to its decline during the Second Temple period, Spinoza writes:

> At that time, accordingly, they could have no wish to promulgate new decrees but merely administered and safeguarded the existing edicts. By no other means than keeping the laws uncorrupted could they safely preserve their liberty against the will of the secular leaders.
> (TTP, XVIII, p. 231 [222])

The ecclesiastics, just as the political authorities, acted in a moral way that did not stem from a moral impulse. In the ancient Hebrew state the ecclesiastics protected the accepted morals not because it was proper to do so, but because in this way they were able to protect the borders of the social space that distinguished them from the boorish multitude on the one hand, and those holding the reins of power on the other.[48]

The biblical prophet, the role models, and the ecclesiastics

Political authority is duty-bound to use revised religion exclusively in order to achieve its original and legitimate intention: securing the stability of society. According to Spinoza, a political authority that seeks to use revised religion for the advancement of the self-centered goals of those who stand at its helm, will find that neglecting the good of the whole will turn revised religion into a double-edged sword in its hands. Indeed, revised religion constitutes fertile ground for the cultivation of religious revolutionaries seeking to seize power from the hands of despotic rulers. Spinoza wishes that the fear of religious revolutionaries in his time would be identical to the fear of a new prophet that prevented the leaders of the ancient Hebrew state from acting according to their whims.[49]

> [T]he fear of a new prophet. If a man who lived a blameless life showed by certain accepted signs that he was a prophet, he had by this fact alone the supreme right of command like that of Moses – which he exercised in the name of God who was revealed to him alone.... There is no doubt that such men could easily draw the oppressed people to themselves, and persuade them of whatever they wanted even by trivial signs. On the other hand, if things were well-run, the leader could stipulate beforehand that any prophet should first appear before him so as to be examined by him, as to whether he was of good morals, whether he had certain and indubitable signs of his mission, and whether what he wanted to say in God's name agreed with accepted doctrine and the common laws of the country. If the signs were unsatisfactory or the doctrine was new, he could rightly condemn him to death, but if all was well, he was accepted solely on the authority and testimony of the leader.
>
> (TTP, XVII, pp. 221–222 [213–214])

A political authority administering a moral policy is awarded by the support of its citizens because it grants them protection from the immoral actions of their fellow citizens. As long as the political authority continues to protect its citizens, they will continue to stand by its side in every confrontation that arises with religious revolutionaries. Contrarily, a political authority that administers an immoral policy not only fails to protect its citizens from their fellow citizens, but is itself harmful to them as well. A political authority such as this is perceived by its citizens to be an enemy that should be subdued at the first opportunity. Therefore, in such a situation it is easy for that man "of good morals" (ibid.) to unite the citizens under his command to revolt against the authorities.

This is to say that Spinoza's position regarding religious uprising from moral motivations is two-sided. We saw above that Spinoza is not prepared to justify such an uprising; however, here we see he claims such an uprising to be unavoidable. If one takes into account that Spinoza's audience in the second part of the TTP (as we will see below) is the political ruler, this position – which determines

28 The first kind of knowledge

that religious uprising from moral motives is illegitimate as well as unavoidable – has greater rhetorical power than its opposite, which determines that such a religious uprising is justified though its occurrence is not necessary. Spinoza is interested in imbuing the ruler with a sense that he is positioned on his side, and therefore opposes any kind of uprising with his quill; however at the same time he is interested in cautioning the ruler from administering immoral policies, and thus presents the occurrence of the uprising as unavoidable if such policies are implemented.

The chronicles of the kings of the ancient Hebrew state are presented by Spinoza as proof of the fact that political corruption lays the foundation for the growth of religious revolutionaries. Therefore, he claims, "prior to rule by kings, there were very few prophets.... But once monarchy was opted for, there were always a large number of prophets" (TTP, XVII, pp. 224–225 [233]). Moreover, the hour of moral weakness of the political authorities is not only the hour of the prophets of truth and morals, but also the hour of the prophets of falsehood and manipulation bent on swaying the people to their side. One way or another, Spinoza warns the political authorities that administering an immoral policy towards its citizens will, in the end, be self-destructive. Understanding the role of the prophet in the ancient Hebrew state as identical to the role of the prophet or the private citizen preaching a faith in the framework of revised religion, might solve the first three contradictions that we revealed earlier.

Regarding the biblical prophet Spinoza is interested in developing a double awareness: appreciation of the prophet's moral excellence and admonishment for his political subversion. Therefore, in the first part of the TTP Spinoza praises the prophet's moral excellence,[50] while in the second part he denigrates his political subversion.[51]

In contrast to the biblical prophet, Spinoza presents the protagonist of revised religion as a figure who combines the ideal of citizenship with the ideal of moral excellence. In the first part of the TTP Spinoza forms the moral component of the role model of revised religion, and in the second part he develops that role model's civil component. The role model of revised religion is a man who, in the event of a clash between the moral law and the political law, would always choose to obey the political law because he understands obedience to the latter as a moral obligation (TTP, XVIII, pp. 232–233 [242–243]). Spinoza thought that the implementation of the ideal of a religious role model that is a hybridization of Jesus and Torquatus would ensure the stability of society.[52]

The role of ecclesiastics, who constitute the embodiment of the role models of revised religion among the masses, is to contribute to the stability of society in two complementary domains. Firstly, they should attempt to assimilate the moral laws into the hearts of the multitude; and secondly, they should advance the civil loyalty of the multitude. The ecclesiastics should also try and convince the multitude to prefer the obligation of obedience to the political authorities over a moral obligation in the event of a clash between the two.

The right to interpret the foundations of faith and the definition of justice in revised religion

Understanding the contradiction between the reduction of the religious to the moral and the reduction of the religious to the political as a constructive contradiction, which fortifies the stability of society, allows us to deal with the two additional contradictions mentioned above in the two parts of the TTP: the contradiction in the answer to the question of who has the right to interpret the foundations of faith (every person or the political authorities alone), and the contradiction in the concept of justice in the framework of revised religion (to give every man his right, or to give every man his right according to what the political authorities have decreed).

It is no coincidence that Spinoza first identifies the foundations of faith with the principles of morals before stating the claim that those in power have to be the *exclusive* interpreters and defenders of religious law (TTP, XVII, p. 228 [238]). In the framework of revised religion, the moral obligation fundamentally precedes the political obligation; indeed the moral obligation stands at the foundation of the political obligation. In other words, the political obligation is in fact the embodiment of the moral obligation:

> For we are obliged by God's decree to treat with piety all persons, without exception and inflict harm on no one. Accordingly, no one is permitted to give assistance to anyone who seeks to cause loss to another, much less to the whole state. Hence, no one can behave piously towards his neighbor according to God's decree, unless he accommodates piety and religion to the public interest. But no private person can know what *is* in the interest of the state other than from the decrees of the sovereign authorities, who alone have the responsibility to transact public business. Consequently, no one can rightly cultivate piety or obey God, without obeying all the edicts of the sovereign authority.
>
> (TTP, XIX, p. 243 [232–233])

It is important for Spinoza that the citizens understand that their obedience to the sovereign stems from moral motives. In fact, in the second part of the TTP, Spinoza does not do away with reducing religion to morals, but simply presents the political authorities as in fact realizing this reduction.[53] Given that the reduction of the religious to the moral in the text of the TTP precedes the reduction of the religious to the political, it is possible to speculate about the system of education in the framework of revised religion – a subject that Spinoza does not directly and systematically treat in the TTP.[54] Thus, it can be assumed that in the framework of revised religion the cultivation of a moral obligation should precede the cultivation of a civil one in the education system.

Spinoza's goal was that the deep internalization of the moral law by the citizens would limit the way in which the ruler could interpret the foundations of faith. Even if the ruler was granted considerable space to maneuver in terms of the interpretation of the foundations of faith, he is not granted unlimited interpretive space in which to maneuver. Therefore, on the one hand the right to interpret the foundations of faith is given to everyone and on the other hand the right to interpret the foundations of faith is given to the ruler. Indeed, in the framework of revised religion, the precise interpretation of the foundations of faith is located in the middle ground between the way in which they are understood by the citizens and the way in which they are understood by the ruler.[55]

Dealing with the contradiction between the two concepts of justice in the two parts of the TTP requires reliance on the following point: the internal logic of the second part, which is based on the reducing rights to power, led Spinoza to equate justice with the law of the state (TTP, XVI).[56] Moreover, an examination of the foundations of the state shows that it is not logically-conceptually possible to attribute injustice to the actions of the political authorities. Despite this, in the second part of the TTP as well Spinoza continues to use the definition of justice from the first part; a definition that does not depend on the decision of the political authorities (TTP, IV, p. 58 [58–59]). In one place Spinoza posits that "we find no traces of divine justice except where just men rule" (TTP, XIX, p. 242 [231]). In another place he turns to answer the question: "who shall have the right to champion piety, if those who hold power choose to be impious?" (TTP, XIX, p. 246 [236]) not by claiming that an impious government is a contradiction in terms, but by claiming that any other institution that achieves superiority can become impious, including the Church. In yet another place Spinoza designates a government legislating laws in matters of opinion as an "oppressive" government (*imperium violentum*) (TTP, XX, p. 250 [239]).

Spinoza uses, in the second part of the TTP, on three different occasions, the concept of justice in the same manner in which it is presented in the first part. It is not reasonable that this is a matter of loose penmanship by a writer as cautious as Spinoza. It is more reasonable to assume Spinoza is indirectly claiming through this three-time repetition that from a practical standpoint the ruler cannot act arbitrarily when he outlines the details of the foundations of faith, which are none other than the moral principles for legislation and policy (TTP, XVII, p. 208 [201]). Similarly, even if justice is determined according to the interpretation of the ruler for the benefit of all, this interpretation is thus limited by the accepted definition according to which justice is "a constant perpetual will to assign each man his due" (TTP, IV, p. 59 [59]).

The ruler cannot escape the moral judgment of his citizens. Even Moses, who was endowed with exceptional political talents, did not stymie the anger of the people when he chose members of his own tribe to serve as priests. Indeed, the Levites, as Walzer put it, had a material interest in sanctity that was difficult to conceal.[57] According to Spinoza, the destruction of the ancient Hebrew state resulted from Moses' immoral preference (TTP, XVII, pp. 225–229 [217–220]).[58] Thus in the second part of the TTP as well, during the course of Spinoza's reducing obedience to God to obedience to the political authorities, he does not avoid equating obedience to God with obedience to the moral laws;

indeed, he posits that obedience to the state must be accompanied by moral criticism of it, a criticism that is presented in the TTP as religious criticism.

Spinoza's return to the reduction of religion to obedience to the moral law during the course of the second part of the TTP – which reduces religion to obedience to the political law – can also explain why Spinoza understood the section on the foundations of faith (Chapters 13–14), in which the reduction of the religious to the moral reaches its apex, to be the core of the TTP. It can also explain why in the TTP he demands of the reader, in an unprecedented way, to read these chapters and to contemplate them again and again (TTP, XIV, p. 185 [180]). It was important for Spinoza, at the end of the first part of the TTP, to emphasize that even if in the second part he would instruct complete obedience to the political authorities and subjugate religion to the authority of the political ruler, the final loyalty of revised religion would *not* be to the political ruler; rather, it would be to the moral decree. For complete obedience to the political ruler is none other than an expression of complete obedience to the moral laws.

Turning to the sovereign

Spinoza was not satisfied with religion's role – even as a revised religion, in guaranteeing the moral behavior of the sovereign. The duty to ensure the stability of society was, in Spinoza's eyes, also laid on the shoulders of the philosophers;[59] the very publication of the TTP is a step that Spinoza as a philosopher took in an effort to fulfill this duty.[60] The TTP is in fact directed towards two different groups: the first part towards potential philosophers, who are still in the grips of theology; and the second part towards those holding the reins of power.[61] Reading the second part of the TTP as directed towards the political ruler illuminates from another angle Spinoza's talent in adjusting his language for his addressee. In order to achieve his goal, Spinoza takes care to couch his call to the ruler to conduct a moral policy in repetitive declarations of the total supremacy of the state.

The title of Chapter 16, which opens the second part of the TTP, is "On the foundations of the state, on the natural and civil right of each person, and on the authority of sovereign powers." Spinoza, who knew well the great interest that the ruler would take in this chapter, immediately presents at the start of the chapter the reduction of the right to power, from which he concludes, "that sovereign power is bound by no law" (TTP, XVI, p. 200 [193]). In the remainder of the chapter he aggrandizes the right of the political authorities to the point that he is forced to distinguish between subject and slave (TTP, XVI, pp. 200–201 [194–195]); and at the end of the chapter he declares that "[s]hould the sovereign refuse to obey God in his revealed law, he may do so, but at his own peril and to his own loss. No civil or natural law forbids him" (TTP, XVI, p. 206 [199]).

Nevertheless, between Spinoza's repeating salutes to the supremacy of the political authorities he urges, again and again, those holding the seats of power to restrict themselves to administering a moral policy; this is not because it is appropriate to do so, but because it is *worth* doing. The political authorities,

Spinoza states, "[t]o protect their position and retain power, they are very much obliged to work for the common good and direct all things by the dictate of reason; for no one has maintained a violent government for long, as Seneca says" (TTP, XVI, p. 200 [194]).[62] Additionally, Spinoza takes care to direct the attention of the sovereign – via a threefold repetition as well as historical examples – to the fact that the greatest danger to the state stems from its citizens and not its enemies (TTP, XVII, pp. 208–212 [201–205]).[63] This continuous fissure in the supremacy of the sovereign reaches its apex in the last chapter of the TTP, in which Spinoza posits:

> So while conceding that they [the sovereign authorities] may by natural right employ a high degree of violence in governing, and arrest citizens or liquidate them for the most trivial reasons, nevertheless everyone will agree that this is not consistent with the criteria of sound reason. Indeed rulers cannot do such things without great risk to their whole government, and hence we can also deny that they have absolute power to do these similar things and consequently that they possess any complete right to do them. For as we have proved, the right of sovereign authorities is limited by their power.
>
> (TTP, XX, p. 251 [240])

In the final chapter, Spinoza assumes that the ruler-reader has already understood that from the equation of power to right presented in the opening of the second part of the TTP (XVI, pp. 195–196 [189–190]), it follows that immoral action of the ruler, in that it harms the ruler's power, completely abolishes his right to perform that action. In his dual-layered writing, Spinoza makes use of the identification of power with right in order to strike a balance between the citizen's political obedience and the preservation of his freedom. On the one hand, when Spinoza addresses the citizen he uses this equating of terms in order to highlight the authority of the ruler, as if saying to the citizen: do not think that the political authorities have only power, but know that they act according to their right, and so you must obey them. On the other hand, when Spinoza addresses the ruler, he uses the same equating of terms in order to highlight the power of the citizens, as if saying to the ruler: do not think that the citizen has only duties, but know that he also has great power; and therefore, in order for the citizen to use his power for your sake and not against you, you must guard his freedom.[64]

The rhetorical consideration in concealing the constructive contradiction

If Spinoza thought that there exists within revised religion a constructive contradiction between obedience to the moral law and obedience to political law, why does he not present this contradiction in a clear and obvious manner? Why does he remain completely silent regarding not only the meaning of this contradiction, but even its very existence? This seems to give the impression that the two parts of the TTP are entirely detached from one another, indeed, that they undermine and negate one another.

The style of a text is a result of the nature of the audience to which it is addressed. The rigid geometric writing of the *Ethics* that was intended for philosophers is not the same as the essay-like writing of the TTP, which at times even reads as a pamphlet (Chapter 15, for example, is worded as a polemical pamphlet against the religious position of Rabbi Jehuda Al-Fakhar, while Chapter 20 is worded as a pamphlet championing freedom of thought and expression).[65] The answer to the question for whom did Spinoza write the TTP and what did he attempt to achieve with its publication, has a decisive implication on the form of his writing in general as well as on the contradiction between the first and second parts.

Throughout the first part, in which Spinoza addresses potential philosophers, the goal – as Strauss has already argued – was the liberation of the potential philosopher from the grasp of theological dogmas in which he was caught.[66] For this purpose Spinoza meticulously analyzes the foundational concepts of revealed religion and demonstrates to the potential philosopher that revealed religion is entirely directed towards the creation, preservation, and cultivation of moral behavior. The second part, which is addressed to the political sovereign or state authorities, is intended to convince those in power to adopt a moral policy for their own benefit. However, even if the two parts of the TTP were written for different audiences, they were directed against the very same group: the theologians of existing religion. In the first part of the TTP, Spinoza denies them all authority in metaphysical matters, and nullifies the very possibility of conducting theology as a science; in the second part he denies them all authority in political matters and transforms them into servants of the state.[67]

The non-philosophical character of the two audiences of the TTP forced Spinoza to present his positions in a simplistic and one-dimensional form. As a result, in the first part of the TTP Spinoza simply equates religious law with moral law, and in the second part he equates religious law with political law. In the first part of the TTP, Spinoza is interested in convincing the potential philosopher that if he should desire that the Holy Spirit reside over him, it is sufficient that he act morally; he has no need to prostrate himself before the dogmatic authority of the theologians (TTP, XV, pp. 192–193 [187–188]). Spinoza therefore preferred not to link the main argument from the second part of the TTP to the first part, according to which the political authorities have a monopoly over the meaning and implementation of moral decrees. Linking this argument to the first part of the TTP would cloud the sense of freedom that Spinoza is trying to instill in the potential philosopher. The latter might sense that Spinoza is removing the yoke of the theologians, while setting in its place the yoke of the political authorities.

In the second part of the TTP, Spinoza aims to convince the political ruler that it is beneficial to him to conduct a moral policy, and it is therefore important for Spinoza to emphasize the supremacy of the political authorities over the religious authorities. The rhetorical power of the second part of the TTP would be weakened if Spinoza had included within it the argument from the first part, according to which religion is reduced to morality without granting the ruler supremacy over religion or morals.[68] Such an integration of arguments would give the reader-ruler the feeling that instead of promoting his interests, Spinoza is inciting the multitude against him behind the guise of religious-moral concerns. The contradiction here is not intended, as with Plato, to impose on the aspiring philosopher the task of extracting the final conclusion from the dialogue on his own.[69] Spinoza's consideration in creating the contradiction between the two parts of the TTP is not educational but rather rhetorical. In order for his two main audiences to internalize his program, Spinoza was forced to prioritize certain matters while blurring or obscuring others in each of the two parts of the TTP. Only a philosopher meticulously reading the entire book would be capable of putting together a complete and comprehensive picture of revised religion in the way Spinoza himself understood it: a religion that demands of its believers the contradictory obligations to the moral law on the one hand, and to the law of the state on the other, in order to ensure the stability of society.

Notes

1 Here, as in the following chapter headings, when "or" appears in italics, it refers to the Latin *sive* or *seu*; this indicates that regarding the matters being discussed Spinoza presents the two contrasting possibilities as equivalent.

2 This problem was accompanied by two secondary problems that Spinoza presents in Letter 30 to Oldenburg: the former's being accused of heresy by the multitude, and the taking root of prejudices in the minds of potential philosophers. See Letter 30, Shirley, p. 185 (citations from Spinoza's letters are taken from Edwin Curley's *Collected Works*; those letters that are not translated by Curley are cited from Baruch Spinoza, *The Letters*. Translated by Samuel Shirley with introduction and notes by Steven Barnone, Lee Rice, and Jacob Adler, Indianapolis and Cambridge: Hackett, 1995. The citation will include the letter number, translator's last name, and page number in the English translation).

3 See Smith, *Spinoza, Liberalism*, p. 2. Epicurus, one of the first Western philosophers to develop a rigorous socio-political critique of religion, garnered Spinoza's rare admiration. See Letter 56 to Boxel, Shirley, p. 276. On the adoption of Epicurean motives in Spinoza's philosophy, see Catherine Wilson, *Epicureanism at the Origins of Modernity*. Oxford: Oxford University Press, 2008, pp. 125–135.

4 In the TTP, Spinoza mocks the Platonic political aspirations of such medieval philosophers as Maimonides (TTP, p. 114 [114]). To quote Pines:

> Apparently he [Spinoza] considers philosophers of this kind as megalomaniacs whose dreams of grandeur could not in the nature of things materialize; an impossibility which he evidently did not deplore. As against this, organized superstition was an indubitable reality; Spinoza was its opponent, but it aroused in him an incomparably greater interest than Platonizing political doctrines.
> (Shlomo Pines, "Spinoza's *Tractatus Theological-Politicus*, Maimonides, and Kant," pp. 12–13)

5 Spinoza assumed that because the *Ethics* was more radical than the TTP, and because the TTP was meant to advance freedom of thought and expression, the publication of the latter would pave the way for the publication of the former. However, the publication of the TTP had the opposite result: the negative reputation that the TTP gained

for Spinoza made the publication of the *Ethics* impossible in his lifetime. See Letter 68 to Oldenburg, Shirley, p. 321. See also Lewis S. Feuer, *Spinoza and the Rise of Liberalism*. New Brunswick: Transaction Books, 1987, p. 148; Steven Nadler, *Spinoza: A Life*. Cambridge: Cambridge University Press, 2001, pp. 333–336; Jonathan I. Israel, *Radical Enlightenment: Philosophy and the Making of Modernity: 1650–1750*. Oxford: Oxford University Press, 2002, pp. 285–287; and Piet Steenbakkers, *Spinoza's Ethics From Manuscript to Print: Studies on Text, Form and Related Topics*. Assen: Uitgeverij Van Gorcum, 1994, pp. 7–8.

6 The fact that Spinoza published the TTP without first publishing his other writings (especially the *Ethics*) indicates that he understood the TTP to be an independent work whose meaning is not derived from its relation to the entirety of his writings. Therefore, following Spinoza, I aim in this chapter to present the model of revised religion in the first kind of knowledge through a focus on the TTP. In the only work that Spinoza published besides the TTP (and prior to it) he presents, as the title indicates, *Descartes' Principle of Philosophy* (1663), and not his own philosophy; however, some of his own positions found their way into this work, as Curley and Israel have shown. See Curley, *The Collected Works of Spinoza*, pp. 221–224; and Jonathan I. Israel, "Spinoza as an Expounder, Critic, and 'Reformer' of Descartes," *Intellectual History Review* 17.1 (2007), pp. 59–78.

7 Following this understanding Spinoza designates the political authority as "supreme powers" (*summas potestates*); for example, see the title of Chapter 19. Spinoza's position in this context is closer to the supremacy of the law. See Chaim Gans, *Philosophical Anarchism and Political Disobedience*. Cambridge: Cambridge University Press, 1992, pp. 24–33.

8 Similarly, the measure of historicity that Spinoza attributes to the condition of nature, as he formulates it in the TTP, is not sufficiently clear. See the TTP, pp. 72–74 [73–75], 189–190 [195–196], 201–202 [195], 212–213 [205]. For a discussion of the differences between the *Political Treatise* and the TTP in this context, see Douglas Den Uyl, *Power, State and Freedom: An Interpretation of Spinoza's Political Philosophy*. Assen: Van Gorcum and Co., 1983, Chapter 3.

9 In one of the rare instances in which Spinoza makes use of metaphor in the *Ethics*, this existential oscillation is presented as follows: "[I]t is clear that we are driven about in many ways by external causes, and that, like waves on the sea, driven by contrary winds, we toss about, not knowing our outcome and fate" (III.59, Schol, II/189).

10 In the same vein, in the opening sentence of the TTP Spinoza declares: "If men were always able to regulate their affairs with sure judgment, or if fortune always smiled upon them, they would not get caught up in any superstition [*superstitione*]" (TTP, Preface, p. 3 [5]). For the philosopher this is a problematic claim since even if the philosopher does not always live a philosophical life, he does not return to superstition but is drawn by his affects. See the *Ethics*, V.20, Schol, II/293. See also Steven Frankel, "Politics and Rhetoric: The Intended Audience of Spinoza's *Tractatus Theologico-Politicus*," *The Review of Metaphysics*, Vol. 52, No. 4 (June 1999), p. 906, footnote 31.

11 On the other hand, from the point of view of the *Ethics*, superstition is a distortion of the true concept of God; Spinoza dedicates the appendix of the first part of the *Ethics* to an analysis of the falsehood in the concept of God among the multitude. See also "Metaphysical Thoughts," Curley, *The Collected Works of Spinoza*, p. 326.

12 Although Spinoza also does not develop a philosophy of history (this being the reason Hegel considered him as philosophically inadequate), he has a key role in the transition from "sacred history" to "secular history" in the modern period. Georg Wilhelm Friedrich Hegel, *Lectures on the History of Philosophy: Volume Three*. Translated by E.S. Haldane and F.H. Simson, London: Routledge, 1955, p. 288; Ben-Shlomo, "Reply to Professor Hampshire," in Rotenstreich and Schneider (eds), *Spinoza: His*

Thought and Work, Entretiens in Jerusalem, The Israel Academy of Sciences and Humanities, 1983, p. 145; and Smith, *Spinoza, Liberalism, and the Question of Jewish Identity*, pp. 84–118. Moreover, as Rosenthal has shown, the imagination in historical narrative fulfills a central role in the war of reason against the affects; not only in a social context, as described in the TTP, but also in a psychological context, as described in the *Ethics*. See Michael A. Rosenthal, "Spinoza and the Philosophy of History," in *Interpreting Spinoza: Critical Essays*. Edited by Charles Huenemann, Cambridge: Cambridge University Press, 2008, pp. 111–127.
13 At most it can be claimed that Spinoza is approaching here what Nietzsche calls "monumental history," i.e., "the knowledge that the great which once existed was at least *possible* once and may well again be possible sometime" (Friedrich Nietzsche, *On the Advantage and Disadvantage of History For Life*. Translated by Peter Preuss, Indiana: Hackett Publishing, 1980, Chapter 2, p. 16).
14 Maimonides also presents idolatry as a result of deterioration in the history of mankind. See the Mishneh Torah, *Book of Knowledge*, The Laws of the Worship of the Stars, Chapter 1. Regarding this matter, Spinoza follows not only Maimonides, as shown by Pines "Spinoza's *Tractatus Theological-Politicus*, Maimonides, and Kant," pp. 8–13, but also Hobbes, as argued by Halbertal. See Moshe Halbertal, *People of the Book: Canon, Meaning, and Authority*. Cambridge, MA: Harvard University Press, 1997, p. 138.
15 Regarding the institutionalization of religion and its domination of the political entity in the ancient Hebrew state, Spinoza posits: "As a result religion [*religio*] degenerated into a fatal superstition [*exitiabilem superstitionem*]" (TTP, XVIII, p. 231 [222]). It is also important here to note the differentiation between superstition and religion.
16 Spinoza's focus on the theological-political problem leads him in the TTP to adopt a more limited definition of religion than the one he presents in the *Ethics* (IV.37, Schol 1, II/236); a definition in whose framework not every action derived from knowledge of God is understood to be religion, but rather only action that is intended to ensure the stability of society.
17 For example, see the TTP Preface, p. 9 [10]; XIV, p. 241 [231].
18 For example, see Spinoza's harsh wording in the opening of the introduction to the *Political Treatise*; also see the TTP, VII, p. 114 [114].
19 In this context see Gideon Katz, *To the Core of Secularism: A Philosophical Analysis of Secularism in an Israeli Context*. Jerusalem: Yad Ben Zvi, 2011 [Heb.], pp. 143–145. Compare to Rebecca Goldstein, *Betraying Spinoza: The Renegade Jew Who Gave Us Modernity*. New York: Shocken, 2006, p. 121.
20 On the philosophical-cultural groundwork of Spinoza's esoteric writing in the TTP, see Strauss, *Persecution and the Art of Writing*, pp. 142–202. By contrast, in the *Ethics* Spinoza presents his philosophy (at least apparently) through a Euclidean model that requires transparency and clarity. Hence in the TTP and the *Ethics* Spinoza is revealed to be a master craftsman of dual meaning and double language as well as clarity and exactness. See Yovel, *Spinoza and Other Heretics*, p. 141. Also see the discussion of Spinoza's misleading writing style in the *Ethics* in Ran Sigad, *Philo-Sofia: On the Only Truth*. Tel Aviv: Dvir, 1983 [Heb.], pp. 56–57; and in his *Truth as Tragedy: Nietzsche, Spinoza, Kierkegaard, and Marcus Aurelius*. Jerusalem: Mosad Bialik, 1990 [Heb.], pp. 124–130.
21 Even without accepting Hermann Cohen's extreme accusation that Spinoza incited the Christian world against Judaism in order to exact revenge on the rabbis of Amsterdam who excommunicated him (see Hermann Cohen, "Spinoza über Staat und Religion, Judentum und Christentum," in B. Strauß (ed.), Jüdische Schriften, Berlin: Schwetschke, 1924, Vol. 3, pp. 290–372; Franz Nauen, "Hermann Cohen's Perception of Spinoza: A Re-appraisal," *AJS Review* 4 (1979), pp. 111–124), it is possible to claim that the philosopher, who set the motto "caution!" for himself, did not take the necessary caution in his presentation of Judaism. As such, as Siedler has shown, the

TTP was deployed as a new philosophical iteration of the old Christian hostility towards Judaism, and served as a transitional link in the history of hostility towards Judaism in an era that was no longer theological-Christian but had not yet been introduced to the anti-Semitic consequences of Darwin. See Meir Siedler, "Baruch Spinoza: The Designer of of the Image of Judaism in the European Enlightenment," *Daat*, 54 (2004) [Heb.], pp. 29–46. At the basis of the reading of the TTP that the European enlightenment adopted for itself are the two following claims: first, Judaism is a solely political religion, and as such is devoid of any spiritual-ethical element; and, second, with the destruction of the ancient Hebrew state there is no need for the continued existence of Judaism.

22 TTP, XIX, p. 247 [237]. These statements are made in the context of Chapter 19, though they refer to the entirety of the TTP.
23 On Spinoza's awareness of the danger involved in publishing the TTP, and the steps he and Jan Rieuwertsz, his publisher, took in order to protect themselves, see Nadler, *Spinoza: A Life*, pp. 269–270. The anonymous publication of the TTP did not prevent the identification of its author as Spinoza. See W.N.A. Klever, "Spinoza's Life and Works," in Garrett (ed.), *The Cambridge Companion to Spinoza*, Cambridge: Cambridge University Press, 1996, pp. 39–40; p. 45; Feuer, *Spinoza and the Rise of Liberalism*, p. 143. However, as Israel has shown, due to Rieuwertsz's well-oiled, underground mechanism of dissemination, the first editions of the TTP enjoyed unprecedented distribution in central and Western Europe in comparison to other banned texts. See Israel, *Radical Enlightenment*, pp. 273–285.
24 See Menachem Lorberbaum, "Spinoza's Theological-Political Problem," p. 207; also see Katz, *To the Core of Secularism*, p. 157.
25 The religious importance that Spinoza grants the direct, unmediated position of the individual facing God is demonstrated in his interpretation of the verse that he adopts as the motto of the TTP:

> "Hereby know that we dwell in him, and he in us, because he hath given us of his Spirit" (John, 4:13).... He [John] even concludes, because no one has seen God, that no one recognizes God or is aware of him other than through love of his neighbor, and hence that the only attribute of God that anyone can know is this love, so far as we share in it.
> (TTP, XIV, p. 181 [176])

Throughout the TTP Spinoza makes this claim even more radical when he states that "the spirit is in truth simply the mental peace which arises in the mind from good actions" (TTP, XV, p. 193 [188]). Here Spinoza comes close to equating God with moral action itself.
26 "[W]e are obliged to carry out absolutely all the commands of the sovereign power," Spinoza claims, "however absurd they may be" (TTP, XVI, p. 200 [194]).
27 In the first part of the TTP, Spinoza posits that the prophets not only "taught nothing out of the ordinary about the divine attributes, but rather had thoroughly commonplace conceptions of God" (TTP, II, p. 35 [37]). Additionally, he notes that "the minds of the prophets were directed exclusively to what is right and good" (TTP, II, p. 29 [31]) and "not for the sublimity and excellence of their intellects but for their piety and constancy" (ibid.).
28 In the first part of the TTP see pages 29–30 [31–32] and 35 [37]; in the second part of the TTP see pages 229 [220], 232 [223], and 234–235 [226].
29 See, for example, TTP, pages 19 [21], 63–64 [64–65] and 69–70 [70–71].
30 TTP, pp. 242–243 [232]. Titus Manlius Torquatus (fourth century BCE) was celebrated in the Roman tradition as an outstanding example of a military hero; he received the epithet "Torquatus" after he succeeded in tearing a necklace (torques) from the neck of a large Celtic soldier. In the TTP, Spinoza alludes to an event that occurred in 340 BCE in which his son, a Roman military officer, decided, in explicit opposition to the

38 *The first kind of knowledge*

command of his father the consul – the supreme commander of the military – to set out on an attack against the enemy. In response, Torquatus executed him with an axe. Cicero, in his book *On Moral Ends*, attributes to the representative of the Epicurean school, Lucius Manlius Torquatus, praise for the act of his ancestor, Titus Manlius Torquatus. The latter is depicted there as one who

> preferred the principle of obedience to those that bore the burden of office over the natural emotion of love for one's own son, and one who was bringing pain upon himself as a consequence of the need to preserve the authority of his military command ... providing for the security of his fellow citizens, and thereby – as he was well aware – for his own.
> (Cicero, *On Moral Ends*, I.35. Translated by R. Woolf, Cambridge: Cambridge University Press, 2001, p. 15)

This praise is consistent with the manner in which Spinoza chose to present Torquatus in the second part of the TTP.

31 According to Spinoza, since the multitude lacks the necessary capabilities for rational understanding – "great caution and perspicacity and supreme mental disciple" (TTP, V, p. 76 [77]) – the holy books, which were written for an entire people and later on for all of humanity, had to supply examples instead of a theoretical explanation of moral truths. However, the stories alone are not enough for the multitude who

> get more pleasure from stories and from strange and unexpected events than from the actual doctrine of histories. This is why, in addition to reading the histories, they also need pastors or church ministers to explain these to them, owing to the weakness of their understanding.
> (TTP, V, p. 78 [79])

32 TTP, pp. 183–184 [178–179]. While Spinoza quite clearly states the seven principles of revised religion (see ibid., pp. 182–183 [177–178]), he rejects a dogmatic position toward their interpretation. Moreover, according to Spinoza, the existence of different interpretations of the foundations of faith is not merely optional; rather, each person has an obligation to adapt the foundations of faith to his own worldview. The principles of revised religion are not as such either true or false; rather, they allow, with a deliberateness that finds expression in their vague and noncommittal formulation, both a false interpretation that suits the comprehension of the multitude, as well as a true explanation matching that of the philosopher. Pines sees in the principles of faith of the TTP a new beginning for the philosophy of religion. In his words:

> As far as I know, he [Spinoza] was chronologically the first philosopher who affirmed on doctrinal grounds that the dogmas which he propounded and recommended, but in no way considered as suprarational, do not and should not fall under the jurisdiction of theoretical reason.
> (Pines,"Spinoza's Tractatus," p. 35)

33 TTP, pp. 237–238 [228–229]. In ancient times, according to Spinoza, in order to achieve complete recognition of their sovereignty, kings "tried to persuade their people they were descended from the immortal gods" (ibid., p. 211 [204]). However, in our days "it is only where men become wholly barbarous [*prorsus barbari*] [that] they allow themselves to be so openly deceived" (ibid., p. 212 [205]). Therefore the equation of obedience to the state with obedience to God should, in our time, be presented in a more sophisticated and less blunt manner.

34 See, for example, TTP, p. 178 [173] and 238 [228–229]. Throughout the whole TTP, Spinoza takes care to point out the different dangers that arise from the ecclesiastics, and consequently adopts a harsh, severe tone. In the first part of the TTP he presents the ecclesiastics as enemies of philosophers and rationality, and in the second part he presents them as enemies of the rulers and the stability of society. After reading the

TTP, Hobbes notes to John Aubrey that he himself would not have dared to write in such a bold way. See John Aubrey, *Brief Lives*. Edited by Andrew Clarke, Oxford: Clarendon, 1898, p. 357.

35 TTP, p. 58 [59], *Justitia enim, ut communiter definitur, est constans et perpetua voluntas jus suum cuique tribuendi*. See also Letter 23, Curley, p. 387.
36 TTP, p. 203 [197], *Justitia est animi constantia tribuendi unicuique, quod ei ex jure civili competit.*
37 Spinoza returns a number of times to the contrast between reason and "[its] certain dictates" and between the "laws of appetite," according to which "everyone is drawn in different directions" (TTP, XVI, pp. 197–198 [191]). See page 45 [46]; see the definition of justice on pages 58–59 [59–60]; also see the differentiation between the wise and the impious on pages 66–67 [67–68].
38 Spinoza claims that the multitude would not be prepared to accept the authority of the philosophers even if it was limited only to the interpretation of the Scriptures (TTP, VII, p. 114 [114]). Despite this fundamental difference between Plato's *Republic* and Spinoza's TTP, it should be noted that the first project of Plato's ideal state, immediately following its physical establishment, is the founding of revised religion. See Michael Morgan, "Plato and Greek Religion," in *The Cambridge Companion to Plato*, Cambridge: Cambridge University Press, 1995, pp. 227–247. On the different incarnations of Platonic insight with respect to the close tie between religion and politics to Hobbes and Spinoza via Maimonides' and al-Farabi's medieval philosophy, see Menachem Lorberbaum, "Making Space for Leviathan: On Hobbes' Political Theory," *Hebraic Political Studies*, Vol. 2, No. 1, Winter 2007, pp. 82–83. See also, Carlos Fraenkel, *Philosophical Religions from Plato to Spinoza: Reason, Religion, and Autonomy*. Cambridge: Cambridge University Press, 2014.
39 Spinoza's turning to the ancient Hebrew state in order to extract from it a political lesson is not obvious, as Biale puts it:

> the assertion that the Jews were, above all, political geniuses was an astonishing claim to make in the seventeenth century. No other people appeared as politically feckless. By the same token, no one thought of the biblical Jews primarily in political terms but instead as religious precursors to Christianity. Thus, Spinoza turned the Bible, or at least the Bible as people understood it in his day, on its head: its contribution to world history was not in the realm of theology but in the realm of politics.
> (David Biale, *Not in the Heavens: The Tradition of Jewish Secular Thought.* Princeton: Princeton University Press, 2010, p. 100)

40 From here on brackets denote additions made by the author.
41 Complete imitation or rebuilding anew of the ancient Hebrew state are not possible; this is not for the explicit reason that Spinoza highlights: "But God has revealed through the Apostles that His covenant is no longer written in ink or on stone tablets but rather on the heart by the spirit of God" (TTP, XVIII, p. 230 [221]), but for another reason; Spinoza believed that the ancient Hebrew state was appropriate for the group of slaves who escaped Egypt, but could not be appropriate for the contemporary European society. Indeed, "it is only where men become wholly barbarous [*prorsus barbari*] that they allow themselves to be so openly deceived" (ibid., p. 212 [205]). Moreover, a complete imitation of the ancient Hebrew state is undesirable because love of the homeland was bought at the cost of hatred towards other peoples (ibid., pp. 223–223 [214–215]). Such hatred leads to international isolation that can benefit only a very few (ibid., p. 230 [221]).
42 Spinoza sides with democracy because "it seems to be the most natural and to be that which approaches most closely to the freedom nature bestows on every person" (TTP, p. 202, [195]). Spinoza claims that the equality which exists in the state of nature is preserved in a democracy because everyone defers their own rights to the rights of the

whole. For various interpretations of Spinoza's attitude towards democracy, see Israel, *Radical Enlightenment*, pp. 271–273; Stanley Rosen, "Spinoza's Argument for Political Freedom," *Cardozo Law Review* 25 (2003–2004), pp. 729–740; and Susan James, "Democracy and the Good Life in Spinoza's Philosophy," in Heunemann (ed.), *Interpreting Spinoza*. Cambridge: Cambridge University Press, 2008, pp. 128–146.

43 In a social context, as Victor Turner has shown in his analysis of Ndembu society, pairs of opposites create a situation in which

> the unity of such a pair is that of a tensed unity or *Gestalt*, whose tension is constituted by ineradicable forces or realities, implacably opposed, and whose nature as a unit is constituted and bounded by the very forces that contend within it. If these mutually involved irrepressibles belong together in a human being or a social group, they can constitute strong unities, the more so if both principles or protagonists in the conflict are consciously recognized and accepted.
> (Victor Turner, *The Ritual Process: Structure and Anti-Structure*. Chicago: Aldine Publishing Co., 1969, p. 83)

44 Contemporary scholars of Spinoza tend to disapprove of his fundamental opposition to rebellion against the ruler, even if he is a tyrant. For example, see Smith, *Spinoza, Liberalism*, pp. 197–198; Curley, "Kissinger, Spinoza, and Genghis Khan," in Garrett (ed.), *The Cambridge Companion to Spinoza*, Cambridge: Cambridge University Press, 1996, pp. 315–355; and Evyatar Levine, "A Note on Obedience to Law According to Spinoza's *Theological-Political Treatise*," *Iyyun: The Jerusalem Philosophical Quarterly* 28 (1978), pp. 292–296 [Heb.]. In this context also see Michael Della Rocca, "Getting His Hands Dirty: Spinoza's Criticism of the Rebel," in Melamed and Rosenthal (eds), *Spinoza's "Theological-Political Treatise": A Critical Guide*. Cambridge: Cambridge University Press, 2010, pp. 168–191.

45 TTP, XVII, pp. 208–212 [201–205].

46 Katz claims that more than trying to train the multitude, Spinoza seeks to urge them towards rational action. See Katz, *To the Core of Secularism*, Chapter 7.

47 This limitation, which the ecclesiastics placed on those holding the reins of power, brought Spinoza to speculate: "Perhaps also a leader abstained from novelties so far as he could, so that he would not be obliged to come before the high priest and suffer the indignity of standing in his presence" (TTP, XVII, p. 222 [214]).

48 Throughout the TTP, Spinoza is consistent in the grounding of his claims in utilitarian-realistic considerations. For example, he presents an intolerant regime as one that acts against itself, and claims that democracy is preferable over tyranny because the goal of the former is something that can be realized. See Smith, *Spinoza, Liberalism*, p. 24; and Julie Cooper, "Freedom of Speech and Philosophical Citizenship in Spinoza's *Theologicao-Political Treatise*," *Law, Culture and the Humanities* 2 (2006), pp. 91–114.

49 Spinoza emphasizes that the prophet is a private individual preaching a faith (TTP, XVIII, p. 232 [224]; XIX, p. 246 [236]). Therefore, despite that "we have no prophets in our day so far as I know," (ibid., I, p. 15 [16]) as he claims, it is important to discuss them in the context of the theological-political problem.

50 In the first part of the TTP Spinoza emphasizes the passive element in the figure of the biblical prophet as a mediator who brings the word of God to the people; and he blurs the active element of the biblical prophet who serves as the advocate of the people who debates with God and who deflects the evil of God's decrees. According to Yochanan Muffs, it is the active element of the figure of the prophet that is prominent in the Bible. Moses, for example, after the sin of the golden calf (Exodus 32) and the transgression of the spies (Deuteronomy 13–14), does not convey to the people God's decree of destruction, but debates God and succeeds in having it reversed. See Yochanan Muffs, *Love and Joy: Language, Law and Religion in Ancient Israel*. New York: Jewish Theological Seminary, 1995 [Heb.], Chapter 1.

51 Spinoza's two-sided relation to the biblical prophets does not fall in line with Levi's claim, according to which:

> seeing ancient Judaism only as a political group also led Spinoza to a doubtful interpretation of the Hebrew prophecy. Unlike the generally accepted opinion among modern historians and interpreters of the Bible (both Jewish and non-Jewish), Spinoza, the secular harbinger in biblical research, did not consider the social and anti-clerical content of the word of the prophets. Loyal to his philosophical viewpoint, which would not disobey the authorities, he saw the prophets principally as revolting against the monarchy and undermining the foundations of the state, as well as endangering its existence and stability.
> (Ze'ev Levi, *Spinoza and the Concept of Judaism*. Tel Aviv: Sifriyat Poalim, 1983 [Heb.], p. 32)

52 Even if in the TTP Spinoza denounces the personality cult of the ecclesiastics of revised religion, he does not denounce the presentation of role models, such as Jesus and Torquatus, in the public domain. See Cooper, "Freedom of Speech."
53 See Katz, *To the Core of Secularism*, p. 146.
54 In other places Spinoza also does not thematically discuss educational issues. On the role of imagination in the educational process according to Spinoza, see Genevieve Lloyd, "Spinoza and the Education of the Imagination," in Rorty (ed.), *Philosophers on Education*. London: Routledge, 1998, pp. 157–172.
55 From the foundations of faith in Chapter 14 of the TTP it is clear that there is no place in revised religion for polytheism. And this is in opposition to Smith's claim, according to which Spinoza opens the gates of the revised religion not only to monotheists but also to pagans. See Smith, *Spinoza, Liberalism*, p. 119. Moreover, despite that Spinoza does not call explicitly for censoring philosophical works, it is clear that for him, if these works clash with the foundations of faith of the revised religion, such censorship is necessary. In this context it can be assumed that Spinoza would have forbidden the dissemination of Nietzsche's writings because they clearly clash with the foundations of faith of the revised religion. In this context Garber presents a radical position according to which Spinoza's philosophy itself does not stand up to its own criteria for the publication of philosophical texts. As such, Spinoza should have, in a fundamental sense, avoided its publication. See Daniel Garber, "Should Spinoza Have Published His Philosophy?" in Huenemann (ed.), *Interpreting Spinoza: Critical Essays*. Cambridge: Cambridge University Press, 2008, p. 185 and on.
56 For a discussion of Spinoza's three different descriptions for the establishment of the state, see Den Uyl, *Power, State and Freedom*, pp. 20–38.
57 See Michael Waltzer, *Exodus and Revolution*. New York: Basic Books, 1985, p. 97.
58 Even the earth that opens its mouth and swallows the slanderers does not quiet the bitter resentment of the people who believed "that those men had been destroyed not by God who was their judge but rather by the craft of Moses" (TTP, XVII, p. 227 [219]). Spinoza derides Moses for preferring his own tribe, and also "must exclaim, in Tactius' words, that at that time 'God did not wish to save them but to punish them.'" (ibid., p. 226 [218]). Additionally, Spinoza posits that he cannot

> sufficiently express [his] amazement that there was so much anger in the divine mind, that He should actually make laws (which are normally designed to protect the honour, safety and security of all the people) to avenge himself and punish them.
> (Ibid.)

Spinoza does not refer here to the biblical god whose existence is negated in the framework of his metaphysics, but rather to Moses who in his anger over the sin of the golden calf anchored in the law a preference for his own tribe. See Biale, *Not in the Heavens*, pp. 98–99.

59 It is possible to distinguish three levels within the activity of the philosopher that parallel the three kinds of knowledge. In the first stage the philosopher realizes himself through the dimension of falsehood. The dimension of falsehood is the dimension of society and politics. Activity in this stage includes the link between the philosopher and the society of which he is a part. In this stage it is possible to locate the publication of the TTP. In the TTP Spinoza uses falsehood, among other things, in order to achieve comfort within the society in which he lives. It can be said that in the first stage the philosopher realizes himself via the multitude. In the second stage the philosopher realizes himself via his fellow man. Activity in this stage is based on the philosopher's relating morally to his fellow man. In the third stage the philosopher fulfills himself by identifying himself, his fellow man, and the society in which he lives with existence in its totality. Spinoza's activity in the framework of this stage is realized through his zealousness for privacy that enabled him to live in relative solitude (see IV.37, Schol 2 II/237; IV.73, Schol, II/265 and also V.30–31 II/299–300).

60 See Letter 30, Shirley, p. 185. Cooper links the anonymous publication of the TTP with the ideal of the anonymity of the philosopher in a democratic society. See Cooper, "Freedom of Speech."

61 Strauss' claim according to which Spinoza's addressee was the potential philosopher still bound by the chains of theology is only appropriate regarding the first part of the TTP. The addressees of the second part of the TTP, as Spinoza himself points out, are "some who hold high positions in my country" (Letter 13, Curley, p. 207). Nevertheless, Strauss is right to point out that Spinoza wrote the TTP in its entirety fully conscious that the multitude would also listen to his ideas. See Strauss, *Persecution and the Art of Writing*, pp. 162–163, p. 184.

62 According to Curley this is an invalid claim. There were tyrants, such as Stalin, whose rule lasted for a long duration; moreover, there were those like Hitler whose rule was short yet who caused massive damage. See Curley, "Kissinger, Spinoza and Genghis Khan," p. 334.

63 Here Spinoza adopts a biblical writing style that contains numerous repetitions of the same claim (behave morally!) accompanied by an abundance of historical proofs to corroborate it. See the TTP, V, pp. 75–78 [76–78]. Spinoza assumes that politicians are not philosophers, and therefore they must be addressed through rhetorical writing that is not based on rational explanation.

64 This conclusion is in opposition with the position of various commentators of the TTP who tend to blur the model of moral religion that Spinoza presents in the first part of the TTP, and claim, based on the second part alone, that Spinoza's revised religion is none other than religion serving as a means to assist in fulfilling the goals of the political authority. In this way they tend to criticize Spinoza for glorifying the authority and supremacy of the state while neglecting its restraint and moderation. Yovel presents this critique as follows:

> Such a program has its dangers. Spinoza leaves too vague the difference between educating and manipulating the multitude; he gives far too little thought to the need for checks and balances that would disperse the concentrated power of the state without compromising its authority or dividing its sovereignty. More generally, he pays little heed to the danger of a despotism of reason, a concept that Spinoza must have deemed incoherent, but which historical experience has since validated and to which Spinoza's theory is not sufficiently immune.
>
> (Yovel, *Spinoza and Other Heretics*, p. 135)

Also see Smith, *Spinoza, Liberalism*, pp. 197–198; and Levi, *Spinoza and the Concept of Judaism*, pp. 11–43. Edwin Curley, who sharpens this critique by focusing on the reduction of the right to power in the TTP, summarizes one of his studies of Spinoza's political philosophy with the following statement: "That the notion of natural right (not coextensive with power) disappears in Spinoza seems to me still to be a defect in his political philosophy, sympathetic though I may be to the arguments which lead to that result" (Curley, "Kissinger, Spinoza, and Genghis Khan," p. 335). This position was shared by Motzkin, who states in reference to Spinoza that "No one has declared with greater freedom or clarity that justice (i.e., right) and power are the same: 'Might makes right'" (Aryeh Leo Motzkin, "A Note on Natural Right, Nature, and Wisdom for Spinoza," *Iyyun: The Jerusalem Philosophical Quarterly* 28 (1978) [Heb.], p. 73). Levine is even more radical when he concludes his paper on obedience to law in the TTP with the following words:

> About twenty years after the publication of Leviathan by Hobbes, Spinoza links the authority of the legislator to a "social covenant with the grace of God." Unlike Hobbes, he does not permit under any circumstances an act which is inconsistent with it. Shaking off the absolute rule of the Church comes about at the price of absolute subjugation to the supreme secular authority, to the ruler and the state: to the law as it is.... Everything is forbidden, unless it is permitted by law, including rebellion, protest, and criticism – all this, as opposed to the true goal of Spinoza, as defined on the title page of the Treatise.
> (Levin, "A Note on Obedience to Law," p. 296)

65 See Lorberbaum, "Spinoza's Theological-Political Problem," pp. 203–204.
66 Strauss, *Persecution and the Art of Writing*, pp. 162–163; see also Eugene Sheppard, *Leo Strauss and the Politics of Exile: The Making of a Political Philosopher*. Waltham, MA: Brandeis University Press, 2006, p. 49 and on.
67 Katz employs Clifford Geertz's distinction between the "work of the text" and "traditionalism" in order to trace how on the one hand Spinoza seeks to undermine institutional religion by uprooting its hermeneutic infrastructure, while on the other hand he seeks to cultivate and enhance the traditional religiosity that emerged organically from the continuous trajectory of society. Institutional religion is closed and in principle is inaccessible to all the members of society, as such it is dependent on the decisions of a small elite that is immune from any criticism. In contrast, the softened religion that Spinoza offers is open, "borne by the layman and not restricted to a text and its interpretation but is cast as a simple concept in the heart of every man" (Katz, *To the Core of Secularism*, p. 151). Therefore, it is important for Spinoza to adapt the existing religion to reason, without imposing upon it an external rational structure alien to it. Thus, he seeks to enhance the tradition already rooted in society and to strengthen it, "to divert accepted models and to create conditions for the crystallization of a more rationally ordered society" (ibid., p. 153).
68 It should be noted in this context that in Chapter 14 on the foundations of faith, there is not the slightest hint of the authority of the ruler over matters of faith.
69 Also see Alexander Koyré, *Discovering Plato*. Translated by Alexandre Rosenfield and Leonora Cohen, New York: Columbia University Press, 1968, Chapter 1; and Alexander Nehamas, "Meno's Paradox and Socrates as a Teacher," in Day (ed.), *Plato's Meno in Focus*, London: Routledge, 1994, pp. 172–207.

Part II
The contradictions in the concept of God in the second kind of knowledge

Introduction

The concept of God in the revised religion belongs to the first kind of knowledge. As such, it is not meant to be a true concept from a rational point of view, but rather an effective concept from a social point of view. Therefore, the concept of God in the revised religion is not destroyed but *constructed* through the contradiction in its being at once positioned as an entirely moral concept on the one hand, and an entirely political concept on the other. Indeed, as we saw in Part I, it is this very theoretical contradiction that in fact succeeds in ensuring the stability of society. By contrast, the concept of God in the second kind of knowledge, which will be the focus of the present part of the book, is meant to be free of any contradiction. The ascent from the first kind of knowledge to the second kind is presented by Spinoza as liberation from falsehood and as the attainment of truth (II.41, II/123). Furthermore, not only does the truth "not contradict the truth" (Letter 21, Curley, p. 376) but it is also "absurd" to claim, as Spinoza explicitly asserts in the *Ethics*, that "a Being absolutely infinite and supremely perfect," namely, God, "would involve a contradiction" (I.P11 Alt. Dem. II/53).

Indeed, in the *Ethics* Spinoza promises to lead us down a strict, logical path to the one and only truth about God or existence in its entirety; a truth that is a necessary condition, even if not sufficient, to attain the blessing of happiness and redemption in the third kind of knowledge. However, as we will see in the following chapters, as soon as we reach out our hand to reason and seek to march in a straight geometric line with meticulous and strict logical consistency, we become entangled in circular reasoning as a flood of logical contradictions bear upon us from every direction. The repetitive textual appearances of contradiction and circular reasoning in the concept of the God of reason, as we will aim to demonstrate, are not the outcome of a philosophical failure on the part of Spinoza; contrarily, the contradictions are an expression of his fundamental understanding of the concept of God. Accordingly, we must clarify in a thorough and in-depth way the position of these contradictions in the second kind of knowledge. In order to do so we will begin the discussion with an examination of the definition of God that Spinoza presents in the *Ethics*.

The idea of God as a true idea

The first part of the *Ethics* is dedicated to a critical analysis of the concept of God, which serves as the organizing concept of theology. Spinoza understands the theological concept of God as false and as belonging to the first kind of knowledge. However, he does not claim that the concept of God in and of itself is a false concept, and as such should be dismissed. On the contrary, Spinoza concludes that the concept of God is indeed true and of the highest importance, but claims it had hitherto been imbued with an incorrect and distorted meaning. Therefore, Spinoza annexes the concept of God to his philosophy in the same way he appropriates other foundational concepts of the philosophical and religious traditions; he apparently accepts their validity but changes their meaning.[1]

Spinoza seeks to transform the idea of God from a false idea to a true one; in other words, an idea that "agree[s] with its object" (*cum suo ideato*) (I, A6, II/47). But what is the object with which an idea of God agrees? What ensures this agreement? The answer to these questions is found in Spinoza's definition of God.

> By God I understand a being absolutely infinite, i.e., a substance consisting of an infinity of attributes, of which each one expresses an eternal and infinite essence.
>
> (I, D6, II/45)

Existence is that object which agrees with the idea of God; the agreement between the idea of God and existence is determined by Spinoza by definition. God is defined as the true idea of existence. The definition casts the existence of God within the mold of a tautology; and indeed it follows from this definition that the existence of God is none other than the existence of existence.[2] Therefore, Spinoza, who attributes to God's existence the "greatest certainty" (I.11, Schol, II/54), claims in the *Treatise on the Emendation of the Intellect* that those who cast doubt on God's existence "have nothing but the name, or they feign something which they call God; this does not agree with the nature of God."[3]

The polemical meaning of the definition of God

Careful writing requires careful reading! This basic rule is valid in all of the territories of the *Ethics*, though it is particularly valid regarding the opening definitions of Spinoza's Euclidean work. Indeed, a careful reading of Spinoza's definition of God reveals that it is not made of one piece but is instead comprised of two different definitions of God: a *traditional* definition at the beginning ("a being absolutely infinite") and a *philosophical* definition at the end ("a substance consisting of an infinity of attributes, of which each one expresses an eternal and infinite essence").[4] The philosophical definition is valid as it bases the concept of God on concepts whose meaning has already been determined by the preceding definitions. Contrarily, the traditional definition of God is invalid as it relies on the concept of being, which has not been defined and will not be defined anywhere else in the *Ethics*. Spinoza's definition of God, therefore, seemingly merely exchanges an undefined concept ("God") for another undefined concept ("a being absolutely infinite").

The insertion of the traditional definition of God in the lexicon of philosophical terms in the *Ethics* is perplexing; yet it is possible to explain this as an inseparable part of Spinoza's continuous and mostly concealed struggle with the theological position. Beyond the validity and consistency of his definition of God, Spinoza prefers to refute the theological concept of God not via rejection of its characteristics (i.e., infiniteness, freedom, perfection and eternalness), but rather via a complete acceptance of them. Therefore, as Spinoza writes: "By God I understand a being absolutely infinite, i.e., a substance consisting of infinity of attributes, of which each one expresses an eternal and infinite essence" (I, D6, II/45). He seemingly turns to us, the readers, stating that the critical analysis he will present during the course of the first part of the *Ethics* will demonstrate that a philosophical definition of God ("a substance consisting of an infinity of attributes") is none other than the true meaning of the theological definition of God ("a being absolutely infinite").[5] Thus, Spinoza seemingly presents the definition of God in the *Ethics* like a Trojan horse at the gate of the theological fortress. Every theologian will definitely accept the definition of God as an infinite being, but no theologian will accept, at least in a simple sense, Spinoza's conclusion that God and nature are equivalent: *deus sive natura* (*Ethics*, preface to Part IV). Identifying the concept of God with the concept of being, guarantees that God's existence will have the absolute certainty that theology demands. However, this certainty comes at a price. The positioning of the concept of existence in place of the concept of God uproots the traditional dichotomy between God and the world from which the different limbs of theology branch out, such as: the idea of creation, the separation of the material world from God and the transcendence of God. Additionally, Spinoza's equating God with existence completely annuls the possibility of conducting the relationship between God and man as it is perceived in the framework of the Scriptures and the theological literature that followed. Therefore, it is possible to claim that through the definition of God in the *Ethics* Spinoza is celebrating his victory over theology in its own conceptual playing field.

On the metaphysical and textual elusiveness of the concept of existence in the *Ethics*

From Spinoza's definition of God one can see the flicker of the polemical characteristic of the entire first part of the *Ethics*, which was dedicated to the presentation of the philosophical concept of God intended to replace the theological concept.[6] Examining Spinoza's understanding of divinity is to examine his concept of existence; indeed, for Spinoza, God and existence are one and the same. However, despite the fact that the concept of existence is the central concept of Spinoza's philosophy, any attempt to clarify its meaning places us in front of a considerable difficulty. The concept of existence appears explicitly or implicitly in all of the definitions of the first part of the *Ethics*; however, as mentioned above, it is not directly defined by Spinoza in the first part, nor anywhere else in the *Ethics* for that matter. The textual elusiveness of the concept of existence in the *Ethics* perfectly expresses its metaphysical elusiveness. On the one hand, the meaning of existence seems to us to be trivial. Our existence, as well as the existence of all things around us, instills in us the sense that we know the meaning of what it is to exist. This feeling is present in our use of the concept of existence in the framework of everyday language, and it grants the concept of existence the status of a coin passing hands in the market of non-critical discourse. On the other hand, when we are required to explain existence, we are revealed to be powerless. To explain something is to relate it to something else, but every time we attempt to explain the concept of existence we get caught up in circular argumentation. Indeed, every thing to which we try to relate the concept of existence already exists. The concept of existence, therefore, is a concept that we adopt from habit alone; and there is nothing more doubtful than habit: "We see therefore, that all the notions by which ordinary people are accustomed to explain nature are only modes of imagining, and do not indicate the nature of anything, only the constitution of the imagination" (*Ethics*, Appendix to Part I, pp. 445–446).

With the definitions of the first part of the *Ethics*, Spinoza marches in two opposite directions. On the one hand, he shines light on the concept of existence via the presentation of its necessary characteristics in the framework of the different definitions; but on the other hand Spinoza takes care to keep the concept of existence in the dark by intentionally avoiding defining it. Come what may of the motivations for this intentional avoidance – and we will attempt to understand them during the course of the discussion – Spinoza is in fact laying on us, the readers, the task of clarifying the meaning of the concept of existence through an analysis of its necessary characteristics and an examination of the relation between them. Actually, because the concept of existence is the organizing concept of the *Ethics*, its elucidation is none other than the elucidation of the meaning of the *Ethics* itself. The interpretive challenge that Spinoza places before the reader betrays the true form of his composition. A kind of philosophical writing that does not provide its conclusions in an orderly way, but rather places the task of extracting its meaning on the reader, is not Euclidean but Socratic.[7] Therefore, Spinoza's Euclidean proclamation on the title page, and his forming the text in a geometric cast, are the means by which he provides the *Ethics*, a profoundly Socratic text, with a Euclidean mask.[8] According to this reading, even if the *Ethics* is a monologue in form, its internal philosophical logic is dialogic.[9] We will now turn to explore Spinoza's concept of God, which is none other than his concept of existence, and we will do so through an attempt to join together all the parts of the *Ethics*. We will begin in the same place in which Spinoza does, the definition of "cause of itself" (I, D1, II/45), which we will examine in the following chapter in the framework of our discussion of Spinoza's concept of causality and the contradictions embedded within it.

Notes

1 See Amos Funkenstein, "Comment on R. Popkin's Paper," in Force and Popkin (eds), The Books of Nature and Scripture: Recent Essays on Natural Philosophy, Theology and Biblical Criticism in the Netherlands of Spinoza's Time and the British Isles of Newton's Time, Dordrecht: Kluwer, 1994, pp. 21–23; Amos Funkenstein, Styles of Medieval Biblical Exegesis. Tel Aviv: Misrad Habitachon, 1990 [Heb.], p. 75. This annexation is conducted in a distinct manner in the first six chapters of the TTP, where Spinoza, through an original interpretation of Scripture, suggests a revolutionary meaning to the three foundational concepts of the revealed monotheistic religion: prophecy, law, and divine providence. See Strauss, Persecution, pp. 165–166. Despite Spinoza's frequent use of scholastic concepts, only in one place in the Ethics (I.24, Cor) does he explicitly declare that he is adopting a scholastic term.

2 Asserting God's existence in his definition turns the demonstrations of God's existence (which appear in the demonstrations and scholium to proposition I.11) into pseudo-demonstrations that again and again reaffirm the concept of God as a concept that connotes existence. In this context Mason posits: "the function of 'proof' – *demonstratio* – is more like one of dismantling a clock to demonstrate how its parts work together" (*The God of Spinoza*, p. 35).

3 Curley, *Collected Works*, footnote to paragraph 54, p. 24. In the TTP Spinoza uses the following example in order to clarify this claim:

> For just as someone who does not comprehend a triangle properly does not know that its three angles are equal to two right angles, so anyone with a confused conception of the divine nature does not see that it belongs to the nature of God to exist.
> (TTP, Annotation 6, p. 262 [252])

This example also appears in Letter 21 to Blijenbergh, Curley p. 375.

4 For a survey of the conception of God as an infinite being in medieval theology see Harry Austryn Wolfson, *The Philosophy of Spinoza*. Cambridge, MA: Harvard University Press, 1983, Vol. 1, pp. 133–141.

5 The full meaning of the concept of God, like the other concepts in the first part of the *Ethics*, is revealed only by taking into account all the logical conclusions that are deduced from it. Indeed, as Hampshire claims:

> In any such deductive system, containing terms endowed by exact definition with meanings which may be remote from their current meanings, the significance of the initial propositions can be understood only in light of their logical consequences in the later propositions; one has to travel round the whole circle at least once before one can begin to understand any segment of it.
> (Stuart Hampshire, *Spinoza*. London: Penguin Books, 1981, p. 55)

6 In the guise of geometrical order Spinoza conducts additional veiled polemics. For example, during the course of the opening of the first part of the *Ethics* that aims at demonstrating the monism of the substance, Spinoza embeds a polemic against the Cartesian camp. Spinoza, as Yovel claims,

> makes use at the beginning of the *Ethics* of a language that apparently recognizes the existence of many substances, and brings a refutation to this position, and then – and only then – does the foundational Spinozian truth burst forth regarding the uniqueness of the substance and the equivalence of god and the world. This indirect path would certainly have been unnecessary had things been written from 'the perspective of eternity,' without the involvement of additional interests, and without the dialectical need to convince others.
> (Yovel's translation of the *Ethics*, p. 44)

50 *The second kind of knowledge*

7 For a discussion of the structure and logic of the Socratic dialogues see Chapter 1 in Alexander Koryé, *Discovering Plato*. It could be that Spinoza was stylistically influenced by Maimonides' *Guide of the Perplexed*. In any case, Spinoza is more Aristotelian than his sworn enemy; indeed, as opposed to Maimonides he does not declare his stylistic tendency and he does not implore the reader to carefully join together the chapters of his work from fear that "that which he [the reader] understood me to say might be contrary to my intention. He thus would harm me in return for my having wanted to benefit him and would repay evil for good" (Maimonides, *The Guide of the Perplexed*. Translated by Shlomo Pines, Chicago: University of Chicago Press, 1974, p. 15). Spinoza stoically risks the danger that his philosophy might be distorted in later generations only so that he would not be dependent on his readers and be forced to seek their interpretive grace; this is a risk even Nietzsche, who praises the isolation of the philosopher, was not prepared to take. For a comparison between Spinoza and Nietzsche on this point see Sigad, *Truth as Tragedy*, pp. 130–132. See also Shai Frogel, *Ethics: Spinoza and Nietzsche*. Jerusalem: Carmel, 2009 [Heb.].

8 For a comprehensive examination of Spinoza's Socratic tendencies see Sigad, *PhiloSofia*, pp. 56–86. In referring to the possibility of applying to the *Ethics* the tools of analysis that Spinoza suggests for Scripture, Curley posits:

> No doubt Spinoza thought these rules applied only to works which, like Scripture, are inherently obscure, not to works which, like Euclid's geometry, are inherently intelligible. No doubt, also, he would have classed his own work with Euclid's. But three hundred years of Spinoza scholarship have amply demonstrated that he was too optimistic about the intelligibility of his work.
>
> (*Collected Works*, pp. xi–xii, footnote 6)

9 In this context it should be noted that in his early work, Short *Treatise on God, Man, and His Well-Being*, which reveals several of the deeper trends in his system that are blurred for various reasons in the *Ethics*, Spinoza integrates substantial dialogues. See Curley, *Collected Works*, pp. 67–73. However, also in the *Ethics* itself Spinoza adopts, in his own way, Hume's position in *Dialogues Concerning Natural Religion* according to which the study of God "seems to lead us naturally into the style of dialogue and conversation" (David Hume, *Dialogues Concerning Natural Religion*. London: Merchant Books, 2009, p. 30). Given the Socratic character of the *Ethics*, Hume's later statements are no less important:

> Concerning these [enquiries of the nature of god], human reason has not yet reached any certain determination: But these are topics so interesting, that we cannot restrain our restless enquiry with regard to them; though nothing but doubt, uncertainty and contradiction, have, as yet, been the result of our most accurate researches.
>
> (Ibid., p. 30)

2 Spinoza's conception of causality and the first two contradictions in the system
(1) infiniteness *or* finiteness;
(2) immanence *or* transcendence

In the preceding chapter it became clear that a proper understanding of Spinoza's conception of God, which is none other than his conception of existence, requires that we take into account the many and variegated references to this issue throughout the *Ethics*. In the present chapter we will examine Spinoza's understanding of causality, which stands at the center of his understanding of existence. Indeed, according to Spinoza, all the details in existence are pinned down in an infinite causal chain in which each one of them constitutes both a cause and an effect (I.36, II/77), while existence in its entirety is the cause of itself (I, D1, II/45)

Spinoza's strict concept of logical causality that is embedded in his axiom of causality (I, A4, II/46) and in its various textual offshoots (Preface to Part IV, p. 543; III.56, Dem, II/184; and I.8, Schol 2, I/49), determines that everything that is in an effect is derived from within the cause because the latter is the essence, nature and definition of the effect. Moreover, as becomes clear at the end of the first part of the *Ethics* (I.33, Schol 2, II/74), from the application of the axiom of causality to the concept of God in that it is the cause of itself, it follows that there is total equivalence between cause and effect.

However, Spinoza's positions on two fundamental issues in his philosophy directly contradict what would seem to follow from applying the axiom of causality to God: first, the existence of finite things following from the infinite (I.28, II/69 in conjunction with II, Def 7, II/85) contradicts the equivalence in the order of magnitude between cause and effect that is required by the application of the axiom of causality to God; second, Spinoza's contradictory answers to the question of whether or not everything that is in the cause is also in the effect – when God is the cause and the world is the effect – leads him to establish in the *Ethics* two concepts alongside each other that also exclude one another, the one immanent (see, for example, I.33, Schol 2, II/74) while the second is transcendent (for example, I.1, II/47). The first concept falls in line with the application of the axiom of causality to God, while the second contradicts it completely. Following the uncovering of these contradictions, at the end of the chapter we will conduct an initial discussion of their status in Spinoza's philosophical system. However, before turning to examine the causal relations between existence in its entirety and the details of

52 *The second kind of knowledge*

existence, it is necessary to examine the causal relations between existence and itself, relations that are presented to us immediately in the very first definition of the *Ethics*.

Cause of itself

Spinoza chooses to open the *Ethics* in a perplexing way. The first definition that he presents to us, the readers, is a concept that philosophically seems utterly unfounded: "cause of itself" (*causa sui*). While cause and effect are concepts that relate to two different objects that are connected by a causal link, the concept "cause of itself," posits the same object as both cause and effect. Abolishing the gap between cause and effect turns the concept "cause of itself," at least seemingly, into a worthless hybrid concept. Moreover, the concept "cause of itself" raises the suspicion that it infiltrated Spinoza's philosophy from theological thought, which Spinoza radically criticized.[1] Spinoza's definition of "cause of itself" only strengthens this suspicion:

> By cause of itself [*causa sui*] I understand that whose essence involves existence, *or* that whose nature cannot be conceived except as existing.
> (I, D1, II/45)

Instead of moderating the paradoxical nature of "cause of itself" by reducing its scope of applicability, Spinoza posits it as a necessary characteristic of existence in its entirety and therefore maximally expands the concept's scope of applicability. The definition of "cause of itself," like Spinoza's other definitions, is not a neutral one.[2] There are embedded, within Spinoza's definitions, basic metaphysical claims through which he seeks to answer traditional philosophical questions, such as the question of God, the question of the good life etc.[3] In the opening definition of the *Ethics*, we already find embedded the claim that the logic of the causality of existence in its entirety is the opposite of the logic of the causality of the details of existence. Indeed, Spinoza makes this point explicitly later on in the discussion:

> [T]his cause, on account of which a thing exists, either must be contained in the very nature and definition of the existing thing (*viz. that it pertains to its nature to exist*) or must be outside it.
> (I.8, Schol 2, II/50)

According to Spinoza, everything that exists is both effect and cause. There is no thing that has no cause. Indeed, "there must be, for each existing thing, a certain cause on account of which it exists" (ibid.).[4] However, there should be a distinction made between the causality of existence and the causality of the details of existence. For every thing in existence there is a cause that is external to it, but the cause of existence in its entirety is within existence itself.[5] The existence of existence is tautological because existence is the cause of itself. Existence is the cause of itself in the same sense that it is the effect of itself. Therefore, it is necessary for the logic of the causality of existence to be the opposite of the logic of the causality of the details of existence inasmuch as existence, in its order of magnitude, is the opposite of the details of existence.[6] This is the philosophical explication we are required to grant to Spinoza's claim, which is presented in the garb of a geometric definition, that one of the necessary characteristics of existence is "cause of itself."[7] Spinoza must describe existence through a concept that in a Nietzschean spirit can be labelled a "threatening logical monster,"[8] because existence in its entirety is a monstrous entity; it is completely different from all other entities known to us in the framework of regular experience, which provides us with fragments of existence rather than existence itself. Therefore, at least at this stage of our inquiry, despite the seemingly non-critical reliance on the concept of "cause of itself," Spinoza's use of it withstands philosophical criticism.

The axiom of causality, its textual offshoots and its application to the concept of God

Spinoza does not limit himself to allotting a special causal logic to existence in its entirety. An examination of the causal relations between existence itself and its details – i.e., between the substance and the modes – reveals the *distinctness* of existence in its entirety to have further far-reaching implications. The nature of the causality between the substance and its modes should be examined in light of Spinoza's basic insight regarding causality, which he presents as an axiom (hereafter: the axiom of causality)

> The knowledge of an effect depends on, and involves, the knowledge of its cause.
>
> (I, A4, II/46)

From this axiom and its textual offshoots (see below), it follows that knowledge of a determined thing depends on knowledge of its cause, since every thing that is in the effect is derived from the cause. Indeed, if we adjoin references scattered throughout the *Ethics* (hereafter: the textual offshoots of the axiom of causality), we can assert that the cause is the nature, essence and definition of the effect:

a   The cause constitutes the nature of the effect: "For nothing belongs to the nature of anything except what follows from the necessity of the nature of the efficient cause" (IV, Preface, II/208).
b   The cause is the essence of the effect from the validity of the equivalence that Spinoza asserts between nature and essence: "essence, *or* nature" (*essentia, seu natura*) (III.56, Dem, II/185).[9]
c   The cause is also the definition of the effect according to Spinoza's definition that equates the nature of a thing with its definition: "the true definition

of each thing neither involves nor expresses anything except the nature of the thing defined" (I.8, Schol 2, II/50).[10]

Moreover, from the application of the axiom of causality to the concept of God, the cause of itself, it follows not only that every thing in the effect is also in the cause, but also that every thing in the cause is also in the effect, as God is both the cause and the effect of himself. Therefore, there exists a total equivalence between God and his decrees, according to *Ethics*, I.33, Schol 2, which we will treat at length in the following sections.[11]

The first contradiction in the application of the axiom of causality to God: an infinite begets a finite

Logically, the application of the axiom of causality to God requires equivalence in the order of magnitude between God and what follows from him. Thus the fact that God is at the point of departure of Spinoza's philosophy should have transformed it into a philosophy of the infinite. If all that exists follows from God, and God is infinite, all that exists must also be infinite. And indeed, the meaning that propositions 21–23 in the first part impose on proposition I.16, the famous proposition pertaining to the things that follow from God, falls in line with the logical demand for equivalence in the order of magnitude between cause and effect. The mediated and immediate modes are infinite in that their causes are infinite. From propositions I.21–23, it follows that God maintains his infiniteness in all of his appearances. God bequeaths his infiniteness to all things that follow from him.[12] However, in the corollary of proposition I.25, Spinoza, not only contradicts the unique axiom of causality of his system, but causes a real logical scandal when he casually posits:

> Particular things are nothing but affections of God's attributes, *or* modes by which God's attributes are expressed in a certain and determinate way.
> (I.25, Cor, II/68)

The scandal here is two-fold: first, Spinoza abruptly informs us of the existence of finite things in his system without any preceding explanation and with a total disregard for his geometric obligation.[13] As we have already seen in knowledge bound by logical necessity, there is no place for finite things, and there cannot be place for them in Spinoza's philosophical system, which is supposed to be a philosophy of the infinite. Thus, it seems that it is not by means of the process of rational consideration that the finite enters Spinoza's philosophy, but by breaking in as though stealing across the border from the territory of everyday experience that is populated with confused and erroneous understandings (II.40, Schol 2, II/122); second, the fact that finite things suddenly appear in an arbitrary way in Spinoza's philosophy does not damage their status. On the contrary, Spinoza asserts that it is by means of finite things that attributes of God, which are infinite in their kind, are expressed (*exprimuntur*) (I, D6, and the explanation there,

II/45). However, a finite thing expressing the infinite is a logical impossibility that has no place in any philosophical system that recognizes the existence of the finite and infinite as excluding one another; all the more so in Spinoza's philosophy, which posits that things that are not connected by a causal link are "[t]hings that have nothing in common with one another" (I, A5, II/46; see also I.3). Consequently, in order for the finite to express the infinite there must be something in common between them, but in order to have something in common, the finite must be the effect of the infinite. Yet from Spinoza's axiom of causality and its textual offshoots, in order to be the effect of the infinite the finite must itself be infinite, which is a contradiction.

Spinoza does not explicitly assert that the infinite is the cause of the finite, though this assertion, and the contradiction within it, stem from the combination of two other assertions in his philosophy. According to one, the cause of every finite thing is another finite thing whose cause is also finite, "and so on, to infinity" (I.28, II/69). According to the second, when several causes beget one effect they should all be understood as one cause (II, D7, II/85). It thus follows that the cause of the finite thing is God in that he is infinite.[14]

Examining the causal relation between the substance and the modes brings up the contradiction as its principal finding. The *Ethics* contains both the claim according to which cause and effect are equal to one another, as well as the claim according to which cause and effect exclude one another, regarding their order of magnitude. The first claim results from the application of the axiom of causality and its textual offshoots to God, and the second claim results from positioning the infinite as the cause of the finite as well as from the accompanying assertion according to which the finite expresses the infinite. On the one hand, we are told it is impossible for the infinite to be the cause of the finite; on the other hand, we are told the infinite is necessarily the cause of the finite. Whatever the explanation for this contradiction may be, and we will attempt to clarify it below, Spinoza lays before us, the readers, as a textual fact, a philosophical work that contains two contradictory conceptions of the relations between cause and effect regarding God. And Spinoza's conception of causality suffers from an internal contradiction not only regarding the order of magnitude of cause and effect, but also regarding his inconsistent answers to the question: is every thing that is in the cause also in the effect in the context of the relations between God and what follows from him? This brings us to the following contradiction in the application of the axiom of causality to God: the contradiction between immanence and transcendence.

The second contradiction in the application of the axiom of causality to God: the contradiction between immanence and transcendence

Spinoza shakes the foundations of Western culture through the application of his axiom of causality to God. Indeed, removing the gap between cause and effect in the traditional causal pair God/world leads Spinoza to establish, for the first time in modern thought, what can be called a "philosophy of immanence."[15] By applying the axiom of causality to God as the cause of the world, it follows that God comes to full realization in the world. There is therefore no transcendent world, nor a transcendent God. This world is all that exists and in it we must anchor every thing that has meaning for us. Applying the axiom of causality to God, therefore, forms the basis of Spinoza's immanent position. However, as we have seen, Spinoza does not fully uphold the application of his axiom of causality to God. In fact, he abandons it, not someplace deep in the forest of the *Ethics*, but immediately in the opening proposition of the book, in which he declares:

> A substance is prior in nature to its affections.
>
> (I.1, II/47)

The preceding of the substance in nature before its affections, which according to definition (I, D5, II/45) are none other than its modes, must assume that the substance contains something that is not within the modes that follow from it. However, this assumption contradicts the application of the axiom of causality to God from which it follows, as we saw earlier, that all that is in God must appear in all that follows from him. Additionally, the first proposition of the *Ethics* that posits that the substance precedes its affectations in nature assumes that it is possible to separate the substance and the modes that follow from it, or, to speak in theological terms, that it is possible to separate God and his decrees. This assumption stands in complete contradiction to Spinoza's claim that such a separation is impossible:

> God was not before his decrees [*sua decreta*], and cannot be without them.
>
> (I.33 Schol 2, II/75)

God does not precede his modes temporally or ontologically. This precedence has no place in the framework of the logical equivalence that arises from the application of the axiom of causality on God's relations with what follows from him. Spinoza, who claims to approach the issue of causal links between God and the world in a philosophical and critical manner, should have utterly rejected the idea of transcendence, the organizing principle of theology. However, as it turns out, Spinoza rejects transcendence with one hand while embracing it with the other. Two additional examples demonstrate Spinoza's grasping of both ends of the rope in this context:

a   While in the second scholium to proposition I.33 Spinoza adheres to an immanent position according to which it is not possible to separate between the substance and its affects, in the demonstration to proposition I.5, he takes the transcendent position, positing that the substance "in itself" (*in se*) is distinguished from its affections.

b   While total equivalence between the cause and the effect, which is derived from the application of the axiom of causality on God, upholds Spinoza's immanent position, in the *Ethics* I.17, Scholium (II/63), Spinoza makes a distinctly transcendent claim:

> [S]ince God's intellect is the only cause of things (viz. as we have shown, both of their essence and of their existence), he must necessarily differ from them both as to his essence and as to his existence. For what is caused differs from its cause precisely in what it has from the cause.
>
> (Ibid.)

God's intellect is not equal to the things that follow from him in that he is their cause.[16] On the contrary, it is entirely different from them. The conception of causality that Spinoza adopts here is in total opposition with the application of his axiom of causality on God:

> [T]he thing that is the cause both of the essence and of the existence of some effect, must differ from such an effect, both as to its essence and as to its existence.
>
> (Ibid.)

From the conception of causality Spinoza adopts here ensues a logical necessity that not only God's intellect, but God himself, is completely different from all the things that follow from him in that he is the cause of both their essence (I.25, II/67) and their existence (I.24, Cor, II/67). However, in the present scholium, Spinoza focuses on refuting the anthropomorphization of the intellect and will of God, which are none other than interchangeable concepts in his philosophy.[17] He therefore claims:

> [I]f will and intellect do pertain to the eternal essence of God, we must of course understand by each of these attributes something different from what men commonly understand. For the intellect and will which would constitute God's essence would have to differ entirely from our intellect and will, and could not agree with them in anything except the name. They would not agree with one another any more than do the dog that is a heavenly constellation and the dog that is a barking animal.
>
> (I.17, Schol, II/62–63)[18]

It appears that the position adopted here by Spinoza, which asserts a total differentiation of the human and divine intellects, is none other than an anti-philosophical position upon which he himself brought down the axe. Indeed this position, as Spinoza himself claims, is liable to reinforce ignorance, to nourish superstition and to encourage "zeal to oppose those who pursue natural philosophy" (TTP, XI, p. 81 [81]).[19] The overlap between the human intellect and the divine intellect, even though it is not complete but rather limited to the basic outlines of existence, is the keystone of Spinoza's philosophy; without it, his entire philosophical system collapses. Reason, Spinoza claims, enables us to come to know existence; and in the theological-like language that Spinoza commonly used: "we get a fuller knowledge of God and God's will as we acquire a fuller knowledge of natural things" (ibid., p. 85 [85]).[20] Spinoza asserts that in the framework of true knowledge there is no difference between the human intellect and God's intellect:

> [T]he human Mind is a part of the infinite intellect of God. Therefore, when we say that the human Mind perceives this or that, we are saying nothing but that God, not insofar as he is infinite, but insofar as he is explained [*explicatur*] through the nature of the human Mind.
>
> (II.11, Cor, II/94–95)[21]

However, in order to escape the claws of the theologians who claim there is a rift between God's intellect and the human intellect, Spinoza is forced to become again entangled in the logical contradiction that an infinite mode (God's intellect) is explained by means of a finite mode (the human mind). I will not repeat here our discussion of the contradiction embedded in this assertion (see previous section). For our purposes it is enough to point out that Spinoza contradicts himself in his answers to the question: is, in the context of the relation between God and what follows from him, everything that is in the cause also found in the effect? In certain places in the *Ethics* he responds positively (I.33 Schol 2, II/74)) and thus, as we saw, adopts an immanent position; in other places in the *Ethics* he responds in the negative (I.5, Dem, II/48; I.17, Schol, II/61) adopting a transcendental position.[22] The recurrence of the contradiction as the principal finding in the study of the issue of causality in the *Ethics* allows for an initial discussion of the status of contradiction in Spinoza's philosophy.

The status of contradiction in Spinoza's philosophy: an initial discussion

Regarding the orders of magnitude of cause and effect, as well as regarding the relations between cause and effect in the context of the relation between God and what follows from him, we discovered that by connecting Spinoza's different assertions we are faced with two groups of inconsistent claims. Yet it is important to note that this is not a matter of a random bundle of incoherent claims. In fact, in the two instances Spinoza's group of claims split into two well-distinguished sub-groups, each of which maintained consistency among its different elements while each one clashed head-on with the other. The first affirmed a specific claim and the second negated that very claim. In the matter of finiteness and infiniteness we found, on the one hand, a group of claims positing that the order of magnitude of the cause (God) must be equal to that of the effect (what follows from God); on the other hand, we found a group of claims positing that the order of magnitude of the cause (God) must be the opposite of that of the effect (what follows from God). In the matter of immanence and transcendence we found, on the one hand, a group of claims positing that each thing found in the cause (God) is also found in the effect (what follows from God); on the other hand, we found a group of claims positing that there is nothing in the cause (God) that also appears in the effect (what follows from God).

If, moving forward, we find that other issues in Spinoza's philosophy are dealt with in a similarly contradictory fashion to that of the subject of causality, the inescapable conclusion will be that Spinoza's philosophy is none other than the philosophy of contradiction. In other words, it is a unique philosophy in that when one gathers together the various claims scattered throughout the text on a particular philosophical issue, it turns out those claims can be assembled as two opposite poles that exclude one another logically. Obviously, we cannot be satisfied with a philosophy structured according to the geometrical method but replete with what can be called "consistent inconsistency," i.e., the consistent appearance of a contradiction every time Spinoza delves to the depths of a philosophical issue. It is still too early to determine the intent and meaning of contradiction in Spinoza's philosophy; however, two possible explanations should be rejected out of hand:

a   Perplexed as we might be by the contradictions that we illuminated in our study, we should not blame our own lack of understanding and suggest that Spinoza's conception of causality is sound yet beyond our ability to grasp. We would then be turning the *Ethics* into a holy text and ourselves into pseudo-theologians who enslave "reason, the greatest gift and the divine light, to dead letters [*mortuis literis*]" (TTP, XV, p. 188 [182], translation slightly altered); indeed, there was no philosopher in the history of Western thought who opposed the consecration of texts, canonical though they may be, more than Spinoza.[23]
b   It is not possible to rid ourselves of the problem of inconsistency in Spinoza's conception of causality by claiming the matter to be merely a local deficiency that does not extend to the entirety of the systematic structure. As causality is the organizing principle of existence in that existence is a cause of itself, the deficiency cannot but affect the entire philosophical system.

The fact that we find within the same text two conceptions of causality that exclude one another and that apply to existence in its entirety, that is to say to God, testifies that the philosophy being conducted in the *Ethics* has two masks. Behind one of them, Spinoza attempts to raise a partition between God and the things that follow from him, and behind the other he is occupied with completely shattering that very partition. In other words, Spinoza's philosophy appears before us simultaneously as a philosophy of transcendence *and* as a philosophy of immanence.

Notes

1   For example, the concept "cause of itself" is discussed by the companion in Yehuda HaLevi's *Kuzari* (*The Kuzari*, translated by Hartwig Hirschfeld, New York: Shocken Books,1974.). See also Wolfson, *Philosophy of Spinoza*, Vol. 1, p. 127 and the references there in footnote 2.

60 The second kind of knowledge

2 The truth of Spinoza's philosophy, Schlanger claims, is meant to reinforce that the "I understand" (*intelligo*) of Spinoza is a general *intelligo* "that is meant to be found in each one of us, and which, in the case of the *Ethics* comes from Spinoza's throat" (Jacques Schlanger, *Gestures of Philosophers*. Jerusalem: Magnes Press, 1997 [Heb.], p. 22).
3 According to Ben-Shlomo's formulation in his introduction to *Short Treatise on God, Man and His Well-Being*:): "at this point [the question of the good life] the Spinozian philosophy opens, at the beginning of the *Treatise on the Emendation of the Intellect*, and it ends in the final part of the *Ethics*" (Baruch Spinoza, *Short Treatise on God, Man, and His Well-Being*, translated into Hebrew by Rachel Hollander Steingardt with introduction and notes by Yosef Ben-Shlomo. Jerusalem: Magnes Press, 1987, p. 68).
4 Spinoza concludes the first part of the *Ethics* with the claim that "Nothing exists from whose nature some effect does not follow" (I.36). It follows that from God there must also be an effect, but that in God there is equivalence between the effect and the cause. To paraphrase the scholium to proposition I.25, it can be claimed that in the same sense that we say God is the cause of himself we should also call him the effect of himself. Wolfson transgresses this foundational insight of Spinozian metaphysics when he claims: "*Causa sui*, like the medieval 'necessary existence,' is primarily nothing but a negation, meaning causelessness, and to Spinoza it is only a shorter way of saying that the essence of substance involves existence" (*Philosophy of Spinoza*, Vol. 1, p. 127). See also Curley's entry for "cause of itself" in the glossary he appends to his translation of the *Ethics* (Curley, *Collected Works*, p. 628).
5 See also *Ethics*, I.33, Schol 1. The exact status of the external cause in Spinoza's system becomes clear only in the framework of the third kind of knowledge. See the last chapter of the present book.
6 See Sigad, "God as Final Cause."
7 Spinoza did not even properly outfit the geometric garb of the first definition of the *Ethics*, since in its framework he uses the concept "essence" (*essentia*), which he does not define until the second definition of the second part of the *Ethics*. In the issue of the "cause of itself," like at other central junctures in the *Ethics*, the reader is required to reconstruct, on his own, the explanations standing behind Spinoza's metaphysical positions. Indeed, in certain cases, like in the case of the "cause of itself," Spinoza does not explain his position, and in other cases, as Yovel claims, "the body of thought that Spinoza expresses is often informed by completely different considerations from those that appear in the formal demonstration, so that the procedure of the demonstration is quite often external to the point at hand" (Introduction to Yovel's translation of the *Ethics*, p. 44). In his discussion of the demonstration of the monism of the substance in proposition I.14, Bennett writes: "In this respect as in some others, I submit, his official apparatus of 'demonstrations' is not a good guide to his [Spinoza's] actual reasons for his metaphysical doctrines" (Bennett, "Spinoza's Metaphysics," in Garrett (ed.), *The Cambridge Companion to Spinoza*. Cambridge: Cambridge University Press, 1996, p. 65).
8 In *Beyond Good and Evil* Nietzsche writes: "The CAUSA SUI is the best self-contradiction that has yet been conceived, it is a sort of logical violation and unnaturalness; but the extravagant pride of man has managed to entangle itself profoundly and frightfully with this very folly" (Friedrich Nietzsche, *Beyond Good and Evil*. Translated by Helen Zimmern, New York: Dover Publications, 1997, Chapter 1, Paragraph 21). See also Sigad, "God as Final Cause," p. 398. Scruton writes: "Seldom has a great work of philosophy begun so forbiddingly" (Roger Scruton, *The Great Philosophers: Spinoza*. London: Routledge, 1999, p. 7).
9 Spinoza presents this equivalence when he posits: "Desire [*cupiditas*] is the very essence, or nature, of each [man]."

10 Spinoza identifies the essence of a thing with its definition: "essentia, seu definitio" (I.33, Schol1).
11 The application of the axiom of causality to God raises a very grave problem: if it is possible to reduce the effect to the cause, what differentiates the cause from the effect? Even though Spinoza does not directly refer to this problem, its solution is couched in the concept of the conatus that he presents only in the third part of the *Ethics*. In order to sustain the continuity of our discussion, we too will postpone treatment of the problem of the relation between the cause and the effect (Chapter 4 below), and its presentation will suffice for now. In *Creative Evolution* Bergson opposes situating causality on one principle and distinguishes between three kinds of causality that are distinct from one another on the level of the quantitative and qualitative link between the cause and the effect. Bergson himself is exempt in the first place from the problem of the relation between cause and effect that arises from Spinoza's axiom of causality, as the former claims that it is not possible to reduce the effect to the cause. Life, according to Bergson, creates at each and every moment something new that is lacking any shared measure with what preceded it. See Henri Bergson, *Creative Evolution*. Translated by Arthur Mitchell, New York: The Modern Library, 1944, pp. 38–39; for his distinguishing between three types of causality see ibid., pp. 81–83.
12 This is the place to point out an additional grave problem in Spinoza's philosophy the discussion of which would deviate from our present topic. Spinoza posits only two infinite elements in every attribute on the metaphysical map of his system: an infinite, immediate mode, and a mediated, finite mode. See Letter 64 to Schuller (Shirley, p. 298). However, this claim is not in line with proposition I.16, which asserts: "From the necessity of the divine nature there must follow infinitely many things in infinitely many modes." In the group of infinite elements in each attribute there must be infinite many elements and not just two. In other words, the fact that Spinoza's system does not have infinite elements deriving from "the face of the whole universe [*facies totius Universi*]" (Shirley, Letter 64, p. 299) contradicts the necessary conclusion that follows from linking the axiom of causality (I, A4) to the final proposition in the first part of the *Ethics* (I.36), and according to which from every infinite mode there necessarily follows another infinite mode.
13 The corollary to proposition I.25 is the first place in the *Ethics* in which Spinoza refers to the existence of finite things; indeed, the definition of the "finite in its own kind" (I, D2) is presented by Spinoza only in order to assert that it does not apply to God.
14 Compare to the examples of the stone in the appendix to the first part of the *Ethics*, p. 443 [II/81–82].
15 See Yovel, *Spinoza and Other Heretics*, pp. 172–186. Also see Yovel's introduction to his translation of the *Ethics*, pp. 20–22.
16 In the *Ethics* Spinoza uses the term "God's intellect" (*intellectus dei*) without defining it. Only in Letter 64 to Schuller does Spinoza explicitly state that the intellect of God is an infinite, immediate mode in the attribute of thought (Shirley, Letter 64, p. 298).
17 In the *Ethics* I.32, Cor 2, it is explicitly stated: "will, or intellect [of God]." See also Letter 19 to Blijenbergh (Curley, p. 357). While in the TTP Spinoza claims that only from the way in which we perceive God is it possible to distinguish between the will and intellect of God, but "God's will and God's understanding [intellect] are in reality one and the same thing in themselves" (TTP, IV, p. 62 [62]), in Letter 54 to Boxel he posits, "it is commonly and unanimously admitted … that God's will, intellect, and essence or nature are one and the same thing" (Shirley, Letter 54, p. 268).
18 The example of the dog as homonym appears in Maimonides, *Treatise on Logic*. Arabic original and three Hebrew translations, edited and translated into English by Israel Efros, New York: PAAJR, 1938, p. 58; also see p. 16.
19 Throughout the entirety of the TTP, either explicitly or implicitly, there is an attack leveled against the anti-philosophical position that claims complete disconnect

62 *The second kind of knowledge*

between the human intellect and the divine intellect. This attack reaches its climax in the sixth chapter, "On Miracles," which is dedicated to refuting the existing of events that are not subordinate to the laws of nature. In the appendix to the first part of the *Ethics*, Spinoza presents the reader with a summary of the attack against the theological position that claims "the judgments of the gods far surpass man's grasp" (ibid., p. 441, II/79).

20 In Spinoza's words in the *Ethics*: "The more we understand singular things, the more we understand God" (V.24). The hierarchy of knowledge that Spinoza posits here is qualitative and not quantitative. See Chapter 3.

21 Spinoza, who posits equivalence between objects of knowledge of finite and infinite intellects (I.30), claims "our Mind, insofar as it perceives things truly, is part of the infinite intellect of God; hence it is as necessary that the mind's clear and distinct ideas are true as that God's ideas are." Indeed, "our Mind, insofar as it understands, is an eternal mode of thinking, which is determined by another eternal mode of thinking, and this again by another, and so on, to infinity; so that together, they all constitute God's eternal and infinite intellect" (V.40, Schol).

22 In fact, as I will attempt to show in the coming chapter, the contradiction between transcendence and immanence is already couched in the contradiction between the definition of the substance (I, D3) and the definition of the mode (I, D5).

23 Spinoza's principal discussion on attributing sacredness to texts appears in Chapter XII of the TTP.

3 The contradictions regarding the essence and perfection of the things that follow from God

In the previous chapter we saw that Spinoza applies two contradictory conceptions of causality to God. The first conception claims complete equivalence between cause and effect, while the second concept differentiates completely between cause and effect. This contradiction, as we saw in the previous chapter, led Spinoza to contradict himself not only regarding the relations between the finite and the infinite in his system, but also to present his philosophy in its entirety simultaneously as immanent and transcendent. The present chapter will explore two additional offshoots of the contradiction between the two conceptions of causality that Spinoza applies to God: the first contradiction relates to the essence of the things that follow from God, an essence which is presented as both including existence and not including it; and the second contradiction relates to the perfection of the things that follow from God, a perfection presented as both complete and as only partial. A fundamental examination of these two contradictions and of the different textual means Spinoza implements in order to simultaneously conceal and reveal them, will enable us to advance the inquiry we initiated in the preceding chapter regarding the place and meaning of contradiction in the *Ethics*.

The first contradiction: the essence of the things that follow from God involves *or* does not involve existence

At the heart of the first part of the *Ethics* Spinoza suggests, in two consecutive propositions, two contradictory answers to the following question: does the essence of things produced by God involve existence? (From here on: the question of the essence of the things produced by God.) In proposition I.24, Spinoza's answer is unequivocally negative:

> The essence of things produced by God [*a Deo*] does not involve existence.
> (I.24, II/67)

This assertion is self-evident. Only the essence of existence in its entirety involves existence in that only it is the cause of itself (I, D1, II/45). Contrarily, in terms of the details of existence, both finite and infinite, "their essence can be the cause neither of their existence nor of their duration, but only God, to whose nature alone it pertains to exist (by I.14, Cor 1)" (I.24, Cor, II/67). Indeed, in the first axiom of the second part of the *Ethics*, Spinoza posits that "[t]he essence of man does not involve necessary existence, i.e., from the order of nature it can happen equally that this *or* that man does exist, or that he does not exist" (II, A1, II/85). By contrast, in the following proposition Spinoza posits:

> God is the efficient cause, not only of existing things, but also of their essence.
> (I.25, II/67)

From this assertion it follows unequivocally that the essence of things produced by God does indeed involve existence. If we adjoin to this proposition Spinoza's axiom of causality (I, A4) and its textual offshoots (Preface to IV; III.56, Dem; and I.8, Schol 2), which claim the cause of a thing is the nature, essence, and definition of that same thing, and if we take into consideration that God's essence involves existence, it logically follows that the essence of things that follow from God involve existence. And indeed, in the scholium of the present proposition Spinoza claims "God must be called the cause of all things in the same sense in which he is called the cause of himself" (I.25, Schol, II/68). The existence of existence in its entirety as a cause of itself, is none other than the existence of its details in that it is their cause.

However, I.25 undermines the first axiom of the second part of the *Ethics* that claims: "from the order of nature it can happen equally that this *or* that man does exist, or that he does not exist." Yet the existence of this man or that, just as the existence of all other things in existence, is necessary precisely in the same way that existence in its entirety is necessary as the cause of itself. "To conceive things under a species of eternity," Spinoza asserts in the fifth part of the *Ethics*, is to conceive of them "insofar as through God's essence they involve existence" (V.30, Dem, II/299).[1] This contradiction regarding the essence of things produced by God also comes up when we adjoin proposition I.25, which claims that God is the efficient cause of both the existence and essence of all things, to Spinoza's claim in the second part of the *Ethics* that "singular things can neither be nor be conceived without God, and nevertheless, God does not pertain to their essence" (II.10, Cor, Schol, II/94). Likewise, the claim that God does not pertain to the essence of the singular things (II.19, Cor, Schol) contradicts not only proposition I.25, but also proposition II.45, which implicitly asserts: "Each idea of each body, or of each singular thing which actually exists, necessarily involves an eternal and infinite essence of God."

Despite the fact Spinoza knew, as we do, that logically God is either the essence of the things that follow from him, or does not pertain to the essence of the things that follow from him, Spinoza posited in the text that God is of the essence of those things that follow from him *and* that God does not pertain to them. Moreover, as will become clear that Spinoza's contradictory answers to the question of the essence of things produced by God appear not only in the *Ethics*, which from the outset was intended for publication, but also in a letter to a close friend and supporter of Spinoza's, Simon de Vries.[2] In Letter 10, which was addressed to de Vries, Spinoza makes two contradictory references to the subject of the essence of the things produced by God; in the letter, just as in the *Ethics*, Spinoza does not acknowledge, to say the least, the existence of a contradiction.[3]

In the first paragraph of this brief letter, it is implicitly stated that since it is not possible to derive the existences of the modes from their definition, experience is required in order to understand them. Yet in the second and final paragraph of the letter, it is stated that the existence of the modes, as well as their affections, are eternal truths; despite the fact Spinoza avoids using the term "eternal truths" regarding the modes in order "to distinguish them (as everyone generally does) from those which do not explain any thing or affection of a thing, as for example, *nothing comes from nothing*" (Curley, Letter 10, p. 196). Thus either the truths of the modes are not eternal truths, meaning that existence does not pertain to their essence, and so experience is required to know them; or they *are* eternal truths, meaning that existence does pertain to their essence, and that "no experience will ever be able to teach us this, for experience does not teach any essences of things. The most it can do is to determine our mind to think only of certain essences of things" (ibid.).[4]

In sum, Spinoza responds to the question of the essence of things produced by God with two contradictory answers anchored in the axioms of his philosophical system. In the first axiom of the second part of the *Ethics*, just as in proposition I.24,[5] Spinoza answers this question in the negative; by applying his axiom of causality (I, A4) to God he answers the same question in proposition I.25 with an affirmative.[6] In fact, the contradiction in the matter of the essence of things produced by God is none other than a variation of the contradiction in the conception of causality that Spinoza applies to God, which was discussed in the previous chapter. The positive answer to the question of the essence of things produced by God reflects the application of the axiom of causality to God, while the negative answer reflects the rejection of the axiom of causality regarding God. Moreover, the contradiction regarding the essence of things produced by God reveals an additional layer of the metaphysical fracturing between immanence and transcendence in Spinoza's philosophy, which was uncovered in the preceding chapter. Indeed, Spinoza's positive answer to the question of the essence of the things produced by God joins the immanent trend in his system, while the negative answer to the question joins the transcendental trend.

The second contradiction: the perfection of the things that follow from God is complete *or* only partial

In the *Ethics* Spinoza suggests two contradictory answers to the question: are all the things that follow from God absolutely perfect, like him? (From here on: the question of the perfection of the things that follow from God.) On the one hand, Spinoza answers in the positive regarding the question of the perfection of the things that follow from God. Indeed, he denies the existence of imperfect things. The differentiation between perfect and imperfect things, as Spinoza claims, does not express the essence of things, but rather only a certain relation between the man who values them and the things being valued. Contrarily, Spinoza claims that both God and the things that follow from him are absolutely perfect (from here on, the conception of non-hierarchical perfection). On the other hand, Spinoza also answers in the negative to the question regarding the perfection of the things that follow from God. Alongside the conception of non-hierarchical perfection, Spinoza puts forth an entirely different conception of perfection claiming that the things that follow from God are different from one another in terms of their perfection, and they thereby establish a hierarchy of perfection in existence (from here on: the conception of hierarchical perfection). An examination of Spinoza's two conceptions of perfection, in the two following sections, will aid us in understanding the place and role of contradiction in his conception of God.

The conception of non-hierarchical perfection

Spinoza's discussion of the concept of perfection, just like his other discussions of pivotal philosophical-theological concepts, is two-fold: in addition to a presentation of the philosophical meaning of the concept, Spinoza also seeks to analyze its non-philosophical meaning. In other words, apart from the analytical perspective, Spinoza also suggests an examination of the genealogical roots of the meaning of the concept and the way in which it creates a reciprocal relationship with the multitude's non-critical picture of the world.[7] At the beginning of the current section I will examine the philosophical meaning of the concept of perfection, and will then trace Spinoza's criticism of the multitude's non-critical understanding of this concept.

From a philosophical point of view, Spinoza posits:

> By *reality* and *perfection* I understand the same thing.
> (II, D6, II/85, emphasis added)

Every real thing is perfect. Not only are God, the infinite attributes and modes (both mediated and immediate) perfect, but the finite modes, down to the very last one, are absolutely perfect as well. Every finite mode is perfect by definition in that it is real. However, the equivalence "reality, *or* perfection" (II.1, Schol, II/86)[8] that Spinoza applies to the modes is not a matter of definition alone. This equivalence stems, by logical necessity, from joining the axiom of causality (I, A4) and its textual offshoots (Preface to IV; III.56, Dem; and I.8, Schol 2) to the nature of God, and God being the cause of the modes. Given that the cause constitutes the essence, nature, and definition of the effect, and because God is "absolutely perfect" (I.11, Schol, II/54) and is also "the immanent, not the transitive cause, of all things" (I.18, II/63) in existence, it necessarily follows that all things in existence are also absolutely perfect. This conclusion is one of the most radical implications of the immanent tendency in Spinoza's philosophy. According to theology there exists a dichotomy between the absolutely perfect God and his world, which is a world of partiality, loss, and malfunction; however,

Essence and perfection 67

Spinoza collapses entirely the theological barrier between God and the world, and claims that every thing, in that it is real, is perfect. The creating being and the created being, to employ theological discourse, are perfect in the same measure in that they constitute, according to Spinoza, the very same existence.[9]

However, as was mentioned above, alongside the analysis of the philosophical meaning of the concept of perfection, Spinoza seeks to examine the internal logic of the non-philosophical meaning of the concept. For this purpose, that is for the purpose of a precise analysis of the two points of view – the true and the false – regarding perfection, Spinoza presents the pair of concepts "negation" (*negatio*) and "privation" (*privatio*) as the organizing concepts of the two points of view, respectively. "Negation," Spinoza claims, "is nothing but denying something of a thing because it does not pertain to its nature," while "Privation is nothing but denying something of a thing which we judge [wrongly] to pertain to its nature" (Curley, Letter 21, p. 378).[10] Equipped with this distinction, between the common language on the one hand and philosophical thought about existence on the other, Spinoza attempts to uncover for us the internal logic of two points of view (the false and the true) regarding the perfection of things that follow from God, through the following example:

> We say, for example, that a blind man is deprived of sight because we easily imagine him as seeing, whether this imagination arises from the fact that we compare him with others who see, or his present state with his past, when he used to see. And when we consider this man in this way, by comparing his nature with that of others or with his own past nature, then we affirm that seeing pertains to his nature, and for that reason we say that he is deprived of it. But when we consider God's decree, and his nature, we can no more affirm of that man than of a Stone, that he is deprived of vision. For at that time vision no more pertains to that man without contradiction than it does to the stone, *since nothing more pertains to that man, and is his, than what the Divine intellect and will attribute to him.* Hence, God is no more the cause of his not seeing than of the stone's not seeing, which is a pure Negation.
>
> (Curley, Letter 21, p. 377)[11]

From a philosophical viewpoint, a blind man is also an absolutely perfect finite mode; indeed, as a necessary effect of God, he has in him everything that needs to be in him. All that can be contained in him is contained in him, and all that is contained in him is contained in him necessarily. If the existence of the blind man could have been different, existence in its entirety could have differed, which would suggest a lack of perfection. However, existence, in that it contains all, is absolutely perfect. Therefore, everything that expresses existence in that it derives from it necessarily, such as the blind man for example, has a special and certain cause to be like this or that; thus, he is absolutely perfect (see also I.33, Schol 2, II/74). It is possible to relate to the blind man as lacking perfection only from our limited point of view, which compares the necessary existence of things in reality to the existence of things as we want them to be. Yet the hierarchy of perfections that we impose on the details of existence reflects only our judgments, which are usually wrong about the benefit these details of existence bring us. The differentiation between perfection and imperfection is relative, just like other differentiations of the power of imagination: "*good, evil, order, confusion, warm, cold, beauty, ugliness*" (Appendix to I, p. 444, II/81). Not only is the same thing perceived by different people in different ways, but the same person perceives, in different contexts, the very same thing in different ways as well. For example, "Music is good for one who is Melancholy, bad for one who is mourning, and neither good nor bad to one who is deaf" (Preface to IV, p. 545, II/208). On the other hand, "[t]he most beautiful hand, seen through a microscope, would appear repulsive" (Shirley, Letter 54, p. 269).[12]

The conception of non-hierarchical perfection, Spinoza claims here, expresses existence as it is and not as we would want it to be. Contrarily, a non-philosophical, hierarchical conception of perfection is erroneous because it incorrectly assumes man to be situated at the center of existence. Not only is man not situated at the center of existence in that he is just one more finite mode in an infinite chain of modes, but existence in its entirety has no center. A center can draw from the boundaries of a thing, but the infinite existence, which has no bounds, has no center.[13]

However, an analytic inquiry into the non-philosophical concept of perfection will not suffice. According to Spinoza, this concept is not pre-determined in human thought, but only appeared at a certain stage in the development of human consciousness and language. Therefore, its proper study requires a meticulous examination of its genealogical roots in addition to an analytic investigation of its meaning. Indeed, in the preface to Part IV of the *Ethics*, Spinoza presents a short, three-tiered genealogy that investigates the transition from a valid to an invalid use of the pair of concepts perfection and imperfection.

In the first stage, Spinoza claims, a valid use of the pair of concepts was made. Perfection and imperfection were determined according to the compatibility or the incompatibility between the mind of a human creator and his creation: "If someone has decided to make something, and has finished it, then he will call his thing perfect – and so will anyone who rightly knows, or thinks he knows, the mind and purpose of the Author of the work" (Preface to IV, p. 543, II/205). Therefore, in the framework that Spinoza calls "the first meaning of these words," whomever sees the creation but "does not know the mind of its maker, [...] will, of course, not be able to know whether that work is perfect or imperfect" (ibid., p. 544). In the second stage, by contrast, an invalid use of the pair of concepts perfection and imperfection was made "after men began to form universal ideas" (ibid.) of artificial things such as houses, buildings, towers, etc. Valuing the creation as perfect or imperfect was detached from the intent of the creator and determined only according to its compatibility or incompatibility with "the universal idea he [the one making the judgment] had formed of this kind of thing" (ibid.). In the third stage, in which we find ourselves today, the non-critical use of the pair of concepts perfection and imperfection is transferred from the domain of artificial things to the domain of natural things. Consequently, Spinoza claims, the multitudes tend to "call perfect or imperfect natural things, which have not been made by human hand" (ibid.); they also blame nature for defects and criticize the latter "when they see something happen in nature which does not agree with the model they have conceived of this kind of thing" (ibid.).

Spinoza dismisses the use made of the pair of concepts perfection and imperfection in the last two stages by relying on the following two explanations.

First, determining the perfection of a thing by comparing it to the universal idea of things of the same kind is wrong. Universal ideas are simply fictions that express the limits of man's capacity of knowledge and the dominance of the deceptions of imagination in his consciousness (II.40, Schol 1, Schol 2, II/120). Concepts of perfection whose standards are universal ideas are none other than "notions we are accustomed to feign because we compare individuals of the same species or genus to one another" (Preface to IV, p. 545, II/207). However, this habit is not metaphysically valid; indeed, God, Spinoza posits with nominalist decisiveness, "does not know things abstractly, and he does not make such general definitions" (Curley, Letter 19, p. 359). A true understanding regarding the perfection of things obliges us to abandon the habit, which is unreliable from a philosophical point of view, to value the perfection of things by comparing them to each other and to reject the hierarchy of perfections presented by the power of imagination. The perfection of a thing is its essence (*Ethics*, "General Definition of the Affects," II/103–104, p. 542), and the essence of a thing, as well as its nature and definition, are its cause (I.8, Schol 2, I/49; III.56, Dem, II/184; Preface to IV, p. 543); and because God, the "absolutely perfect" (I.11, Schol II/54), is "the efficient cause, not only of the existence of things, but also of their essence" (I.25, II/67), it follows necessarily that all things in existence are, like God, absolutely perfect.[14]

Second, in the last two stages the perfection of things, both natural and artificial, was determined according to their compatibility with the purpose for which they were created. However, God *or* nature, Spinoza claims,

> exists for the sake of no end, he also acts for the sake of no end. Rather, as he has no principle or end of existing, so he also has none of acting. What is called a final cause is nothing but a human appetite insofar as it is considered as a principle, *or* primary cause, of some thing.
>
> (Preface to IV, p. 544)

The only causality in nature, and this includes man who is but one of its parts, is the efficient cause (I.16, Cor 1, II/60). Indeed, final causality is presented by Spinoza as a product of the imagination that is nourished by man's ignorance regarding the reasons that stimulate his appetite and determine him to action.[15]

Along with a new understanding of the perfection of the things that follow from God, Spinoza also suggests a new understanding of the perfection of God himself. As opposed to the Epicurean position that identifies God's perfection with his total passivity, Spinoza claims that God's perfection is realized fully in his infinite action.[16] Epicurus avoided attributing action to God because he erroneously identified action with yearning and the disadvantage of the one who acts.[17] However, according to Spinoza, for whom the concept of action is central, action expresses perfection and not a defect; indeed, to act is to be a cause. That which expresses defect is not action but affect (III, D2, II/84). Therefore, despite that God's perfection is static, "God can pass neither to a greater nor a lesser perfection" (V.17, Dem, II/291), this static state is not expressed by passivity but by *activity*. God's action, in that it is deductive, does not lessen or increase his perfection, but rather expresses it, since "there is no cause, either extrinsically or intrinsically, which prompts God to action, except the perfection of his nature (I.17, Cor 1, II/60).

The conception of the hierarchy of perfections

The conception of non-hierarchical perfections does not fully exhaust Spinoza's stance regarding the perfection of the things that follow from God. Alongside this conception, in different contexts and in unambiguous language, Spinoza situates an entirely different idea of perfection (which will from here on be called: the conception of the hierarchy of perfections). According to this conception, the things that follow from God are different from each other in their perfection, and as such they establish a hierarchy of perfections in existence. This is opposed to the conception of non-hierarchical perfections that views the details of existence, in terms of their perfection, as equal to one another and to existence in its entirety, meaning equal to God. However, in the framework of the conception of the hierarchy of perfections, the perfection of every detail in existence is distinguishable from the perfection of every other thing, and inferior to the perfection of existence in its entirety *or* God.

In the following, I aim to clarify the conception of the hierarchy of perfections through an examination of the different contexts in which it appears. I will begin with an investigation of the way in which the conception of the hierarchy of perfections is embedded within Spinoza's panpsychic position; I will continue with a presentation of the basic structure of the hierarchy of perfections through a study of Letters 35 and 36 to Hudde, and will conclude with an examination of the existential meaning with which Spinoza imbues his ethical notion of the ascent and decline of man on the rungs of the ladder of perfections.

Spinoza's panpsychism is a necessary consequence of his parallelism. Since every body has an idea in the attribute of thought, as well as infinite other expressions in an infinite number of other attributes, and because the idea of every thing is its mind, just as the mind of man is the idea of his body (II.13, II/96), it necessarily follows that all beings are "animate" (*animata*) (II.13, Cor, Schol, II/96).[18] Nevertheless, Spinoza dulls this radical panpsychic conclusion (which states every being has a mind) at the moment he presents it by means of a hierarchy that does not stem from any previous definition, axiom, or proposition in the *Ethics*:

However [although man is animate along with all other individuals], we also cannot deny that ideas differ among themselves, as the objects themselves do, and that one is more excellent than the other, and contains more reality, just as the object of the one is more excellent than the object of the other and contains more reality.

(II.13, Cor, Schol, II/97)[19]

Even if every thing has a mind, one mind does not resemble another. The difference between minds is like the difference between their bodies. The degree of the reality and perfection of the body, just like the degree of the reality and perfection of the mind to which it corresponds, is determined according to the following principle:

And in proportion as the actions of a body depend more on itself alone, and as other bodies concur with it less in acting, so its mind is more capable of understanding distinctly.

(Ibid.)[20]

The degree of reality and perfection of a thing is determined according to its capacity for independent action.[21] Just as Spinoza is satisfied, at this stage of the discussion, with only presenting the principle of independent action in a "completely general" way, we too will postpone treatment of the meanings and implications of this principle.[22] Whatever the exact content of the organizing principle of the hierarchy of reality and perfection may be, the very fact of the existence of this hierarchy glaringly contradicts the foundational principles of Spinoza's metaphysics. As we saw extensively in the previous subsection, from the definition of God, the axiom of causality and its textual offshoots, and the propositions dedicated to a description of the derivation of the modes from God, there is a logical necessity for complete equivalence between the perfection of God and the perfection of the things that follow from God. The ladder of perfections, as we saw, is a product of the power of imagination; as such it has no place in the framework of critical philosophical thought.

Spinoza is consistent in his disapproval of the ladder of perfections of the power of imagination, but is inconsistent in the alternative he offers to it. The first alternative rejects all hierarchisation and, as we saw in the previous sub section, attributes absolute perfection to all things in existence. The second alternative, however, does suggest a hierarchical ordering of perfections, albeit a hierarchy of reason which radically differs from the hierarchy of perfections of the power of imagination. In the framework of this alternative hierarchisation, he demands a new ranking of things, one determined by reason, as shown in the quote above. An additional example of this hierarchy of perfections can be found at the end of the appendix to Part I of the *Ethics*, in Spinoza's response to the classic theological problem: how can it be that an absolutely perfect God created a world lacking perfection?

> For many are accustomed to arguing in this way: if all things have followed from the necessity of God's most perfect nature, why are there so many imperfections in nature? Why are things corrupt to the point where they stink? So ugly that they produce nausea? Why is there confusion, evil, and sin?
>
> As I have just said, those who argue in this way are easily answered. For the perfection of things is to be judged solely from their nature and power [*potential*]; things are not more or less perfect because they please or offend men's senses, or because they are of use to, or are incompatible with, human nature.
>
> (Appendix to I, p. 446, II/83)

Spinoza here does not dismiss the existence of the hierarchy of perfections, but only calls to establish it anew from a rational perspective of the "nature and power" (*potentia*) of things; that is, from the perspective of the capacity of their independent action (Preface to IV), and not by the way in which those same things "please or offends men's senses" (Appendix to I, p. 446, II/83).[23] On the other hand, Spinoza clarifies in this context that the claim according to which "[t]he more reality or being each thing has, the more attributes belong to it" (I.9, II/52; see also I.10, Schol), should not be understood as stipulating a hierarchy of reality and perfection that exists between beings whose number of attributes constitute a rising arithmetic sequence; rather, it is only a claim that paves the way for the demonstration of God's existence (I.11, II/52). In other words, the only object of proposition I.9 is God. And in Spinoza's words in Letter 64 to Schuller:

> The axiom in the scholium to proposition 10 ["[t]he more reality or being each thing has, the more attributes belong to it"][24] as I have indicated towards the end of the said scholium, derives from the idea we have of an absolutely infinite Entity, and not from the fact that there are, or may be, entities having three, four, or more attributes.
>
> (Shirley, Letter 64, p. 299)

However, even if Spinoza does not claim anywhere that entities with more or fewer attributes exist, he does repeatedly claim that entities with more or less "reality *or* perfection" (II.1, Schol, II/86) exist. Letters 35 and 36 to Hudde provide an important explanation of the characteristics of this hierarchy of reality and perfection, namely that the hierarchy of perfections is not made of one infinite continuum, but consists of three distinct degrees or levels of perfection reserved for the substance, attributes and modes respectively. The levels of perfection differ from each other in that the order of magnitude of the capacity for self-existence of the substance, attributes and modes differ. Indeed, Spinoza claims in that same correspondence, "it can only be the result of its perfection that a Being should exist by its own sufficiency and force" (Shirley, Letter 35, p. 204).

Essence and perfection 73

God stands alone on the first degree of perfections:

> there can only be one Being whose existence pertains to its own nature.... Nor can it exist outside God; for if it were to exist outside God, one and the same nature involving necessary existence would exist in double form, and this, according to our previous demonstration, is absurd.
>
> (Ibid.)

Only God's nature, Spinoza claims, contains existence within it. Therefore, only God's perfection, which is the capacity for self-existence, is absolute. The infinite many attributes are situated at the second degree of perfections. Despite that the attributes do not include within themselves existence in its entirety, each attribute contains completely "a definite kind of being" (Shirley, Letter 36, p. 208), is closed off within itself, and in its own sphere "exists by its own force" (ibid.). Therefore each one of the attributes is "perfect only in its own kind" (ibid.).

The difference between the first two degrees of perfection reflects the difference between the first two degrees of being, namely, that of the substance and that of the attributes respectively. Every attribute has one certain perfection (in the domain of thought, extension, etc), and no attribute can "express all the perfections" (Shirley, Letter 35, p. 204). Only "God *or* all God's attributes" (I.19, II/64), claims Spinoza from logical necessity, "possess all perfections" (Shirley, Letter 35, p. 205, translation slightly altered). At this point, Spinoza is in fact adjoining the concept of perfection to the concept of infinity. The difference between the substance and the attributes, from the viewpoint of perfection, goes back to the difference between the substance and the attributes from the viewpoint of infinity. Just as the substance is absolutely infinite while the attributes are only infinite in their kind (I, D6, Exp, II/46), the substance is absolutely perfect while the attributes are perfect in their kind. This concealed adjoining of the concept of infinity with the concept of perfection in the letters to Hudde is explicitly formulated in the *Ethics* when Spinoza claims that God is "absolutely infinite, *or* perfect" (I.11, Schol, II/54). It follows from this claim that the attribute, by contrast, is an infinite *or* perfect entity only in its kind.

The modes are situated at the third and final degree of perfections. Their definition as dependent entities lacking the ability to exist on their own (I, D5, II/45) makes their existence imperfect.[25] However, as was already shown (in the scholium to II.13), the imperfection of the modes is not complete and unified, but partial and variegated. In the human sphere, given that the imperfection of people is the source of their misery, and additionally, because every person, just like every other mode, is situated in a different place in the infinite hierarchy of the perfections of the details of existence, each and every person must, by metaphysical necessity, be miserable in his/her own way.[26] However, although the imperfection of humans creates an infinite ladder of perfections, the position of humans on that ladder is not determined. Contrarily, humans incessantly ascend and descend on the ladder of perfections: "We see, then, that the Mind can undergo great changes, and pass now to a greater, now to a lesser perfection" (III.11, Schol, II/49). The movement of the mind on the ladder of perfections occurs at the same time as an identical movement of the body that corresponds to it. Indeed, according to Spinoza's parallelism it must be the case that "the Mind passes to a greater or lesser perfection when it happens that it affirms of its body (or some part of the body) something which involves more or less reality than before" ("General Definition of the Affects," II/203, p. 542). Moreover, the discussion of man's movement on the ladder of perfections stands at the center of Spinoza's philosophy, which aims to "lead us, by the hand, as it were, to the knowledge of the human Mind and its highest blessedness [*beatitude*]" (Preface to II, II/84).[27] Man's ascent on the ladder of perfections, which Spinoza equates with the increase of his "power of acting" (*agendi potentiam*) (Preface to IV, p. 546, II/208), his knowledge (II.49, Schol), his joy ("General Definition of the Affects," II, II/191), and his participation in the divine nature (VI.45), is the *one and only* thing that ensures man will be "more perfect and blessed" (V.31, Schol, II/300; also see V.27, dem).[28]

Why does the absolutely perfect *natura naturans* ("what is in itself and is conceived through itself" I.29, Schol) create the *natura naturata* as a hierarchy of perfections? Why doesn't it create it in its image, absolutely perfect? Spinoza's answer is presented at the conclusion of the appendix to Part I of the *Ethics*:

> But to those who ask "why God did not create all men so that they would be governed by the command of reason?" I answer only "because he did not lack material to create all things, from the highest degree of perfection to the lowest;" or, to speak more properly, "because the laws of his nature have been so ample that they sufficed for producing all things which can be conceived by an infinite intellect" (as I have demonstrated on P16).
>
> (Appendix to I, p. 446, II/83)

Not only, therefore, is the hierarchy of perfections *not* in opposition to the complete infiniteness of God, it in fact necessarily follows from God's infiniteness and fully expresses it. Indeed, to be infinite, Spinoza posits, is to contain all, "from the highest degree of perfection to the lowest" (ibid.). Therefore, if all humans were guided "by the command of reason" (ibid.) the perfection of God would be damaged since it would not include humans that are not guided by the command of reason. Just as both circles and spheres follow from God's perfection by the same necessity, humans guided by the command of reason as well as humans not guided by it follow from God's perfection. Therefore, "to ask God why he did not also give [Adam] a more perfect will is as absurd as to ask him why he did not give the circle all the properties of the sphere" (Curley, Letter 19, p. 360).

The assertion that the infinite necessarily contains imperfection leads us, via Spinoza's adjoining of the concept of the infinite to the concept of perfection (I.11, Schol), to assert that perfection necessarily contains imperfection. In other words, from perfection there necessarily stems imperfection. This contradiction,

Essence and perfection 75

as we can see from the repeated adjoining of the concept of the infinite to that of perfection, is none other than a new formulation of the contradiction according to which the finite necessarily follows from the infinite, which we examined in the previous chapter.

When, in the appendix to part I of the *Ethics* quoted above, Spinoza explains this contradiction (of a perfect entity creating imperfect entities), he directs us to yet another contradiction, earlier in the text, put forth in proposition I.16 (the famous proposition regarding the things that follow from God which will be discussed at length in the following chapter). In that proposition, Spinoza breaks through the definition of God or the substance as a being closed within itself (I, D3, II/45), and claims that from God there follow "infinitely many things in infinitely many modes" (I.16, II/60).

It can thus be concluded that from Spinoza's perspective the contradiction of imperfection following from perfection is one and the same as the contradiction of modes following from God. Indeed, the totality of God forces him to derive modes from within himself. Consequently, as modes are through another (I, D5, II/45) and the substance is in itself (I, D3, II/45), God must simultaneously be both himself and not himself. Similarly, in the case of perfection, God's totality requires him to derive from within his complete and unified perfection infinitely imperfect entities in infinite modes and, consequently, to be at once both perfect and imperfect. In the both cases, the contradiction itself does not destroy the concept of God, but reinforces the complete otherness of that which is totally other in essence.

On the concealment of contradictions in the *Ethics*

In order to conceal the contradictions in the *Ethics*, Spinoza employs the skill of esoteric writing that he acquired when composing the TTP. Indeed, on the surface, he completely denies the existence of any contradictions in his philosophy through the use he makes of the Euclidean model. Yet, beneath the surface, Spinoza takes the pains of directing us again and again, as if fearing it might escape our attention, to the variety of contradictions in his system, going as far, I argue, as presenting contradiction as the central and essential finding of his metaphysical inquiry.

Spinoza's silence regarding the logical contradictions in his system is deafening in light of his readiness to reveal other deviations that he makes from the geometric procedure. In order to clarify the difference between systematic faults that Spinoza was ready to admit to, and the contradictions which he denied, we will now turn to examine two places in the *Ethics* where the reader encounters explicit and blatant deviations from the geometric procedure:

a   Immediately after positing "the human Mind is a part of the infinite intellect of God" (II.11, Cor, II/94), Spinoza requests from his readers, via a special scholium that he sets aside for this purpose, something that has no place in the framework of a geometric system:

76 *The second kind of knowledge*

> Here, no doubt, my readers will come to a halt, and think of many things which will give them pause. For this reason I ask them to continue on with me slowly, step by step, and to make no judgment on these matters until they have read through them all.
>
> (II.11, Cor, Schol, II/95)

In this scholium Spinoza demands interpretive fairness from his readers under the auspices of an ad hoc principle positing that, to quote Hampshire, "one has to travel round the whole circle at least once before one can begin to understand any segment of it".[29] This is despite the fact that Spinoza knew very well, as we do, that in a system written in a geometric order, the propositions should be based on what has been claimed before them, not what will be determined after them.

b   An additional deviation from the geometric procedure Spinoza chose to expose can be found in the scholium to corollary II.17. In this scholium Spinoza explicitly admits that a logical necessity cannot be attributed to the explanation he suggests for the creation of the "images of things" (*rerum imagines*):

> This can happen from other causes also, but it is sufficient for me here to have shown one cause; still, I do not believe that I wander far from the true [cause].
>
> (II.17, Cor, Schol, II/105)

However, one who adopts the Euclidean method must aim for the truth as an archer targets the bull's eye; and it is not enough to think that one has not "wandered far" from the truth. Indeed, as Spinoza himself claims, only "[i]n the common round of life we have to follow what is probable, but in speculative thought we have to follow what is true" (Shirley, Letter, 56, p. 277). Since the *Ethics* is dedicated to a description of God's action, and since God does not act optionally but only in a necessary way (I.17), there is no place in the *Ethics*, nor could there be, for possible causes. However, regarding the creation of the images of things, Spinoza openly and plainly presents a possible cause presented as such.

Nevertheless, there is a fundamental difference between the deviations presented here, which Spinoza only admits to half-heartedly, and the contradictions of depth that are the focal point of my argument, and which Spinoza completely denies. While the above deviations only create local and fixable defects in specific issues in Spinoza's system, the logical contradictions of depth bring the entire structure of the system to the point of collapse. Reorganizing the order of propositions in the text could correct the first deviation from the geometric procedure (II.11, Cor, Schol), while exchanging the explanation of the creation of the images of things lacking logical necessity with an explanation that *does* have logical necessity would correct the second deviation (II.17, Cor). Thus, though Spinoza's partial admissions to these deviations might damage the Euclidean reputation of the *Ethics*, they are meant to point to the critical reader weaknesses in the system, which he or she is supposed to complete and amend. Moreover, from a rhetorical standpoint, Spinoza acquires the confidence of the reader by uncovering his own helplessness in certain territories of his own philosophy. Spinoza instills the reader with the sense that he or she is party to an unwritten covenant of transparency whose foundation is the deep cooperation between lovers of truth. It is as though he turns to the reader between the lines and obligates himself: whenever I do not succeed in completely adhering to the geometric procedure, I will make you aware of this, hoping you, the reader, might be able to repair what came out faulty by my hand.

Contrarily, Spinoza's admission to the existence of logical contradictions in his philosophy would seemingly bring total ruin upon his system. Moreover, attempting to purify the system of the various metaphysical contradictions in the second kind of knowledge would leave us perplexed, facing two philosophical systems which are, from a logical standpoint, mutually exclusive and between which we would not be able to decide: one system would be transcendental, Parmenidean and eternal. In its framework absolute perfection would be attributed to all details of existence. The second system would be immanent, Heraclidean and unfolding in time. It would, furthermore, posit a hierarchy of perfections of the details of existence. However, despite that within his Euclidean procedure Spinoza does not admit to the existence of contradictions in his philosophy, nor can he except at the cost of the system itself, he does take great pains to direct our attention to those very contradictions. In fact, as will be shown below, Spinoza utilizes four different textual techniques to emphasize the contradictions in the *Ethics*.

The first technique is the textual adjoining of claims that are logically mutually exclusive (I.24 and I.25).[30] The second technique is basing one claim on another claim that contradicts it (V.40, Dem).[31] The third technique is directing the reader from one contradiction to another (the demonstration attached to propositions I.16[32] and V.22[33]). And the fourth technique is casting the two contradictory positions into one unified statement, and sometimes while vigorously denying the contradiction between them (I.10, Schol).[34]

Furthermore, the way in which Spinoza chooses to unfold his philosophy not only leads to the realization of the existence of contradictions in his metaphysics, but also points to the central place they hold within it. Regarding the issue of perfection Spinoza direct us, just before the curtain closes on the first part of the *Ethics*, to the inconsistent characteristic of existence, and brings us back to the opening definition of the book: "cause of itself." By this textual closing of the circle, Spinoza turns to us as though between the lines, and presents contradiction as the principal and constitutive finding of his metaphysical inquiry. Indeed, contradiction accompanies that inquiry from the "cause of itself" (I, D1) at the outset, to the way in which things follow from God (I.16), the essence of the things that follow from God (I.24 and I.25), as well as additional issues that will be dealt with in the coming chapters, all the way through to the question of perfection (end of the Appendix to Part I).

78 *The second kind of knowledge*

Therefore, in the framework of the second kind of knowledge, whenever we use reason to understand existence, we find, given that the law of contradiction is the most basic law of reason, that reason is turned against itself over and over again. However, turning reason against itself is likely to send us back to the first kind of knowledge from which we sought to escape by adopting the natural light. At this point of the discussion the reader still finds his or herself perplexed: is Spinoza's journey from the domain of imagination to the domain of reason fundamentally doomed to total failure? If that is the case, why does Spinoza conceal this failure from us? Or could it be – and this possibility becomes quickly apparent – that Spinoza quietly marches along a path whose full examination demands of us an especially careful reading of his work?

Notes

1 For a more comprehensive discussion of the precise meaning of this claim, see Chapter 8 below.
2 It should be emphasized here that De Vries is not counted among those correspondents whom Spinoza took care to exclude from his philosophy, such as Casearius (see Curley, Letter 9, p. 193). On the contrary, both Spinoza's early and later biographers unanimously thought Spinoza and De Vries to be very close. Nadler, who surveys this biographical convention, takes part in it while also noting that in the letters between the two he finds "a personal warmth and intimacy rare in Spinoza's extant correspondence" (*Spinoza*, p. 162). In Letter 8, De Vries writes to Spinoza:

> Sometimes I complain about my lot, because the distance between us keeps us apart for so long.... But though our bodies are separated from one another by such a distance, nevertheless you have often been present in my mind, especially when I meditate on your writings and hold them in my hands.
>
> (Curley, p. 190)

According to Colerus' biography, De Vries, who was a wealthy merchant with a particular interest in philosophy and science, offered Spinoza a large stipend that would have allowed him to devote his time entirely to philosophy, though the latter refused to accept. Spinoza also dissuaded De Vries, when the latter was on his deathbed, from appointing Spinoza as his only heir, claiming that this would deprive De Vries' brother of his due. In addition, when De Vries bequeathed his fortune to his brother on Spinoza's advice, leaving only a monthly allowance for his friend, Spinoza only took half, claiming he had no need for a large sum. For different versions of this episode, see Nadler, *Spinoza*, pp. 259–263; also see Klever, "Spinoza's Life," p. 59, note 57.
3 Letter 10 was written in 1663, before Spinoza turned 32. At the time, a collegium was organized for group learning and study of the drafts of the first part of the *Ethics* in Amsterdam. In the name of the members of the collegium, De Vries sent to Spinoza, who at the time lived in Rijnsburg, questions of clarification and criticism that received responses from the young philosopher. See Letter 8 to De Vries, Curley, p. 190.
4 The letter not only contradicts itself but also the *Ethics*. Spinoza's claim at the start of the letter that we are not dependent on experience in order to clarify the essence of the attributes is not in line with the demonstration to proposition II.1 or the demonstration to proposition II.2 of the *Ethics*. In these passages, Spinoza expressly relies on the existence of individual modes, which is revealed to us through experience, in order to clarify the essence of the attributes that those modes express.

5 In fact, the first axiom of the second part of the *Ethics* is an individual case of proposition I.24. However, as we saw more than once, Spinoza is not punctilious to say the least, in his strictness in following the formal requirements of the Euclidean method. Here, as in other parts of the *Ethics*,

> the division between axioms and propositions is not obvious: there are axioms that would have been more appropriate as propositions, and there are propositions [...] that in fact function as axioms.
>
> (Yovel, Introduction to the *Ethics*, p. 44)

6 The reliance on the axiom of causality appears in the demonstration to proposition I.25.

7 For example, Spinoza's discussions in the TTP of the concepts of revelation and free will open with a short philosophical criticism, followed by a detailed examination of their meaning for the existing religion and for the revised religion. The first two chapters of the TTP are dedicated to an examination of the concept of revelation. The philosophical preface of this examination begins on page 13 and ends on page 14 (15–17 in the Latin), where Spinoza explicitly declares that he is passing from pure rational inquiry to an inquiry conducted in the framework of the existing revealed religion: "Truly, however, whatever we are able to say about them must be derived from Scripture alone" (ibid., p. 15 [17]). The philosophical preface to the discussion of the vocation of the Hebrews, which is carried out in the third chapter of the TTP, can be found at the top of page 43, "True joy and happiness lie in the simple enjoyment of what is good." The discussion on the theological meanings of the concept begins in the same paragraph, when Spinoza explains how Scripture uses the concept of vocation in order "to encourage [the Hebrews] to obey the law" (ibid., p. 43 [45]).

8 Spinoza does not fulfill the requirements of the geometric method when he makes use of this equivalence in the first part of the *Ethics* (I.11, Schol), before presenting it in the framework of the sixth definition of the second part. See also Spinoza's claim at the end of the third part: "we understand by perfection the very essence of the thing" ("General Definition of the Affects," pp. 542–543).

9 Indeed, Blijenbergh, who presents himself as a "Christian philosopher" (Curley, Letter 20, p. 361), claims that the non-hierarchical concept of perfection is none other than nihilism in the veil of a mechanism. "See what an opening we give to all the godless, and the godlessness [via the non-hierarchical concept of perfections]. We make ourselves like logs, and all our actions just like the movements of a clock" (ibid., p. 369). See also ibid., pp. 366–368. It is difficult to think that God, Blijenbergh claims, "wills equally, and in the same way, knavery and virtue" (Curley, Letter 22, p. 384). However, Blijenbergh is mistaken here because he does not take into account the concept of hierarchical perfections, which we will discuss in the following section, in the framework of which Spinoza asserts moral action to be a necessary condition for man's ascent on the ladder of perfections. For an extensive discussion of the Blijenbergh-Spinoza correspondence see Chapter 7.

10 Spinoza is not consistent in the use he makes of this distinction. In Letter 50 he uses the concept of negation as meaning absence when he identifies negation with limitation and being without a figure (Shirley, Letter 50, p. 260), whereas in Letter 36 he uses the concept of absence as connoting negation (Shirley, Letter 36, p. 207). Letter 36 is inconsistent in terms of its content as well as its use of concepts, as we will see in the following sub-section.

11 In another letter to Blijenbergh, Spinoza asserts: "in philosophy we understand clearly that to ascribe to God those 'attributes' which make a man perfect is as bad as if one wanted to ascribe to man those which make an elephant or an ass perfect" (Curley, Letter 23, p. 388).

12 From Letter 54 to Boxel. During the course of the correspondence between the two Spinoza takes care to praise Democritus, whose writings were burned by "those who

have thought up occult qualities, intentional species, substantial forms and a thousand more bits of nonsense" (Shirley, Letter 56, p. 279). Indeed, Spinoza's attack on the distinctions made by the power of imagination echoes Democritus' claim: "by convention sweet and by convention bitter, by convention hot, by convention cold, by convention color; but in reality atoms and void' (DK 68B9) (C.C.W. Taylor, 'The Atomists,' in Long (ed.), *The Cambridge Companion to Early Greek Philosophy*, Cambridge: Cambridge University Press 1999, p. 190.). Also see Paul Cartledge, *Democritus: The Great Philosophers*. London: Routledge, 1999, pp. 10–11.

13 For Spinoza's indirect criticism of cosmologies that assumes existence has a center, see Letter 54 to Boxel (Shirley, p. 267). It is important to emphasize that the claim according to which man does not stand at the center of existence belongs to the second kind of knowledge, and Spinoza will revise it in the context of his discussion of the intellectual love of God in the third kind of knowledge. See the last chapter, Chapter 8.

14 This claim regarding the perfection of all the details of existence is a variation of the claim that was presented at the beginning of the present sub-section.

15 The essence of Spinoza's criticism against the final causes appears in the appendix to Part I of the *Ethics*. In this context it should be noted that the concept of the final cause, like other concepts in Spinoza's philosophy, is an ambiguous concept. Spinoza rejects the partial, human meaning of the concept of finality, while adopting, albeit implicitly, its total, divine meaning. For an extensive discussion of the place, function, and importance of the final cause in Spinoza's philosophy, see Sigad, "God as Final Cause." Also see the discussion of the final cause in the context of the concept of the conatus in Chapter 5.

16 Epicurus claimed that "A blessed and eternal being has no trouble himself and brings no trouble upon any other being" (Diogenes Laertius, *Lives of Eminent Philosophers*. Translated by R.D. Hicks, Cambridge, MA: Harvard University Press, 1958, Book 10, Section 139, p. 663).

17 The passivity of the Epicurean god already faced heated criticism in the ancient period in Cicero's *The Nature of the Gods*, which Spinoza knew well. Velleius, who represents the Epicurean school in the dialogue, claims: "The god is wholly inactive, he has no round of tasks to perform, and no structures to set up" (Cicero, *The Nature of the Gods*. Translated by P.G. Walsh, Oxford: Clarendon Press, 1997, p. 21). Cotta, representing the skeptic's viewpoint in the dialogue, claims:

> "God," says Epicurus, "has no concerns." Like boy-favourites, he clearly likes nothing better than the idle life. But even these boys in their idleness seek enjoyment by playing some physical sport; do we want God to be so idle and sluggish as to make us fear that he cannot be happy if he bestirs himself? That maxim of his not merely deprives the gods of the movements and action appropriate to divinity, but also makes humans lazy, the assumption being that even God cannot be happy if he is doing something.
>
> (Ibid., p. 39)

18 Spinoza's panpsychism is the metaphysical lining of his disapproval of the conception of man as a "dominion within a dominion" (*Ethics*, Preface to Part III, p. 491). However, here too, as in the issue of the center of existence, it is important to emphasize that Spinoza's disapproval of the conception of man as a "dominion within a dominion" belongs to the second kind of knowledge, and Spinoza will revise it in the framework of the third kind of knowledge. See Chapter 8.

19 Spinoza's panpsychic hierarchy is fitting for the scientific project of the modern era that sought, among other things, to prove that distinctions made from non-philosophical-scientific viewpoints as qualitative distinctions are in fact quantitative distinctions that can be explained physically and mathematically. See Hampshire, *Spinoza*, p. 73.

Essence and perfection 81

20 See also V.40. Spinoza "demonstrates" this proposition by means of II, D6, which contradicts it, as we saw at the beginning of the previous sub-section.

21 In fact, the principle of independent action is not the only principle that Spinoza presents as an organizing principle of the hierarchy of perfections. In the appendix to the first part of the *Ethics*, during the course of the polemic against final causes, Spinoza presents another principle as the organizing principle of the hierarchy of perfections: "the more something requires intermediate causes to produce it, the more imperfect it is" (I, Appendix, p. 442). However, this principle, which contradicts not only Spinoza's principle of independent action, but also his claim of God as the nearest cause of all the things that follow from him (I.28, Schol), is neglected by Spinoza at the margins of the hierarchy of perfections, and does not stand at its center. Indeed, in the framework of his different discussions of the conception of the hierarchy of perfections, as we will see below, Spinoza brings up again and again the principle of independent action, and not the principle of the number of mediating causes, as the organizing principle of the hierarchy of perfections.

22 During the course of the discussion it will become clear that the conatus is the precise and systematic expression of this principle. See Chapter 5.

23 Of course, exchanging the imaginative hierarchy with the rational hierarchy does not solve the theological problem but rather requires its reformulation: how is it, that from a rational viewpoint, imperfect things can follow from an absolutely perfect being? Spinoza answers this question immediately in the following paragraph in the appendix (ibid., p. 446) to which we will refer in the discussion below.

24 Spinoza is referring here to Schuller's third criticism in Letter 63 (Shirley, p. 295).

25 In the correspondence with Hudde, Spinoza does not explicitly refer to this rank of perfection; the exchange of letters between the two is dedicated to clarifying the nature of that which necessarily involves existence and not to a typology of the perfection of the different elements of existence. However, the existence of the third rank of perfection is necessarily required from the principle of the potential of self-existence that is the basis of the distinction between the first two kinds of perfection.

26 Tolstoy famously opens *Anna Karenina* by noting that while all happy families are alike, unhappy families are each miserable in their own way (Leo Tolstoy, *Anna Karenina*. Translated by Constance Garnett, New York: Modern Library Classics, 2000, p. 1). However, despite the fact both Spinoza and Tolstoy concur regarding the impossibility of explaining one kind of misery through another kind, it seems that they disagree regarding the existence of a hierarchy of objective misery. While Tolstoy unequivocally denies the existence of a strict hierarchy of misery, Spinoza, as is evident from the considerations presented here, not only affirms its existence, but even provides a metaphysical ground to it. In this context see Henri Troyat, *Tolstoy*. Translated from the French by Nancy Amphoux, New York: Penguin Books, 1967, pp. 661–662.

27 See Hampshire, *Spinoza*, pp. 64–68. At the beginning of the *Treatise on the Emendation of the Intellect* Spinoza also presents ascent on the ladder of perfections as his central philosophical interest. Indeed, his desire to find something that would "continuously give me the greatest joy" (ibid., p. 7) is according to the definition of joy (*Ethics*, "General Definition of the Affects," II) a desire for "passage from a lesser to a greater perfection" (ibid.).

28 Indeed, in the framework of the third kind of knowledge, as we will see below, man succeeds in breaking the bounds of his definition as a mode, and becomes the "cause of himself." See Chapter 8.

29 Hampshire, *Spinoza*, p. 55

30 We discussed these propositions at the beginning of the present chapter. Della Rocca is overly swayed by the geometric style of the *Ethics* when he claims it is not reasonable to assume Spinoza would contradict himself proposition after proposition. See Della Rocca, "Spinoza's Metaphysical Psychology," in Garrett (ed.), *The Cambridge*

82 *The second kind of knowledge*

Companion to Spinoza. Cambridge: Cambridge University Press, 1996, p. 199. While in the specific example Della Rocca discusses, i.e., the relation between propositions III.6 and III.7, there is indeed no contradiction, I will show in Chapter 5 that the demonstrations to these two propositions do contradict them. In this context see also the discussions of Letters 21 and 23 to Blijenbergh in Chapter 7, as well as the discussion of propositions V.31; V.32; V.24; V.25, Dem; V.23, Schol; V.36 in Chapter 8.

31 See the discussion in the previous section.
32 See the discussion in the following chapter.
33 See the discussion in Chapter 8.
34 See the discussion in the following chapter. See the discussion of I.21 in Chapter 6 below, the discussion of the scholium to proposition I.25 in the previous chapter, and the discussion of the scholium to II.13, L7 in the following chapter. Also see the discussion of the scholium to proposition II.45 and the corollary to II.8 in Chapter 6 below.

4 The contradiction between static unity and dynamic multiplicity in existence

Spinoza seemingly thinks of existence as a frozen, static unity. Indeed, from the identification of existence with the concept of substance, it necessarily follows that existence is a barren wasteland of infinite existence. Existence is barred and closed within itself, nothing comes and nothing leaves, and there is nothing new within it. However, in complete contrast to this strict Parmenidean portrait, Spinoza also suggests a Heraclitean portrait of existence in which existence is considered to be an entity with infinitely many parts that is caught in an infinitely flowing stream. The infinite multiplicity of existence is a multiplicity of both attributes and of modes (finite and infinite), and its dynamic character prevails not only in the logical domain but also in the domains of space and time. At the beginning of the present chapter I aim to uncover the contradiction in the conception of existence as static unity and its conception as dynamic multiplicity, after which I will clarify the meaning and intent of this contradiction. At the end of the chapter I will discuss the contribution of the contradiction between static unity and dynamic multiplicity to a better understanding of the fundamental status of contradiction in Spinoza's philosophical system.

The conception of existence as a static unity

The departure point of Spinoza's philosophy is existence in its entirety. Indeed, logically, it is *only* existence, in its total infiniteness, which fits his definition of the substance as "what is in itself and is conceived through itself, i.e., that whose concept does not require the concept of another thing, from which it must be formed" (I, D3, II/45). Moreover, consistent logical thought about the concept of reality, which is in fact the concept of substance, leads Spinoza to the conclusion according to which:

> A substance which is absolutely infinite is indivisible.
>
> (I.13, II/55)

Spinoza demonstrates this proposition by negative proof. If it were possible to divide the substance, either the parts of the substance would preserve its nature, or the parts of the substance would not preserve its nature. If the parts of the substance preserved its nature then they too, just like the substance itself, would be absolutely infinite; but the existence of infinite many substances is absurd, as was proven in proposition I.5.[1] On the other hand, if the parts of the substance would not have preserved its nature, i.e., if the parts of the substance were not absolutely infinite, the division of the substance would have put an end to its existence; but this is also absurd and should be rejected outright since the substance necessarily exists, as was demonstrated in proposition I.11.[2] From here it necessarily follows that "[a] substance which is absolutely infinite is indivisible" (I.13).

This conclusion posits that reality is an indivisible entity. Yet even if this would be completely valid from a logical viewpoint, from an experiential viewpoint it would be entirely unfounded. Indeed, in experience existence appears before us not only as a divisible entity, but rather as one that is in fact divided into infinitely many parts. For what can be divided more than material? Material is the paradigm of division. Here, it seems, Spinoza should have been perplexed. The Euclidean manner of inquiry leads him to territories that are entirely foreign to human experience. An existence that does not contain parts is not known to us and cannot be known to us. Therefore, as a philosopher for whom knowledge is at the heart of his interests, and especially as a man of science occupied with empirical experiments,[3] Spinoza should have utterly rejected the conclusion that existence in its material domain is indivisible. In spite of this, and without hesitation, Spinoza makes the following claim with the determination of one presenting a tautology:

> [n]o substance, and consequently no corporeal substance, insofar as it is a substance, is divisible.
>
> (I.13, Cor, II/55)

The indivisibility of the attribute of extension, which is called here in Cartesian terms "corporeal substance," is one of the more radical implications of Spinoza's strict conception of unity. Spinoza adopts the term "corporeal substance" from the lexicon of his opponents for two reasons: first, because this term serves well his attempts to win over, through the use of rhetorical means, philosophers from the Cartesian camp. Thus, as we saw earlier, Spinoza continues to use terms known to and accepted by his intended audience, while pouring into them new and revolutionary content;[4] and, second, Spinoza also utilizes for the purpose of his own philosophical system the appropriation of the Cartesian term "corporeal substance" regarding the indivisibility of the attribute of extension. Prominently couched in this term is the essential affinity between the attribute of extension and the substance; Spinoza seeks to base the indivisibility of the attribute of extension on this affinity. In fact, joining the essential affinity between attribute and substance to the differentiation between the infiniteness of the substance and the infiniteness in its kind of the attribute demonstrates that, from a metaphysical perspective, the attribute should be understood as a "miniature substance." Indeed, in order to distance the substance from its attributes, Spinoza never makes use of the term "miniature substance" in order to signify the attribute. Despite this, in several places he relies on the insight that is couched in this term.

For example, earlier in the *Ethics*, in the demonstration to proposition I.10, Spinoza depends upon this insight in order to claim that the attribute, just like the substance, must be conceived through itself.[5] Whereas here, in the corollary to I.13, he posits, although indirectly, that "corporeal substance," in that it establishes the essence of an absolutely infinite substance that is "indivisible" (I.13), is itself also indivisible.

In the demonstration to the corollary of I.13, Spinoza once again enlists a logical consideration in order to reinforce his unified stance.[6] This time he presents the division of the material substance as standing in contradiction to its necessary infiniteness.[7] A material substance, in that it is a substance, is infinite, whereas the parts of a material substance, in that they are parts, are finite. Thus the division of a corporeal substance transforms it from infinite to finite, "which implies a plain contradiction" (I.13, Schol, II/55).[8] Hence every substance, in that it is a substance, is necessarily infinite, as is shown in proposition I.8.[9]

The turn to philosophers from the Cartesian camp is especially evident in Spinoza's claim that regarding the indivisibility of the corporeal substance, "[a]ll those who know that clear reason is infallible must confess this – particularly those who deny that there is a vacuum" (I.15, Schol, II/59, p. 423). The denial of the existence of a vacuum is a Cartesian position that Spinoza adopts and labored to explain in his book *Descartes Principles of Philosophy*.[10] According to Spinoza, the impossibility of a vacuum does not concord with the division of the corporeal substance into parts really (*realiter*) distinct from each other: "Truly, of things which are really distinct from one another, one can be, and remain in its condition, without the other" (ibid.).[11] However, given that "all [nature's] parts must so concur that there is no vacuum" (ibid.), the annihilation of one of the parts would force all other parts to readjust as all parts must be "so fitted together that there is no vacuum" (ibid.). This negates the possibility of the parts being really (*realiter*) distinct from one another. It therefore necessarily follows that "corporeal substance, insofar as it is a substance, cannot be divided" (ibid.).

Spinoza presents the choice between the divisibility and indivisibility of corporeality as the choice between falsehood and truth; yet he does not present it as an easy decision to take. Each one of us is necessarily saturated by "random" or "vague" experience (*experientia vaga*) that teaches us over and over, in all of its might and infinite apparitions, about the divisibility of corporeality:

> If someone should now ask why we are, by nature, so inclined to divide quantity, I shall answer that we conceive quantity in two ways: abstractly, *or superficially*, as we [commonly] imagine it, or as a substance, which is done by the intellect alone [without the help of the imagination]. So if we attend to quantity as it is in the imagination, which we do often and more easily, it will be found to be finite, divisible, and composed of parts; but if we attend to it as it is in the intellect, and conceive it insofar as it is a substance, which happens [seldom and] with great difficulty, then (as we have already sufficiently demonstrated) it will be found to be infinite, unique, and indivisible.
>
> (I.15, Schol, II/59, pp. 423–424)[12]

86 *The second kind of knowledge*

Here, just as at other junctions of knowledge and action, we are called upon to favor the intellect over the power of imagination, even if this preference demands special effort on our part. For example,

> we conceive that water is divided and its parts separated from one another – insofar as it is water, but not insofar as it is corporeal substance. For insofar as it is substance, it is neither separated nor divided. Again, water, insofar as it is water, is generated and corrupted, but insofar as it is substance, it is neither generated nor corrupted.
>
> (Ibid., p. 423)

The difference between the parts of water is merely the difference in the mode (*modaliter*), and is thus not a true distinction; in the Cartesian terms[13] which Spinoza here adopts, it is a distinction between different qualities of the same thing that is determined by the power of imagination alone, not by the intellect.

In Letters 35 and 36 to Hudde, Spinoza also maintains a strict Parmenidean stance by binding the indivisibility of the substance to its absolute perfection. To divide a thing means to impose a defect on it, to set a limit for it, or to attribute to it a change that "it might undergo from external causes through its lack of force" (Shirley, Letter 35, p. 204). However, "if we were to ascribe any imperfection to such a Being [who involves necessary existence], we would at once fall into a contradiction" (ibid.). Further, "we are always reduced to saying that this nature which involves necessary existence does not exist, or does not exist necessarily" (ibid.). In other words, the substance, in that it involves existence, is absolutely perfect; in that it is absolutely perfect it cannot be divided. Additionally, in these letters to Hudde Spinoza binds the indivisibility of the substance to its eternity. Given that the substance is eternal, "[i]t is simple (*simplex*), and not composed of parts" (ibid., p. 203). The parts of a thing precede it, both chronologically and from an ontological perspective; and, "[i]n the case of that which is eternal by its own nature, this cannot be so" (ibid.), in that its existence is timeless (I, D8, Exp, II/48), and necessary (V.30, Dem, II/299).

Spinoza sees fit to especially stress that the simplicity of the substance reinforces its unity and prevents its division. In order to remove any doubt he explicitly and unequivocally states: "by simple I mean only that which is not composite or composed of parts that are different in nature, or of other parts that agree in nature" (Shirley, Letter 36, p. 206).[14] Thus Spinoza dismisses all attempts at division, of one type or another, of the substance. The static state of the substance is necessarily derived from its unity. Indeed, a dynamic state expresses change, and change expresses multiplicity that in fact contradicts the absolute unity of the substance. Moreover, if the substance is dynamic, not only would its complete unity be shattered, but its supreme perfection too would be undermined and its necessary existence would come to an end (ibid., p. 205). It follows that in the substance, in that it is a unified, perfect, and necessary being, no change can take place.

Two conclusions with far-reaching consequences arise from the conception of existence as a frozen, static unity: first, the substance, and only the substance, gives us the true idea (I, A6) of existence. Indeed, only substance connotes the one, unified and desolate unit of absolutely infinite existence. Existence is one and its concept is one. In existence *or* in the substance there are not, nor could there be, attributes and modes because they connote multiplicity; and, second, because the substance is indivisible in that it involves necessary existence (I.13, Dem), and in that it is absolutely infinite (I.13, Cor, Schol), eternal and absolutely perfect (Letters 35, 36, to Hudde), and because what cannot be divided also cannot be explained in that every explanation makes distinctions and divisions, the Spinozistic notion of substance, just like the Parmenidean entity, cannot be known.[15] Here, Spinoza once again leads us on his twisting path to the transcendent territory of his philosophy. He again behaves as "The Lord whose oracle is at Delphi [and who] neither reveals nor conceals, but gives a sign" (22B93 DK).[16] On the one hand, Spinoza never explicitly claims that the substance has no attributes or modes, nor does he declare there to be no way to know the substance. On the other hand, in several places in the *Ethics*, he directs us to precisely these insights.

These insights are not hidden in the side-alleys of the *Ethics*; they are inscribed on the gate to the city that Spinoza erects with logos. All that the reader must do in order to recognize them is to go back and carefully read the definitions of the fundamental metaphysical trio of the system, while keeping in mind the way Spinoza defines definitions. The substance is defined by Spinoza as "what is in itself and is conceived through itself, i.e., that whose concept does not require the concept of another thing, from which it must be formed" (I, D3). The attribute is defined as "what the intellect perceives of a substance, as constituting its essence" (I, D4), while the mode is defined as "the affections of a substance, *or* that which is in another through which it is also conceived" (I, D5). Spinoza's definition of definition determines that the definition of a thing connotes the essence and nature of the defined thing (I.8, Schol 2, Section I.; I.33, Schol 1; and III.56, Dem). Therefore, the absence of the attributes and the modes from the definition of the substance proves that they are not essential to it. Moreover, they do not exist in the substance. If they did, they would exist contingently and not necessarily since they are not essential to it; but this cannot be, since all that exists, exists by necessity and not by contingency (I.29). It follows from this that substance does not and cannot have attributes or modes.

The definition of the substance buttresses the fortress of the Being closed within itself, resists any attempt to make distinctions in it or to know it, and protects the purity of static unity from the multiplicity and dynamic state of the attributes and modes. This transcendence of the substance returns and appears both in the opening proposition of the first part of the *Ethics*, i.e., "a substance is prior in nature to its affections" (I.1), and in Spinoza's related assertion according to which considering the substance truly and in itself (*in se*) requires a detachment from the affections (I.5, Dem). Since we already discussed these claims at length in Chapter 2, there is no need to treat them here; it will suffice to simply take note of them. The definition of the attribute joins the transcendent trend that permeates the definition of the substance. The attribute, as we saw, is defined only as "what the intellect perceives of a substance, as constituting its essence" (I, D4), and not as what it in itself (*in se*) constitutes of the essence of the substance.[17] Thus the essence of the substance is beyond the attributes and cannot be perceived even by the infinite intellect, as the latter is an immediate, infinite mode in the attribute of thought (Shirley, Letter 64). That is to say, existence, in that it is a static unity, is not known to man given that he is but a finite fragment of it; it is not even known to itself, given that a unified substance cannot be grasped by a multiplicity of attributes, or a multiplicity of modes, even if they are infinite as the mode of infinite intellect is.

If the concept of God itself (I, D6) was not invalidated by the multiplicity of attributes contained within it, we would be permitted to declare: not only does man not know God, but even God does not know himself.[18]

Dynamic multiplicity versus static unity

Although Spinoza declares his obligation to the conception of existence as a static unity several times and concerning various areas of his philosophy, this does not prevent him from comprehensively adopting the opposite stance, which conceives of existence as a dynamic multiplicity. The majority of Spinoza's work in metaphysics, epistemology, science, and ethics is dedicated to mapping the infinitely many details of existence by tracing the organizing principles of the dynamic state in which they are situated.[19] Moreover, Spinoza sees no need to conceal his adoption of the concept of dynamic multiplicity, the metaphysical opponent of the concept of static unity, and he openly declares his loyalty to the former. For example, in the second part of the *Ethics* Spinoza awards the stamp of reason to "common notions" (*notions communes*) that signify what is common to all things equally in the part and in the whole (II.37, II/118) when he situates them in the framework of the second kind of knowledge (II.40, Schol 1, II/122).

Here, too, the perplexed reader of the *Ethics* finds himself standing at a crossroads leading to opposite metaphysical destinations that have no place in a Euclidean system. On the right is the path leading to existence as a static unity, on the left the path leading to existence as dynamic multiplicity, and in the center stands Spinoza, one hand pointing to the right while the other points to the left. Where should the reader turn? If in one place Spinoza teaches him that, "no corporeal substance, insofar as it is a substance, is divisible" (I.13, Schol), in another place Spinoza not only attributes parts to a corporeal substance, but also explicitly claims "that each part pertains to the nature of corporeal substance, and can neither be nor be conceived without" (Shirley, Letter 32, p. 194). Which path will the reader choose? In one place Spinoza teaches him that the whole is a simple thing that "is not composite or composed of parts that are different in nature, or of other parts that agree in nature" (Shirley, Letter 36, p. 206). In another place he claims that the whole is divided into parts that agree with each other according to their nature; in his words: "I consider things as parts of a whole to the extent that their natures adapt themselves to one another so that they are in the closest possible agreement" (Shirley, Letter 32, pp. 192–193).

The contradiction in the matter of unity and multiplicity joins a long line of contradictions in other fundamental issues within Spinoza's metaphysics, which we discussed in the previous chapters. Without lessening the importance of uncovering an additional contradiction of depth in Spinoza's philosophical system, in this instance the significance of the contradiction lies not only in its existence but also in the way in which it is presented. Indeed, the special way in which Spinoza chooses to present the contradiction in the matter of unity and multiplicity has crucial importance in terms of understanding the essential status of contradiction in his philosophical system. In the previous issues we discussed, contradiction came up only when we joined together two separate statements made by Spinoza, even if textually he took care to connect them in one way or another, as though from fear that the contradiction between them would escape us;[20] yet, in certain places regarding the question of unity and multiplicity, Spinoza casts the two contradictory stances within one single statement. For example, during the course of the discussion on the relation between the substance and its attributes Spinoza posits:

> it is far from absurd [*absurdum*] to attribute many attributes to one substance.
> (I.10, Schol, II/52)[21]

This is a fascinating claim; Spinoza presents the contradiction in the matter of unity and multiplicity while at the very same time denying that contradiction. However, before clarifying this, we will look at an additional statement that appears during the course of Spinoza's discussion of complex individuals:

> the whole of nature is one Individual [*Individuum*], whose parts, i.e., all bodies, vary in infinite ways, without any change of the whole Individual.
> (II.13, L7, Schol, II/102)

In the first passage, Spinoza equates unity with multiplicity, and in the second passage he equates the static with the dynamic. In the first passage Spinoza posits the equality of opposites in *natura naturans*, and in the second passage he asserts that same equality in *natura naturata*. Moreover, from the isomorphism that Spinoza claims can be found in individuals in nature as well as in nature in its entirety (II.13, L7, Schol), it follows that each and every individual in nature carries within it the contradiction between static unity and dynamic multiplicity that nature in its entirety carries. The repetition of the same contradiction in the most universal and the most particular sheds light on Spinoza's famous claim in the last part of the *Ethics*, "The more we understand singular things, the more we understand God" (V.24, II/296).[22] The finite and the infinite contradict each other but, in that they carry within them that very same contradiction, they are identical. Therefore, understanding one is the same as understanding the other. This is the hidden meaning of the laconic, almost provocative demonstration that Spinoza appends to this proposition: "This is evident from I.25, Cor" (V.24, Dem). In the corollary to proposition I.25, for the first time in the *Ethics*, the

90   *The second kind of knowledge*

dialectic relations between the finite and infinite are determined, and in the framework of these relations the finite expresses the infinite in that it both contradicts the latter and is identical to it.[23] Furthermore, from proposition I.16, we understand that the very same contradiction contained in the definition of God (I, D6) – the contradiction between unity (the complete unity of the substance) and multiplicity (the infinite multiplicity of the attributes) – is also the internal logic of the eternal abundance that follows from him, in the framework of which multiplicity (the infinite multiplicity of the modes) follows from unity (the complete unity of the substance).

It does not follow from the definition of the substance (I, D3) that it has infinitely many attributes, or that infinite many modes derive from it. The opposite is true, as we saw in the previous section; the strict Parmenidean definition of the substance determines it to be an entity that does not and could not have attributes and modes. Only from the definition of God that shatters the unity of the substance in *natura naturans* through infinite many attributes, follows the shattering of the unity of the substance in *natura naturata* through infinite many modes. Indeed, according to Spinoza's axiom of causality (I, A4) and its textual offshoots (Preface to Part IV; III.56 Dem; I.8 Schol 2), as a result of the *natura naturans*, the *natura naturata* necessarily maintains within itself the identity of opposites of its cause. This is the full meaning of proposition I.16, in which Spinoza pegs the flow of infinite many modes to the "divine nature," which, in accordance to the equivalence between the definition of a thing and its nature (I.8, Schol 2, Section I), is God. It is determined in this proposition, as is shown in the explanation that Spinoza appends to it, that from the contradiction between complete unity (of the substance) and infinite multiplicity (of the attributes) contained in the nature of God, there follows the contradiction between the complete unity (of the substance) and the infinite multiplicity (of the modes) that follow from God. Moreover, in the demonstration to proposition 16, Spinoza pins the infinite flow from God on his infinite many attributes (I, D6), which, according to proposition I.9, grant him infinite reality.[24] That is to say: Spinoza teaches us that just as the multiplicity of attributes in *natura naturans* does not destroy but rather constructs the absolute being, the multiplicity of modes in *natura naturata* does not destroy but constructs that very same being. To put it differently, as Spinoza does later on in the discussion: "God must be called the cause of all things in the same sense in which he is called the cause of himself" (I.25, Schol, II/68). Meaning, in the same sense that one sees God as static unity, one must also see God as dynamic multiplicity.

The meaning of the contradiction between unity and multiplicity and its contribution to understanding the fundamental status of contradiction in Spinoza's system

From all that we have seen up to this point, it can be concluded that the contradiction between the conceptions of static unity and dynamic multiplicity appears at three central junctions in Spinoza's philosophy: the relation between substance

Static unity or dynamic multiplicity? 91

and the attributes; the relation between the substance and the modes; and the relation between the modes, in that they are individuals, and themselves. Thus, the contradiction between static unity and dynamic multiplicity completely subsumes all of existence, its general principles and details, strata, branches and different components.

As noted, Spinoza does all he can in order not to admit the existence of this contradiction. In the beginning, he denies it in a weak voice when he lets slip, as though incidentally, in the scholium to proposition I.10 that, "it is far from absurd to attribute many attributes to one substance." Later on, he once again is not satisfied in just denying the existence of the contradiction, and even seeks to drape it in the garb of a Euclidean axiom when he loudly declares in proposition I.16 – in which he derives one appearance of the logical contradiction between unity and multiplicity (the relation between the substance and the modes) from another of its appearances (the relation between the substance and the attributes) – "This proposition must be plain to anyone [*manifestum*]" (I.16, Dem).[25] Yet in I.10, Schol, and in I.16, Dem as well, if something is at all "plain to anyone," it is not Spinoza's innocence from being "absurd," but in fact his undeniable guilt. Moreover, the appearance of the logical contradiction in the matter of unity and multiplicity within one and the same claim (as in I.10, Schol and II.13, L7, Schol), which was discussed earlier, is absolute proof of Spinoza's guilt of betraying logic, or being "absurd," and that he did so not in error, but intentionally.

A reader who would attempt here (I.10, Schol; II.13, L7, Schol) to defend Spinoza and to present him as one who accidentally encountered contradictory positions in the matter of unity and multiplicity, would find himself taking on against his will, even if opaquely, one of the following two grave charges: Spinoza does not understand what a logical contradiction is and/or Spinoza does not understand his own ideas. In the first case, he declares faith in logic without understanding it, while in the second case he is utterly lost in a meaningless maze of words, which he erected with his own hands while absolutely convinced that he was sheltered by the security of his magnificently built Euclidean castle. Either way, one who seeks to defend Spinoza ends up accusing him.[26] There is no doubt this interpretive possibility is particularly radical; it seems to present one of the great thinkers of Western philosophy as a rather incompetent thinker. Nevertheless, we should not reject it just because it is not in line with the reputation of Spinoza and his writings. Otherwise we would make Spinoza holy and his writings sacred, which would certainly be against the spirit of a philosopher who declared a war, on both the metaphysical and the social-political fronts, against those who enslave "reason, the greatest gift and the divine light, to the dead letters [*mortuis literis*]" (TTP, XV, p. 188 [182] slightly rephrased). Indeed, truth, in that it is universal, is completely indifferent to the reputation of any cultural hero. It is better that we remain with the truth and without Spinoza, rather than remain with Spinoza but without the truth.

It might seem that Spinoza's philosophy is positioned as a city without a wall facing this interpretive attack; it lacks organized, explicit theoretical defense that would prevent the logical contradiction revealed in it to lead to its destruction. Nevertheless, in its present state it is still capable of holding on and repelling the interpretive attack against it. To paraphrase the French politician Talleyrand regarding Russia, it can be said that even if Spinoza's philosophy is not as strong as it seems, it is also not as weak as it seems. Ultimately, this interpretive attack suffers a decisive defeat that is twofold: *Firstly*, its adoption leads the interpreter to betray his obligation to interpretive fairness, which determines that only when he has no other choice is he permitted to judge his subject as lacking all meaning.[27] However, in the case of the contradiction between unity and multiplicity, as I aim to show, presenting Spinoza's position as lacking all meaning is not the only possibility, and therefore there is no basis for the exclusivity granted to this interpretation. *Secondly* – and this is more grave – this interpretation exempts itself, with intolerable ease, from a serious and exhaustive treatment of a philosophy whose true meaning, for internal systematic and fundamental reasons, must be concealed.[28] Every philosopher deserves to have his writings analyzed with interpretive fairness, and all the more so a philosopher whose writings serve as a prime example of concealment and double-language.[29]

It follows from this that Spinoza is not a dubious philosopher who sins against logic by error or arbitrariness. The opposite is correct: Spinoza is a philosopher who from the first line punctiliously maintains the laws of logic, and it can surely be assumed that if he comes to a logical contradiction, he does so intentionally and for good reasons.[30] Paradoxically – something unavoidable to one who wishes to simultaneously reveal and conceal things – Spinoza admits to the existence of the logical contradiction in the matter of unity and multiplicity through his open denial of it (I.10, Schol; I.16, Dem). The complete non-validity and almost full exposure of this denial testifies to the fact that it is merely an *apparent* denial that serves as a hidden admission to the existence of the contradiction. When Spinoza claims in proposition I.10 that "it is far from absurd to attribute many attributes to one substance," he is not concealing the contradiction but rather handing it over to us;[31] and this is precisely his intent.[32] Between the lines, Spinoza seeks to turn our attention to the existence of the logical contradiction between unity and multiplicity, and to make known to us that it is has not escaped him, nor has its philosophical justification. Concealing the existence of the contradiction in the matter of unity and multiplicity carries with it the concealing of its meaning. Therefore, whoever seeks to uncover the meaning of this contradiction must connect the chapters of the *Ethics* together, and adjoin the following two textual data: *Firstly*, the object of the contradiction in the matter of unity and multiplicity, just as that of every other contradiction of depth in Spinoza's metaphysics, is God.[33] *And secondly*, an unbridgeable metaphysical chasm separates God and all that follows from him.[34] Therefore it is possible to defend Spinoza's philosophy by adopting the claim according to which the absolute other must operate according to a completely other logic.[35] While in the framework of a conventional logic contradiction destroys its object, in the framework of a divine logic, contradiction must construct its object. In other words, to be different in essence from a logical point of view means to be constructed by contradiction itself. Therefore, it could be that what appears before us as an arbitrary violation of the general logic of things, is in fact a careful, measured concealment of the private logic of God.

Spinoza does not explicitly formulate this claim because of considerations of esotericism we will expand upon below.[36] Nonetheless, he returns and directs us again and again, in the various issues discussed in the present part of this book, to both the contradictions embedded in the concept of God, as well as to the status of God as absolutely other from all that follows from him. As such it can be concluded that the contradiction in the concept of God is a result of his total otherness. The text therefore can be saved by a principle that does not explicitly appear in it, though it is embedded within it at the very least as a legitimate interpretive possibility.

The contradiction between static unity and dynamic multiplicity reflects an ancient theological-ontological dilemma: does God's supreme perfection cast him in the mold of a simple, static being? Or does that perfection come to fruition in the infinite dynamic multiplicity of the beings created by him? Or, and this of course, is a paradox, does God, in that he is absolutely perfect, contain within himself the two mutually exclusive logical possibilities?[37] Spinoza chooses the latter option and does so from the following consideration: if God were only static unity, the absence of dynamic multiplicity would diminish his perfection; and the contrary: if God were only dynamic multiplicity, he would lack static unity. Therefore, in order to establish his complete perfection he must contain both of these mutually exclusive logical possibilities.

Spinoza, who equates unity with dynamicity, seems to opt for a Christian point of view. In the framework of the idea of the trinity God is understood as one that is three. Yet the similarity is only very partial. The Christian choice of the number three is, from a Spinozistic perspective, dogmatic and lacks any rational justification, and should therefore be rejected outright. Revising the Christian conception of the trinity, Spinoza claims that God is total unity that is infinite multiplicity. This revision of the Christian concept of the trinity grants us an additional explanation for Spinoza's position (which will be discussed in the afterword) according to which in theology truth is given through a mist of uncertainty.

It should by now become clear to us why contradictions appear again and again in the heart of Spinoza's philosophy; just as the concept of God is constructed through the contradiction between unity and multiplicity, it is also constructed through every other contradiction of depth in Spinoza's philosophy. However, despite that Spinoza chooses contradiction – the mother of all sins in the domain of logic – as his philosophical companion on his path to God, in order to conceal it he continues to wave, throughout the way, the flag of Euclidean thought.

Notes

1 Proposition I.5 posits: "In nature there cannot be two or more substances of the same nature *or* attribute." According to Bennett, the demonstration to this proposition negates the multiplicity of substances that have one mode or those that have infinite modes, but not a multiplicity of substances that have an infinite though different composition of attributes. See Bennett, *Spinoza's Ethics*, p. 64. See also Gilead Bar-Elli. "God and Nature: Spinoza's Problem of Existence and Monism," *Iyyun* 60 (2011) [Heb.], pp. 148–49. While deviating from the geometric order, Spinoza appends an additional demonstration to proposition I.5 in the second scholium of proposition I.8.

94 *The second kind of knowledge*

2 Spinoza is referring here to the proof of God's existence, while relying on the equivalence between the substance and God (I, D6; I.14, Cor 1). However, it would have been preferable here to refer to proposition I.7, which claims: "It pertains to the nature of a substance to exist," not only because this proposition precedes the proof of God's existence (I.11), but also, and principally, because Spinoza grants it, in the most explicit way, a status equal to that of an axiom (I.8, Schol 2; again, while deviating from the geometric procedure).

3 Spinoza was versed in optics, chemistry, anatomy, and hydraulics, among other things. For example, see Letters 6, 13, and 41. As such, when discussing his philosophy, it should be recalled, as Klever posits: "His [Spinoza's] philosophy was not a kind of 'arm-chair philosophy,' far away from the center of natural science. On the contrary, he conceived and practiced a type of philosophy which was continuous with what we call today 'natural science'" ("Spinoza's Life and Works," p. 28).

4 We discussed this in chapters 1 and 3. On Spinoza's attempt to win over Cartesian philosophers by rhetorical means see Yovel's introduction to his translation of the *Ethics*, p. 44.

5 In an earlier version of the *Ethics*, a section of which appears in a letter from 1663, Spinoza almost completely equates the two when he determines them in the framework of one definition:

> By substance I understand what is in itself and is conceived through itself, i.e., whose concept does not involve the concept of another thing. I understand the same by attribute, except that it is called attribute in relation to the intellect, which attributes such and such a definite nature to substance.
>
> (Curley, Letter 9, p. 195)

6 Textually, Spinoza presents this demonstration in the scholium to the corollary to proposition I.13.

7 Given that in the demonstration to the proposition itself (I.13) the division of the substance is presented as standing in contradiction to its necessary existence, and given that in the first scholium to proposition I.8 the infinity of the substance is linked to its necessary existence, the demonstration of the corollary to proposition I.13 is in the form of a variation of the demonstration to the proposition itself. However, as we will see immediately, it is an incomplete variation.

8 In Bennett's adroit words: "It [the extended substance] cannot be split from side to side, because it is infinite in all directions and has no sides, and it cannot have pieces taken away from it because there is nowhere for them to go" (*Spinoza's Ethics*, p. 66).

9 The logical equivalence should have led Spinoza to present a claim parallel to the one presented in the demonstration to proposition I.13, and in its framework he would have been required to dismiss the possibility that the parts of the corporeal substance would be infinite just like the substance itself. Here, the reader can complete the procedure of demonstration I.13, corollary on his own, and by relying on proposition I.5, dismiss the possibility that grants infinity to the parts of the corporeal substance.

10 See ibid., Part II, propositions 2 and 3. Also see Descartes, *Principles of Philosophy*, Part II, paragraph 16.

11 Here, Spinoza is following Descartes, who claims: "we can perceive that two substances are really distinct simply from the fact that we can clearly and distinctly understand one apart from the other" (René Descartes, *Principles of Philosophy*, Part I, paragraph 60, in *The Philosophical Writings of Descartes*, Three Volumes, edited and translated by John Cottingham, Robert Stoothoff, and Dugald Murdoch. Cambridge: Cambridge University Press, 1985, *p.* 213). This distinction became, in Spinoza's independent philosophical framework, an axiom that claims: "Things that have nothing in common with one another also cannot be understood through one another, *or* the concept of the one does not involve the concept of the other" (I, A5).

12 As in the corollary to proposition I.13, Spinoza is referring here to extension "insofar as it is a substance." In fact, Spinoza conceives of the attribute of extension, like the other attributes, as a "mini-substance" as we suggested by relying on I, D4, and the alternative explanation to proposition I.6.
13 See Descartes, *Principles of Philosophy*, Part I, paragraphs 60–61.
14 "Simple: refers to a thing that is not comprised of many things but is only one," Ibn Tibbon states in his *Explanation of Alien Words* that he appends to his classic translation of Maimonides' *Guide to the Perplexed* (Maimonides. *Moreh Nevuchim* [*The Guide of the Perplexed*], translated to Hebrew by Shmuel ibn Tibbon. Jerusalem: Mossad HaRav Kook, 1981), which Spinoza knew well. For a discussion of the theological and philosophical manifestations of the conception of God as a simple being, see Gerard J. Hughes, *The Nature of God*. London: Routledge, 1995, pp. 34–63.
15 See the eighth fragment of Parmenides according to the Diels-Kranz system, especially line 22 and line 50 and on (Daniel Graham, *The Texts of the Early Greek Philosophy: The Complete Fragments and Selected Testimonies of the Major Presocratics*. Cambridge: Cambridge University Press, 2010, p. 217 and p. 219).
16 Heraclitus. *The Art and Thought of Heraclitus*. Translated and edited by Charles Kahn. Cambridge: Cambridge University Press, 1981, p. 45. It seems that in this fragment Heraclitus is hinting at his own concealed style, which already in the ancient period garnered him the title "The Obscure" (Ibid, p. 95).

Spinoza as well, as we will see further on, was already perceived by those of his own time period, such as Blijenbergh and Leibniz, as an enigmatic and confusing philosopher. See chapter 7 and the afterword below.
17 Mason, who extensively surveys the disagreements among interpreters regarding the definition of the attribute, notes that the four concluding words of the definition, *tanquam ejusdem essentiam constituens* ("as constituting its essence") fueled more controversies than any other thing that Spinoza wrote. See Mason, *The God of Spinoza*, p. 46 and p. 96. Mason himself, who claims that Spinoza completely identifies the substance with its attributes, is not able to explain the appearance of the intellect in the definition of the attribute. See ibid., pp. 45–50.
18 Here, Spinoza is adhering to an even stricter version of divine transcendence than the theologians. While in the framework of theological transcendence the knowledge of God is inaccessible only to man and not to God himself, in the framework of Spinozian transcendence even God does not know himself. As is known, Spinoza also adhered to a more radical version of divine infinity than the theologians, in the framework of which he attributed to God the corporeality that the theologians denied him. See I.15, Scholium.
19 The references here are extremely numerous, and I will only discuss the main contexts in which Spinoza supports the conception of dynamic multiplicity. Spinoza's physics and moral theory reinforce this conception. Indeed, Spinoza's physics grants an axiomatic status to the multiplicity of bodies and the dynamic state in which they exist (II.13, A1 and A2), while his moral theory, which is based on a conception of man as a complex individual, grounds the attempt of every individual to be more than what he is in maintaining the proportions between the parts of his body, as well as between the parts of his mind. See II.15, Dem; IV.39; and IV.60.
20 In the previous chapter we presented four textual techniques that Spinoza uses to make prominent the contradictions in the *Ethics*.
21 For a discussion of Spinoza's concept of *absurdus* in his political theory, see Menachem Lorberbaum, "Republic in Hebrew: On the Hebrew Translation of Spinoza's Political Terminology," p. 200.
22 This claim indeed belongs to the third kind of knowledge, as follows from the demonstrations to propositions V.25 and V.26. However, as we will see in the following, the logical contradiction is not abolished in the ascent from the second to the third kind of knowledge. On the contrary, it only becomes stronger because of the existential dimension added to it. See chapter 8 below.

96 *The second kind of knowledge*

23 In Chapter 2 we discussed at length the corollary to proposition I.25.
24 Proposition I.9 is presented in Letter 64 to Schuller as a proposition whose singular object is God. On the special importance of this proposition for the monism of Spinoza's system see Bar-Elli, "God and Nature," p. 151 and on.
25 It does not follow from here that proposition I.16 is "a new axiom in the form of a proposition," as Yovel claims (footnote 1 to proposition I.16 and p. 44 in Yovel's introduction to the *Ethics*). The opposite is correct: proposition I.16 is a new proposition in the form of an axiom. Indeed, as we saw at the end of the previous section, even if in this proposition Spinoza presents a new procedure in his metaphysics, this is not a procedure detached from the procedures that preceded it, but rather a procedure that necessarily derives from the dialectical logic of the system, which was presented and enhanced in what came before proposition I.16.
26 The correspondence between Spinoza and Blijenbergh presents a rich and colorful portrait of an interpreter who, in tracing the logical defects in Spinoza's philosophy, went from being the system's advocate to its prosecutor. See chapter 7 of the present book.
27 Quine demonstrates the principle of interpretive fairness in the following way: "when to our querying of an English sentence an English speaker answers 'yes and no,' we assume that the queried sentence is meant differently in the affirmation and negation; this rather than that he would be so silly to affirm and deny the same thing" (W.V.O. Quine, *Word and Object*. Cambridge, MA: MIT Press, 1960, p. 59). In the framework of this example, the interpreter assumes that if the speaker were completely precise and exhaustive in his language, there would not have been a contradiction in his answer. Spinoza, however, does not need this kind of interpretive fairness, as his language is precise and deliberate and the contradictions in his system aren't some kind of linguistic misunderstanding. Spinoza demands another kind of interpretative attention, in the framework of which, through explanations that will become clear during the course of our inquiry, the contradictions in his system will receive complete recognition.
28 The philosopher's obligation of concealment applies both to the socio-political sphere, which I discussed in the chapter 1, as well as in the metaphysical sphere, which I will discuss in the afterword.
29 The explanation of the claim according to which the *Ethics* as well as the TTP were written in double, concealing language was presented in the introduction. Also see Strauss, *Persecution and the Art of Writing*, pp. 186–190.
30 Yovel supposes that in the background of the Latin phrase *sed mea haec est ratio*, which Spinoza makes use of in the preface to the third part of the *Ethics*, there is situated not only Micio's monologue from the play *Adelphi* by Terence, as several editors have noted, but also the flowery Hebrew phrase *ta'ami v'nimuki imi* ("I have my own reasons"). On Latin phrases and epigrams from Terence's plays that infiltrate Spinoza's writings, as well as the active part that he played as a young man in the presentation of these plays at the municipal theater in Amsterdam as part of his Latin studies in the Van den Enden school, see Klever, "Spinoza's Life," p. 21. Also see Nadler, *Spinoza*, pp. 109–110, 155. Also see the discussion in chapter 8.
31 When Spinoza declares regarding proposition I.16 – in which he derives one appearance of the logical contradiction between unity and multiplicity (the relation between the substance and the mode) from another appearance of it (the relation between the substance and the attributes) – "This proposition must be plain to anyone (*manifestum*)" (I.16, Dem) he is not solving the contradiction but merely emphasizing it.
32 In the TTP Spinoza also deploys this technique. As we saw in chapter 1, his recurring, explicit and unexplained denials of the existence of the contradiction between philosophy and theology only serve to stress the depth of the contradiction between these two foundational projects, as can be seen from the different discussions of truth and falsehood in the TTP.

33 All the chapters in the present part present this textual datum, and as such a flood of references is unnecessary here.
34 Spinoza proclaims this chasm in the opening proposition of the *Ethics*: "A substance is prior in nature to its affections" (I.1), and he returns to point it out in several different contexts in his philosophy, which we discussed in chapter 2.
35 See Sigad, "God as Final Cause," p. 398 and the references there.
36 See the afterword.
37 This theological-ontological difficulty is always on the horizon of Spinoza's discussion, as Mason points out:

> Although abstract, this was an issue where religious intuitions – or perhaps temperaments – had been divided: in contrast with the less schismatic issues of the numerical unity, the infinity or the eternity of God. Even mystical insights could point with equal force in opposite directions – towards simplicity and towards multiplicity – maybe creating the temptations to smother the issue in a blanket of ineffability or divine unintelligibility.
> (The God of Spinoza, p. 47)

However, Spinoza does not adopt, in any context, the equivalence of opposites of the mystics. Indeed, he does not use it as a means to exempt himself from rational inquiry into God. On the contrary, as we will see in the following, Spinoza's insistence on opposites expresses his complete loyalty to reason, as well as his readiness to follow its footsteps even when it leads him to the territory of contradiction. Spinoza's equivalence of opposites is philosophical, not mystical, and it shares in common only a name with the equivalence the mystics make. See the afterword.

5 The conatus of God and the five contradictions embedded within it

(1) static – dynamic;
(2) efficient causality – final causality;
(3) substance – mode;
(4) finiteness – infiniteness;
(5) the contradiction between good and evil in God

At the center of Spinoza's system is the principle of conatus, which connotes the desire of every thing to persevere in its being. The importance of this principle – one of the foundational principles of the *Ethics* – is not cast in doubt. Despite this, many do not take heed of the logical contradictions embedded within the principle; and even more problematic are those who attempt to blur the contradictions throughout the text by means of distorted translations of its definition (III.6), translations that aim to be more successful than the original from a logical standpoint. In contrast, I will seek in the present chapter to uncover the contradictions entrenched in the principle of the conatus, analyze these contradictions, and suggest a proper translation of the definition of conatus to replace the flawed translations that exist. In total, as will be seen, there are five contradictions embedded in the conatus. Some of them are known to us from other territories of Spinoza's philosophy, and some of them we are encountering here for the first time.

The general status of the conatus in Spinoza's system

Spinoza's psychology is completely subordinate to his metaphysics. Indeed, Spinoza maintains the strict naturalist position that claims man to be merely a fragment of nature, and as such his body and mind are completely subordinate to the general laws of nature. Human existence, Spinoza argues, is not conceived in nature "as a dominion within a dominion" (Preface to Part III, p. 491 [II/137]).[1] Indeed, the principle of conatus is situated at the foundation of Spinoza's psychology, and it is a general metaphysical principle applied not only to humans but also to all the other things in nature. This principle – one of the more fascinating and fruitful in Spinoza's philosophy – is presented at the beginning of the third part of the *Ethics*:[2]

> Each thing, as far as it is in itself (*in se est*), strives to persevere in its being.
> (III.6, II/146, my translation)[3]

Spinoza presents the principle of striving in the framework of a proposition, and he even appends to it a demonstration, which will be discussed shortly. Yet, the conatus really functions in Spinoza's philosophy as an axiom. It is adjoined to the proposition that is "evident through itself" (III.4, Dem, II/145), and according to III.9, it belongs to the core of those foundational concepts of nature that Spinoza calls "common notions" (*notiones communes*). These concepts, including the conatus, denote what is common to all things and equal in a part and in the whole (II.38).[4] The principle of striving, Spinoza loudly declares, is one that "everyone must acknowledge" (Appendix to Part I, p. 440).[5]

As we shall see later on, however, not everyone acknowledges the principle of striving. Nevertheless, in a context external to Spinoza's system, proposition III.6 that claims that everything strives to persevere in its being is certainly reasonable, even if doubt can be cast on the exclusivity and totality Spinoza demands for it,[6] as is proven by suicide, for example.[7] Contrarily, in a context internal to Spinoza's system, proposition III.6 is not acceptable nor can it be. When its full meaning is considered along with all that follows from it, it is revealed to be one of the more scandalous propositions in Spinoza's philosophy given that five contradictions are embedded within it.

The first contradiction in the conatus: static or dynamic

Spinoza's non-Euclidean conduct in the *Ethics* is especially radical in the demonstrations that he appends to propositions III.6 and III.7. Not only do the "demonstrations" not prove the propositions,[8] but they instead contradict them. While in these propositions the conatus is identified as static, in the demonstrations that accompany them it is identified as dynamic. Proposition III.6 posits that the principle of striving connotes the desire of every thing "to persevere in its being" (*in suo esse perseverare*), while proposition III.7, which joins it, equates this desire with the actual essence of each thing. Essence is identical to definition (I.33, Schol 1). By definition, every thing seeks to entrench itself within itself, and nothing seeks its own destruction. Indeed, the definition of each thing necessitates its essence and does not negate it (III.4, Dem). Thus each thing seeks to continue and to exist exactly as it is; and this static state impressed on its essence is the organizing principle of its existence. Contrarily, in the demonstrations to propositions III.6 and III.7, the conatus is presented as the aspiration of each thing to shatter the borders of its existence, not to maintain them. Every singular thing, Spinoza reminds us in the demonstration to proposition III.6, expresses in a certain and determined way (*certo et determinato*) the essence of God. However the essence of God is identical to his power, the power of God is identical to his existence, and the existence of God is identical to the action of God.[9] Therefore, every singular thing expresses in its own way the divine equation:

$$\text{essence} = \text{power} = \text{existence} = \text{action}.$$

Hence the conatus is not merely the striving to exist, but the striving to act. Indeed, to exist means to act. To act means, first, to oppose that which seeks to negate one's own existence (according to III.6, Dem) and, second, to be the cause of other things (according to III.7, Dem). The first meaning of action, as will become clear shortly, completely merges with its second meaning; to oppose those things that seek to negate one's existence means to transform oneself from their affect to their cause. Striving to act is thus striving to be a cause. To remove all doubt, Spinoza explicitly and unambiguously posits complete equivalence between the essence, "the power, *or* striving [*potentia sive conatus*]" of each thing and between the action "either alone or with others" of each thing (III.7, Dem). It follows that each thing strives to be more than what it is, and this dynamic state, impressed on its essence, is the organizing principle of its existence. Here we are facing a metaphysic of war of all against all (*bellum omnium contra omnes*) that posits that everything in nature strives, from metaphysical necessity, to dominate all other things, which also from the very same necessity, strive to dominate. The war that the conatus incites in nature is a total war that has no end or recess. It is a war that invites destruction to all that face it, and each thing indeed does face it: "There is no singular thing in nature than which there is not another more powerful and stronger. Whatever one is given, there is another more powerful by which the first can be destroyed" (IV, Pos 1, II/210).[10] From this it follows that despite claiming the conatus to be the one and only principle of all things in nature, Spinoza imbues it with two different and opposed meanings. The first is static perseverance and the second is dynamic action. Moreover, as we saw from a textual standpoint, Spinoza takes care to make obvious the contradiction between the two meanings of the conatus when he posits the first meaning in the propositions III.6 and III.7, and the second meaning in the demonstrations he attaches to them.[11]

The second contradiction in the conatus: efficient cause *or* final cause

Not only does Spinoza contradict himself when he presents the conatus as both the preserving of static existence and the action of dynamic causality, but in the equation of the conatus with dynamic causality he embeds another contradiction when he identifies the conatus with both the efficient cause (*causa efficiens*) and the final cause (*causa finalis*). From a textual standpoint, here too the contradictory meanings of conatus appear one after another during the course of the demonstration to proposition III.7. However this time it is an especially scandalous contradiction, as a result of which the final cause that had been done away with in one of the foundational acts of Spinoza's philosophy returns. Spinoza held the axe that modern philosophy had laid to medieval philosophy, seemingly rejecting the notion of a final cause so prevalent in medieval thought, which had inherited it from Aristotle.[12] As is clear from the in-depth and meticulous philosophical analysis of the issue Spinoza conducts in the appendix to the first part of the *Ethics*, the notion of a final cause is dubious from an epistemological viewpoint, damaging existentially, and dangerous socio-politically. In addition to being completely erroneous, it sets man up for a life of misery and enslaves him to the theologians and their prejudices. Therefore, the reader is perplexed by the sudden appearance of the final cause in the discussion of the conatus as a true cause that is entirely equivalent in terms of its value, weight and function in Spinoza's philosophy to the efficient cause, which contradicts it.[13]

Equating the conatus with the efficient cause is simple from a textual standpoint, and necessary from a philosophical one. In the demonstration to proposition III.7, the action, which is identical to the essence of each thing, i.e., its conatus, is characterized as causal action, when it is clear from the reference to proposition I.36 contained in this demonstration that the intent is efficient causality. From the demonstration to proposition I.36 it is evident that the essence of each thing expresses in a certain and determined way the essence of God (according to I.25, Cor), and "God is the efficient cause of all things" (I.16, Cor 1, II/60); thus the efficient cause is the essence of all things. Moreover, the conatus denotes the essence of the thing (III.7),[14] the essence of the thing is identical to its nature (III.56, Dem), and "nothing belongs to the nature of anything," Spinoza firmly states, "except what follows from the necessity of the nature of the efficient cause" (Preface to Part IV, p. 545). Spinoza's philosophy, at least on the surface, is a philosophy of efficient causality. "God *or* nature" (*deus sive natura*), Spinoza claims when he presents his famous and daring equivalence,[15] "acts from the same necessity from which he exists," and "[a]s he exists for the sake of no end, he also acts for the sake of no end" (ibid., p. 544). In Spinoza's philosophy, as it seems, there is no place for final causality beyond the realm of imagination and error. Throughout the *Ethics*, Spinoza only makes four direct references to the final cause (*causa finalis*), and in each one it is decried as a destructive error.[16] "[A]ll final causes," Spinoza concludes, "are nothing but human fictions [*figmenta*]" (Appendix to Part I, p. 442).

Nevertheless, Spinoza does not hesitate to equate the conatus of each thing, which is presented in proposition III.7 as the essence of each thing, with the final cause. This equation is obvious from a textual standpoint, but as noted it is completely unfounded given Spinoza's obligation to the Euclidean procedure. Textually, equating the conatus with the final cause appears from joining the following three claims:

a   In the scholium to proposition III.9 Spinoza equates striving (*conatus*) with appetite (*appetitus*).[17]
b   In the seventh definition of Part IV he equates appetite (*appetitus*) with the end (*finem*).[18]
c   In the demonstration to proposition III.7 Spinoza twice posits that power and striving are equivalent (*potentia sive conatus*).

The conatus, as we have already seen, is none other than the striving to act; and the striving to act is none other than the striving to be a cause. However, this cause, as it becomes clear here, is a final cause. The end of a thing, equal to its essence, is to persevere (III.7) *or* to increase its being (III.7, Dem)[19] in light of infinite many external causes seeking to reduce or abolish its existence (IV, A1). Therefore, the conatus is the *potentia* through which each thing moves from power to action. Moreover, because the essence of God is existence (I.20), and because the essence of each thing is the striving to exist, each thing, according to its essence, strives to be God. God, in Spinoza's philosophy, is not only the first cause of all things (I.16, Cor 3), but also their final end. Just as the finite stems from the infinite, it also strives for it. Spinoza therefore postulates the equivalence of the efficient cause and the final cause and embeds this contraction in the concept of conatus that is positioned at the heart of his philosophy. In doing so, he demonstrates to us again not just that he is not deterred from logical contradiction, but that he chooses it willingly.

The conatus of God, the collapse of the dichotomy between the substance and the mode and the collapse of the logical gap between the infinite and the finite (the third and fourth contradictions in the conatus)

The concept of the conatus appears only in the third part of the *Ethics* in the framework of the psychological infrastructure Spinoza develops for his theory of morals and salvation. In the first part of the *Ethics,* aptly titled "On God," there is no mention of the conatus, at least not on the surface;[20] this is therefore, a possible explanation for why in interpretations of Spinoza's philosophy, as we will see in the following section, we often find the erroneous notion that only individual things that follow from God have a conatus, but that God himself has no conatus. However, the claim that the conatus denotes *only* the essence of the singular things that follow from God but not the essence of God himself, not only does not fall in line with the internal logic of Spinoza's system, but also is entirely erroneous given Spinoza's explicit statements to the contrary.

The first time he brings up the concept of the conatus (III.6) Spinoza immediately claims that it denotes the striving of "each thing" (*unaquaeque res*) to persevere in its being.[21] Taking into account God is a thing, a free thing (*res libera*) and an eternal thing (*res aeterna*) according to both his definition and the definition of freedom and eternity (I, D6; D7; D8), God also has a conatus.[22] Just as proposition I.36 that claims "[n]othing exists from whose nature some effect does not follow," is applied not only to things that follow from God but to God himself, so proposition III.6 that claims "[e]ach thing, as far as it can by its own power, strives to persevere in its being," is applied not only to things that follow from God but to God himself. Regarding God, this striving is determined for success: "No thing can be destroyed except through an external cause" (III.4, II/145), and beyond God there is nothing (I.15), so therefore nothing can destroy God. For the individual things that follow from God this striving is doomed to fail, since for every individual thing that follows from God there exists always and necessarily "another more powerful [thing] by which the first can be destroyed" (IV, A1, II/210). Hence the same conatus nests within God and within all the individual things that follow from God. Moreover, Spinoza makes a special textual effort in order to emphasize that when he claims "each thing" to have a conatus he also refers to God. In the definition of the conatus (III.6), he positions the definition of the substance as "what is in itself [*in se est*]" (I, D3), which is none other than God in that God is the unique substance (I.14, Cor 1, II/56):

> Each thing, as far as [*quantum*] it is in itself [*in se est*], strives to persevere in its being.
>
> (III.6, II/146, my translation)[23]

A careful reading of the definition of the conatus that takes into account the meticulous use Spinoza makes of the systematic idiom "what is in itself" (*in se est*) on the one hand, and the hierarchy of things found in themselves that Spinoza posits through the use of the expression "as far as" (*quantum*) on the other, leads to the conclusion that not only God has a conatus, but also that only God's conatus is absolute because only God exists absolutely and necessarily in himself. The conatus of individual things that follow from God is only partial, and its measure is that of the existence of individual things in themselves. As we saw, the striving to exist is the striving to act, and the striving to act is the striving to be a cause. Therefore, the greater a thing's conatus, the more that thing corresponds to the definition of God in the sense that "God must be called the cause of all things in the same sense in which he is called the cause of himself" (I.25, Schol, II/68).[24] In other words, what acts more and is less acted upon is more within itself than within another thing. Moreover, given that every individual thing expresses in a certain and determined way the essence of God, which is identical to his power, existence, and action,[25] every individual thing has a conatus to some degree. It follows from the definition of conatus that, apart from God, each thing exists within itself to some degree and in another thing to some degree. Therefore, from a systematic standpoint, two conclusions with far-reaching consequences arise from the definition of the conatus: first, negation of the dichotomy that was determined in the definitions of the first part of the *Ethics* between "what is in itself" (I, D3) and "that which is in another" (I, D5), i.e., the negation of the dichotomy between the substance and the modes; and, second, transforming the definition of the mode to a partial one in that nothing, according to the definition of the conatus (III.6) and the adjoined demonstration,[26] exists absolutely within another thing; i.e., each thing exists, to some degree, in itself.[27]

This being the case, the modes are entities that can be situated on the rungs of the ladder at the top of which rests the substance that exists entirely within itself, and on the bottom of which should be, if it were to exist, whatever exists entirely in another thing. In fact, this ladder, which can be called the ladder of the conatus, is none other than the ladder of perfections that we discussed at length above, in that the principle of self action is determined by Spinoza to be the organizing principle of both (III.11, Schol).[28] Therefore, the place of humans on the ladder of the conatus, just as on the ladder of perfections, is not set but changes frequently in a way that reflects their self action. Spinoza's *Ethics* teaches man, as we saw in Chapter 3, that his ascent on the ladder of the conatus *or* perfections is a function of the expansion of his power to act, his true knowledge, his joy, and his participation in the divine nature, which are all completely identical. The human conatus reaches its apex in the third kind of knowledge, which we will discuss below; indeed, in the framework of this unique and rare action, the conatus of man becomes equivalent to the conatus of God, even while being different from the latter, since man remains a mode. However, in the second kind of knowledge as well, and even in the first, man's conatus is not entirely depleted; all that exists, as long as it exists, possesses a conatus to some degree or another. Man, therefore, exists both in another thing and in himself, and the exact relationship between these two types of existence is prone to constant change, though he is never a thing that exists *absolutely* in another thing (according to III.6 and its demonstration). The equivalence determined in the third part of the *Ethics* (III.6) between the conatus of a thing and that thing's existence in itself (*in se est*) sheds light on Spinoza's earlier claim at the end of the scholium to proposition II.7:

> So of things as they are in themselves [*in se sunt*], God is really the cause insofar as he consists of infinite attributes. For the present, I cannot explain these matters more clearly.
>
> (II.7, Schol, II/90)

In the second part of the *Ethics* Spinoza still does not present the concept of the conatus, and therefore was not able to explain to us in what sense God is the cause of "things as they are in themselves" (*in se sunt*). Seemingly, only God exists in himself, while all that follows from him is – according to the definition of the mode – "that which is in another [thing]" (I, D5). Only in the third part of the *Ethics* does Spinoza clarify that the conatus, which is shared by God and all the things that follow from him, enables things to exist in themselves, even if only partially, according to the definition of the conatus itself (III.6)[29] Indeed, as we saw, only God's conatus is unlimited in that there is no external thing that can contradict it, while the conatus of all individual things that follow from God, such as man, is caught in constant oscillation between overcoming, weakening and persevering until it is completely subdued by external causes the power of which is "infinitely" greater than his own (IV.3 II/212)[30]

Additional textual evidence of the existence of God's conatus and the relation between it and the conatus of the things that follow from him can be found in the TTP.[31] In the discussion conducted in the TTP on the metaphysical foundations of the state, Spinoza repeats, almost word for word, the definition of the conatus from the *Ethics*:

> [I]t is the supreme law of nature that each thing strives to persist in its own state so far as it is in itself [*in se est*].
>
> (TTP, XVI, p. 195 [189], my translation)[32]

Furthermore, Spinoza explicitly argues, in the same passage in which this definition appears, for complete equivalence between the conatus, right (*ius*) and power (*potentia*), both regarding God and the things that follow from him:

> For it is certain that nature, considered wholly in itself, has a sovereign right to do everything that it can do, i.e., the right of nature extends as far as its power extends. For the power of nature is the very power of God who has supreme right to [do] all things. However, since the universal power of the whole of nature is nothing but the power of all individual things together, it follows that each individual thing has the sovereign right to do everything that it can do, or the right of each thing extends so far as its determined power extends. And since it is the supreme law of nature that each thing strives to persist [*conatur perseverare*] in its own state so far as it can, taking no account of another's circumstances but only of its own, it follows that each individual thing has a sovereign right to do this, i.e., (as I said) to exist and to behave as it is naturally determined to behave.
> (Ibid., pp. 195–196 [189])

It is absolutely clear from this passage that God has not only an unlimited conatus, just as he has unlimited right and power, but also that God's conatus *is* the conatus of all the things that follow from him. The striving of all the details of existence to persevere in their state is the same as the striving of existence in its entirety to persevere in its state.[33]

However, the existence of the conatus of God and the relation between it and the conatus of the things that follow from him can be demonstrated not only without the last excerpt from the TTP, but even without relying on the unique use Spinoza makes of the phrase "in itself" (*in se est*) when defining the conatus in the *Ethics* (III.6). Indeed, the existence of the conatus of God and the relation between it and the conatus of things that follow from him, is necessarily derived from the place and role of the conatus in Spinoza's philosophy, as can be seen from the following considerations, which are internal to his metaphysics;[34] the conatus, as we saw, is a common concept (III.9). As such, it connotes "[t]hose things which are common to all, and which are equally in the part and in the whole," and which "can only be conceived adequately" (II.38, II/118). Moreover, as a common concept the conatus must connote not only that which is shared by all things in *natura naturata*, but also what is shared by them and the *natura naturata* in its entirety, in that it is "one Individual [*Individuum*], whose parts, i.e., all bodies, vary in infinite ways, without any change of the whole Individual" (II.13, L7, Schol, II/102). If the conatus did not connote *natura naturata* in its entirety it would not be a common concept: first, because it would not have connoted what is shared by all things; and, second, because it would not have appeared "equally in the part and in the whole" (II.38).

Moreover, on the one hand the conatus is the actual essence of each thing (III.7, and its demonstration); therefore, the conatus is the essence of the *natura naturata*. On the other hand, the cause of a thing also connotes its essence; indeed, according

106 *The second kind of knowledge*

to Spinoza's axiom of causality (I, A4) and its textual offshoots (Preface to Part IV; III.56, Dem; I.8, Schol 2), as we saw in the second chapter, in God there exists complete equivalence between the cause, essence, nature, and definition of the thing. Therefore the *natura naturans* also connotes the essence of the *natura naturata* in that it is its cause (I.29, Schol). The essence of the *natura naturata*, therefore, is identical to both the conatus and the *natura naturans*, which are necessarily identical to one another. It follows that just as the conatus connotes the essence of the *natura naturata* it also connotes the essence of the *natura naturans*. And this is so despite that the *natura naturata*, given that it is a mode, is different from the *natura naturans*, which is a substance and attributes. Locating the conatus in the *natura naturans* injects the definition of the "cause of itself" with the meaning of both an efficient cause and a final cause. From these two causes the *natura naturata* is created (the universe). The conatus, therefore, connotes the most private and intimate essence of every finite thing, though that very same essence is also completely general in that it is shared not only by all the things that follow from God, be they finite or infinite, but also by God himself given that he is their cause. The appearance of the same conatus in both the most general and most private aspects of existence, grants additional meaning to Spinoza's claim that "[t]he more we understand singular things, the more we understand God" (V.24). The finite and the infinite contradict each other, but given that they contain in them the same conatus, they are thus identical to one another. Therefore, the knowledge of one is also the knowledge of the other.[35]

Translations that attempt to blur the contradictions embedded in the definition of the conatus

The concept of God is the organizing concept of Spinoza's system. Therefore, attributing to God the conatus with all of the contradictions embedded in it, is likely to lead to the collapse of the whole Euclidean structure, which would explain why there is an aversion among Spinoza's interpreters to attribute the conatus to God.[36] It could also be that this aversion led translators of the *Ethics*, "to renovate" the definition of the conatus in their translations in order to match it to the Euclidean appearance of the system. The common ground in these translations, which seek to be more "successful" than the original from a logical standpoint, is the intentional exchange of the systematic idiom *in se est* – through which Spinoza embeds the definition of the substance in the definition of the conatus – with idioms that are not systematic and that blur the immanent link between the two definitions from which it follows that God has a conatus.

Many of the prevailing translations of the phrase *quantum in se est* in the definition of the conatus (III.6) that do not preserve the systematic meaning of the phrase *in se est* from the definition of the substance (I, D3):

1   In Curley's translation of the *Ethics*, which has become the standard English translation of the work, the translation is "as far as it can by its own power" (E IIIP6).[37]

2   Caillois translated to French as "selon sa puissance d'être."[38]
3   Blumenstock translated to German as "so viel an ihm liegt."[39]
4   In his Hebrew translation of the *Ethics* Klatzkin translated as "ad kama sh'hu b'rshuto."[40] According to Yovel, "the expression *in se est* does not appear here in the systematic sense as in part I ('exists in itself'), since the systematic sense applied only to God, and here the expression is used in a common way" (slightly rephrased).[41]
5   Contrarily, Elwes[42] and White[43] preserve the systematic meaning of the phrase *quantum in se est* – "insofar as it is in itself" – in their translations, and this is also the preference of Parkinson[44] and Della Rocca.[45]

In the context of the analysis of the status of contradiction in Spinoza's philosophy, the conatus fulfills a double role. On the one hand, it follows from the principle of the conatus that everything that exists contradicts itself in the very character of its existence in that it contains static and dynamic states, efficient cause and final cause, finiteness and infiniteness. However, on the other hand, the conatus itself is also a principle by means of which Spinoza claims that no thing contradicts itself regarding its striving to exist because each thing acts in every context in order to increase its existence. Spinoza's choice to adhere to the principle of the conatus without positing an oppositional principle in his system is especially significant in light of the central place occupied in modernity by the idea that along with man's striving to increase his being, the opposite is also true: man strives for destruction and self-annihilation.[46] God's conatus, however, as we will see in the following, embodies not only elements that reinforce and construct, but also those that lead to destruction and ruin.

The fifth contradiction in the conatus: the contradiction between good and evil in God

The pair of concepts "good" and "evil" belongs to the conceptual apparatus that Spinoza develops during the course of the comprehensive study that he conducts on human nature. This pair of concepts receives in the *Ethics* two different, oppositional meanings. The first meaning is false, and connotes what the imagination presents to us in error as beneficial or damaging (Appendix to Part I),[47] whereas the second meaning is the true one, and it connotes what is known to us by supreme rational certainty to be beneficial or damaging (IV, D1; IV, D2).[48]

Spinoza identifies our true good with what promotes the perseverance (*conservation*) of our existence, i.e., (according to IV, D8) with what increases the power of our action (*potentia agendi*); since our power of action *is* our conatus (according to III.7, Dem),[49] Spinoza identifies the good – in the true sense of the concept – with what increases or strengthens our conatus. While all the true appearances of the concept of good in the *Ethics* relate to man, all the appearances of the concept of good in the *Ethics* that relate to God are false. For example, the true definition of the concept of good (IV, D1) is presented from a human viewpoint,[50] while the theological claim according to which "God does all things for the sake of good" (I.33, Schol 2, II/76) is presented as absurd in that it subordinates God to what exists outside of him.[51] Therefore, the reader is liable to get the impression that the concept of good, in its true and precise sense (i.e., increasing the conatus), belongs only to the human realm, while all of its uses in the divine realm are in the imagination and therefore illusory.[52] However, from a philosophical point of view, not only is the concept of good applied both to the divine sphere and the human sphere, but only in the divine sphere is its application full and complete, while in the human sphere its application is necessarily partial and limited.

Man, as has already been shown, does not establish in nature a "dominion within a dominion" (*Ethics*, Preface to Part III, p. 491). Therefore, just as the conatus is a general metaphysical principle which applies not only to man but also to all other individuals in nature, as well as to nature in its entirety, i.e., God, the concept of "good" in its true meaning, relates not only to man but also to all other individuals in nature, including nature in its entirety, i.e., God.

Lack of discussion is not proof of non-existence. It should not, for example, be concluded from the fact Spinoza does not discuss the minds of inanimate things, plants, and animals that according to him they lack minds. Similarly, it should not be concluded from the fact Spinoza does not discuss the application of the concept of good on inanimate things, plants, and animals that according to him the concept of good, in its true and exact meaning, does not apply to them as well. Just as the relations between the mind and body of man connote "things ... [that] are completely general and do not pertain more to man that to other Individuals, all of which, though in different degrees, are nevertheless animate" (II.13, Cor, Schol, II/96, p. 458), so too the concept of good, which connotes the increase of the conatus both in the body and mind of man, is a general concept that refers not only to man, but also to the rest of the individual things in nature. Spinoza does not discuss the appearances of the concept of good beyond the bounds of the human condition not because he thinks that this concept has no existence in the non-human territories of reality, but because in the *Ethics* he does not seek to discuss all things that follow from God but rather only man, focusing on that which can "lead us, by the hand, as it were, to the knowledge of the human Mind and its highest blessedness" (Preface to Part II, p. 446).

However, even if Spinoza's discussions of the concept of good in the *Ethics* are conducted in the human domain, the organizing principles of these discussions refer to existence in its entirety. For example, the claim according to which "those things are good which bring about the preservation of the proportion of motion and rest the human Body's parts have to one another" (IV.39) relies on two general principles in Spinoza's philosophy. The first principle is a physical principle that determines that maintaining the nature of a complex body requires maintaining the relation by which the parts of the complex body transfer their movement to one another.[53] The second principle is the conatus, which, as we saw, posits that the nature of each thing strives to shatter the bounds of itself and to be more than what it is.[54] Therefore, the things that maintain the relation between movement and rest among the parts of a complex body, such as the human body (according to proposition II.13, A1), preserve its nature and thereby increase its conatus; thus they are good for that body.

In general, therefore, it can be claimed that X is good, if and only if, there exists a Y whose conatus is increased because of X. Therefore, for Spinoza, the claim that X is good does not connote X in and of itself but rather its relation to Y, i.e., X being the cause for the increase of Y's conatus.[55] However, the divide cast in the framework of Spinoza's conception of good between that which makes better (X) and that which is made better (Y) completely collapses when the object of discussion is not what follows from God but God himself, as can be seen by examining the relations between *natura naturans* and *natura naturata*.[56]

The *natura naturans*, according to proposition I.16 (the well-known proposition of the things that follow from God), is the cause of the existence and action of the *natura naturata* and all that is contained within it; since the conatus of the *natura naturata* exists in constant increase, as we saw earlier, *the natura naturans* is good for the *natura naturata* in that it is the cause of increase of the latter's conatus. However, the *natura naturans* and the *natura naturata* are not two distinct entities but are in fact one: God. Therefore God is good for himself in that he connotes what makes good and what is made good simultaneously. To paraphrase the scholium to proposition I.25, it can be claimed that in the same sense God is thought to be the cause of himself, he is also good for himself in that he is the cause of the increase of his own conatus.

When Spinoza identifies virtue (*virtus*) with power (*potentia*), which is posited in the definition of virtue (IV, D8), he is referring to man but not only to man.[57] Given that the power of God is his essence (I.34), his conatus is his essence (according to III.7, Dem); and because "God acts from the laws of his nature alone, and is compelled by no one" (I.17, II/61) in that "God alone is a free cause" (I.17, Cor 2), God being the cause of himself and God possessing virtue are one and the same. It follows that just as in the human realm a distinction should be made between the false meaning and the true meaning of the concept "good," in the divine realm there should also be a distinction made between the two opposite meanings of this concept; one of these meanings Spinoza rejects and the second meaning he accepts. Spinoza rejects the theological equivalence of good with a static pattern into which God attempts to cast himself; and in this context he presents the claim that "God does all things for the sake of good" (I.33, Schol 2) as an absurd claim in that it subordinates God to what exists externally to him. However, Spinoza must accept the equivalence between divine good and the infinite volcanic eruption of the divine conatus. In this context (and only in this context), Spinoza had to accept the claim that God does all for the sake of good given that the aim of all his actions is to increase his own conatus. Indeed, within God's conatus, which expresses God being a cause of himself, like the conatus of every individual thing that follows from God, there exists complete equivalence between the efficient cause and the final cause, as we saw earlier.

God, therefore, is good, but God, in Spinoza's philosophy, is not only good but also evil. This is so not only because the concepts of good and evil are presented by Spinoza in proposition IV.68 as correlative concepts (*correlata*),[58] but also, and principally, because God and the individual things that follow from him are also correlative concepts in Spinoza's philosophy (according to I.33, Schol 2);[59] good dominates in the divine sphere and evil dominates in the sphere of the individual things that follow from God.[60] Good dominates in the divine sphere because God's conatus only increases in that nothing external can contradict him. The origin of evil, according to Spinoza, is always external (according to Chapter 6 in the appendix to Part IV of the *Ethics*), and because there is nothing external to God (I.15), nothing is evil to God. God's conatus overflows without interruption. In the divine sphere all is good in a complete way and out of complete necessity. By contrast, evil dominates in the sphere of individual things that follow from God. The conatus of each individual thing that follows from God, as we saw earlier, is caught in perpetual oscillation between increasing, diminishing, or persevering (IV, Pos 1; III.11, Schol) until it is subdued by external causes the power of which is "infinitely" greater than that thing's power (IV.3)

Yet God's conatus is not detached from the conatus of the individual things that follow from him; in fact, as we saw earlier, it is completely equivalent to it. Therefore, good and evil do not refer to two separate and detached entities, but to the same entity: God. Consequently the incessant increasing and overflowing of God's conatus is pinned to and based on the incessant extinction and annihilation of the conatus of the individual things that constitute God. Therefore, good and evil in God grasp each other's heel metaphysically while logically they contradict each other.[61] Moreover, this contradiction between good and evil in God is directly connected to the previous contradictions that we located. For example, the contradiction between good and evil in God is parallel to the contradiction between the entirety of *natura naturata* and its parts, which is parallel to the contradiction between the infinite and finite, which is parallel to the contradiction between staticity and dynamicity. It is in this context that Spinoza claims that the *natura naturata* is "one Individual, whose parts, i.e., all bodies, vary in infinite ways, without any change of the whole Individual" (II.13, L7, Schol). Good refers to the infinite, and evil refers to the finite, but the finite is part and parcel of the infinite. Therefore, not only does good refer to the infinite, but also to evil. As we saw, because of God's complete otherness, the law of contradiction applies to him in the opposite way it does to the individual things that follow from him. Therefore, just as the concept of God is not destroyed but rather constituted from the contradiction between the infinite and the finite and the contradiction between static and dynamic states,[62] so too it is not destroyed by the contradiction between good and evil but is constructed from it. God's otherness is absolute, and therefore it must contain both the logical domain and the moral domain. Given that God is an absolute concept, he must also contain all in the moral domain; consequently, God is not only good or evil, and it is certainly not the case that he is neither good nor evil. God, as completely other, is both absolutely good and absolutely evil in an absolutely equivalent way.

Notes

1 In Bennett's words: "The whole truth about human beings can be told in terms which are needed anyways to describe the rest of the universe, and ... men differ only in degree and not in kind from all other parts of reality" (*A Study of Spinoza's Ethics*, p. 36). It is important to note that this conception, which does not assign man a special place from a metaphysical standpoint, belongs to the second kind of knowledge, and Spinoza will revise it in the framework of the third kind of knowledge. See Chapter 8.
2 Spinoza indirectly raises the principle of striving as early as the appendix to the first part of the *Ethics*. All men, Spinoza asserts there – seemingly in an impressionistic manner, though he is in fact adhering to his own systematic terms – "want to seek their own advantage, and are conscious of this appetite [*appetitum*]" (p. 440). In the scholium to proposition III.9 Spinoza identifies the appetite (*appetitus*) with striving (*conatus*), and there he also defines desire (*cupiditas*) as "appetite together with consciousness of the appetite."
3 *Unaquaeque res, quantum in se est, in suo esse perseverare conatur.* The translation here is my own. I will discuss the translation of this proposition below.
4 The common concepts, according to the second scholium of proposition II.40, belong to the second kind of knowledge.
5 As we saw, Spinoza posits this claim regarding the appetite (*appetitus*), which, as noted, he identifies with the conatus.
6 In fact, the conatus enables Spinoza to stealthily insert into his system the Aristotelian understanding of the substance, which he abandoned at the gates of the *Ethics*, and therefore the conatus is in line with common sense. As Scruton claims, the conatus "causes an organism to stand apart from its surroundings, in a persistent and active self-dependence" (*Spinoza*, p. 26). However, Scruton is mistaken when he attributes the conatus to organisms alone, and not to inanimate objects (ibid., p. 24). Indeed, as a common concept the conatus signifies the essences of all the things in nature, whether they are alive or inanimate. Hampshire offers a more precise formulation of the link between the concept of the conatus and common sense:

> It [the conatus] implies that our ordinary distinctions of sub-systems within the single physical system of Nature do have some justification in reality, although these sub-systems are never to be represented as genuinely independent substances; for this would imply that their states can be understood without reference to the order of causes in the all-inclusive system.
>
> (*Spinoza*, p. 77)

7 According to Spinoza, suicide expresses, always and necessarily, the increase of external causes and their overcoming of man, whether or not they are revealed or hidden to the eye. See IV.20, Scholium, as well as IV, A1. Sigad claims,

> One who relies on suicide as proof against the conatus casts his imaginings on Spinoza because he identifies the external appearance of man with the logical meaning "conatus," and man's empirical appearance does not indicate his essence, since man's behavior, the emotional in general and the suicidal in particular, presents his explicit subordination to external causes, his enslavement to them, and the loss of his essence.
>
> (*Truth as Tragedy*, p. 142)

From a systematic standpoint, as Berger explains, for Spinoza "the mind cannot cause the death of the body, nor the opposite, since the body and the mind are two aspects of the same essence – the striving to continue to exist – while death always follows from external causes" (Natalia Berger, "From the Fear of Death to the Love of Live: Death and Eternity in Spinoza's Works," M.A. Thesis at Tel Aviv University, 1992

[Heb.]). For a discussion of other contradictory examples, at least seemingly, of the principle of the conatus, see Della Rocca, "Spinoza's Metaphysical Psychology," pp. 200–202.
8 Spinoza appends similar demonstrations to propositions I.11 and II.3. See the introduction to the present part of the book, as well as the following chapter.
9 In the demonstration to proposition III.6 Spinoza directs us to the corollary to proposition I.25, which states that individual things express God's attributes, i.e., the essence of God (according to I, D4). He also directs us to proposition I.34 that identifies God's essence with his power, and which signifies, according to the demonstration appended to it, God's existence and his action. The equivalence between God's existence and his action appear in the scholium to proposition I.25, where it is presented from the viewpoint of causality: "God must be called the cause of all things in the same sense in which he is called the cause of himself." From a systematic standpoint, in this scholium Spinoza teaches us, as we saw in the previous chapter, that the difference between the proposition of the things that follow from God (I.16) and the definition of the cause of itself (I, D1), is only a difference of phrasing, while in terms of content the two are completely identical.
10 "Life ... is like an effort to raise the weight which falls. True, it succeeds only in retarding the fall," Bergson claims in a variation of Lalande's claim according to which all things march toward death despite the momentary resistance that organisms seem to exhibit. See Bergson, *Creative Evolution*, p. 269. Also see footnote 1 there. In an entirely different philosophical climate, Schopenhauer writes:

> Every breath we draw wards off the death that is constantly intruding upon us. In this way we fight with it every moment, and again, at longer intervals, through every meal we eat, every sleep we take, every time we warm ourselves, etc. In the end, death must conquer, for we became subject to him through birth, and he only plays for a little while with his prey before he swallows it up.
> (Arthur Schopenhauer, *The World as Will and Idea*. Translated by R.B. Haldane and J. Kemp. New York: AMS Press, 1977, Part A, paragraph 57, p. 402)

11 Additionally, Spinoza also inserts the contradiction between the two meanings of the conatus in the demonstration to proposition III.7; here, he identifies the "power of each thing, *or* the striving by which it does anything, or strives to do anything," with "the power, *or* striving, by which it strives to persevere in its being," while both the first and second meanings of the conatus are identical in this demonstration to "the given, *or* actual, essence of the thing itself, q.e.d."
12 Spinoza, who disapproves of "speculations" and "Aristotelian trifles" (TTP, p. 8, p. 18), is counted among the pioneers of science and modern philosophy who were completely convinced, as Strauss claimed, "that they were achieving a progress beyond all earlier philosophy or science, a progress condemning to oblivion all earlier efforts" (Strauss, *Persecution*, p. 253).
13 See Sigad, "God as Final Cause."
14 In this proposition it is indeed asserted that the conatus connotes "the actual essence of the thing," while in the demonstration there is explicit equivalence between the actual essence of the thing and its given essence. Spinoza posits here: "the given, *or* actual, essence of the thing itself."
15 The editors of the Dutch edition of the *Ethics* (Nagelate Schriften; NS) published immediately after Spinoza's death in 1677, obscured for precautionary reasons this explicit equivalence. Nevertheless, this equivalence is couched in several other places in the *Ethics*, such as I.20, I.25, and I.29 Scholium. Indeed, this erasure did not prevent the boycott declared on this edition nearly concurrently with its appearance. On the Dutch edition of the *Ethics* see Jonathan I. Israel, *The Dutch Republic: Its Rise, Greatness and Fall 1477–1806*. Oxford: Oxford University Press, 1998, pp. 921–922.

16 The first three references appear in the appendix to the first part, and the fourth appears in the preface to the fourth part in the framework of a discussion – presented by Spinoza as completing that which was begun in the appendix. See the *Ethics*, pp. 440, 441, 442, and 544 in Curley, *Collected Works*.
17 When the desire to persevere in its being refers to "the Mind and Body together, it is called Appetite" (III.9, Schol).
18 "By the end for the sake of which we do something I understand appetite" (IV, D7).
19 The equivalence posited here between persevering in its being and the increase of being relies on the discussion carried out in the previous section.
20 Moreover, from the corollary to proposition I.24, it follows that things created from God do not and cannot have a conatus. Indeed, in this proposition it is explicitly claimed that the essence of things derived from God does not contain duration, which is identified with the conatus according to III.8 and II, D5.
21 Here Spinoza uses *res* and not *individuum*, and thus we have an additional demonstration that an interpretation that reduces the conatus only to individuals, such as Scruton's that was presented earlier, is mistaken. See Curley's remarks regarding Bennett who also maintains this reductive position. Edwin Curley, *Behind the Geometrical Method: A Reading of Spinoza's Ethics*. Princeton University Press, 1988, p. 163, footnote 23. For a critical discussion of the link between Spinoza's conception of the conatus and the place of complex individuals in his system see Della Rocca, "Spinoza's Metaphysical Psychology," pp. 206–210.
22 The second corollary to proposition I.17 can also be adjoined to the definition of freedom, from which it follows that God is the only free thing. I will discuss the definition of eternity and the relation between it and God's conatus in the following chapter.
23 *Unaquaeque res, quantum in se est, in suo esse perseverare conatur*. The translation here is my own.
24 For a discussion of the relation between the conatus and the "cause of itself" see Nancy K. Levene, *Spinoza's Revelation: Religion, Democracy, and Reason*. Cambridge: Cambridge University Press, 2004, pp. 3–5.
25 As we saw in the previous section in the context of our discussion of the contradiction between static and dynamic states in the conatus.
26 The demonstration clarifies that the proposition refers to all things as they are, and not only to a part of them, as can be understood from a reading of the proposition alone. It can be demonstrated that all things have a conatus relying on other references, such as I.25, Cor; I.36; and of course III.7, which claims that the conatus is "the actual essence of the thing."
27 See Arne Naess, *Freedom, Emotion and Self-Subsistence: The Structure of a Central Part of Spinoza's* Ethics. Oslo: Universitetsforlaget, 1976, pp. 73–74, as well as the discussion of Naess' position in Charles E. Jarrett, "Review of Naess (1976)," *Journal of the History of Philosophy* 17, 1979, pp. 345–348.
28 Also see II.13, Cor, Schol, and our discussion in Chapter 3 regarding the principle of independent action that organizes the ladder of perfections.
29 Yovel, who does not credit Spinoza with conjugating the systematic phrase *in se est* in the scholium to proposition II.7, assumes that "Spinoza hints here at the existence of modes that transcends the attributes – i.e., the existence of some mode, without the characteristics of such and such an attribute – such is his intent with the expression 'as they are in themselves'" (Yovel's translation of the *Ethics*, p. 133, footnote 1). However, Spinoza himself explicitly states, both in the *Ethics* as well as in his letters, that it is not possible to perceive modes lacking any characterization by some attribute in that "each being must be conceived under some attribute" (I.10, Schol). See also Letter 9 to De Vries, Curley, p. 193.
30 The distinction between God's conatus and man's conatus is completely hidden by proposition III.37 and its demonstration. Man's conatus is presented as being in a state

114 *The second kind of knowledge*

of constant increase in that it is not only increased by joy but even by sadness, which is in complete contrast to the definition of sadness as a mere diminishment or delay of man's action (according to III.11, Schol). In Spinoza's words in the demonstration to proposition III.37: "the greater the Sadness, the greater the power of acting with which the man will strive to remove the Sadness." Given that it is not possible to count this contradiction with the constructive contradictions in Spinoza's system, dealing with it is particularly difficult, and it is possible that we face an intractable deficiency in the system. In this context see Aliza Tessler, "On the Relation Between Emotion and Knowledge in Spinoza's Thought," M.A. Thesis at Tel Aviv University, 1994.

31 Curley supposes that the writing of the TTP – which deals extensively, if not systematically, with human behavior – causes Spinoza to develop and enhance the principle of the conatus that in the 1665 draft of the *Ethics* still had not claimed a central place in the system. See Curley, "Notes," p. 152.

32 *Lex summa naturae est, ut unaquaeque res in suo statu, quantum in se est, conetur perseverare*. Shirley translates "each thing endeavors to persist in its present being, as far as in it lies" (Baruch Spinoza, *Tractatus Theologico-Politicus*. Translated by Samuel Shirley, E.J. Brill, 1989, p. 237). Elwes translates it as "each individual should endeavor to preserve itself as it is" (Benedict De Spinoza, *A Theological-Political Treatise and A Political Treatise*. Translated by R.H.M. Elwes, New York: Dover Publications 1951, p. 200). These translations blur both Spinoza's use of the systematic term *in se est* from the definition of the substance (I.D3), as well as his use of the concept of the conatus based on the Latin verb *conare*, which beginning with the *Ethics* becomes one of the central concepts of his system. Elwes went even further from the original, when he mistakenly exchanges a thing (*res*) for an individual (*individuum*). Silverthorne and Israel, who translate it as "each thing strives to persist in its own state so far as it can," (*Theological-Political Treatise*, pp. 195–196) also do not maintain Spinoza's use of the systematic term *in se est* from the definition of the substance (I.D3).

33 The concept of the conatus appears openly in this paragraph. It is not in line with Ben-Shlomo's claim regarding this passage, as well as regarding the entirety of the TTP, that "Spinoza is still not identifying here power with each thing's striving (*conatus*) to exist in its being, though he does identify it with the natural right" (footnote 296 on p. 243 of the Hebrew translation of *Short Treatise on God, Man, and His Well-Being*).

34 The following demonstration appears with slight changes in Sigad's "God as Final Cause," pp. 377–378.

35 In the previous chapter we discussed proposition V.24 in the context of another contradiction, that between static unity and dynamic multiplicity in existence.

36 Curley, for example, opposes maintaining the systematic meaning of the phrase *in se est* in the definition of the conatus because he believes there to be a total disconnect between the definition of the conatus and the definition of the substance, which is identical in his opinion to the cause of itself. Curley writes:

> Someone who does not accept my understanding of the definition of substance, and who thinks that *esse in se* means the same thing in IIIP6 as it does in the definition of substance, owes us an explanation of how it can be that every finite thing in *some degree* satisfies the definition of substance (as *quantum* implies).
>
> ("Notes," p. 134)

Spinoza himself answers Curley when he posits, in the demonstration to proposition I.36, "Whatever exists expresses the nature, *or* essence of God in a certain and determinate way (by P25C), i.e., (by P34), whatever exists expresses in a certain and determinate way the power of God, which is the cause of all things." There is no need to reject the correct equivalence Curley posits between the definition of the substance and the definition of the cause of itself in order to understand that the more an individual thing acts and is less acted upon, the more it is appropriate to the definition of God that is none other than the definition of the substance in that God is the only substance (according to I.14, Cor). Moreover, when Spinoza presents the benefit of his philosophy he explicitly claims that it teaches us that we "share in the divine nature, and that we do this the more, the more perfect our actions are, and the more and more we understand God" (II.49, Schol, p. 490 [II/135]).

37 Curley, *The Collected Works*, p. 498. Elsewhere, Curley explains his reasons for this choice in translation: "I preferred a translation which seemed to me to pick up the resonances of Cartesian and Newtonian formulations of the principle of inertia" ("Notes," p. 134). However, as I attempted to show in the present chapter, the principle of the conatus should not be equated with that of inertia, since for Spinoza, as opposed to Descartes and Newton, the striving of each thing to persevere in its being is none other than the striving of each thing to burst beyond the bounds of itself. Moreover, as Yovel rightly claims, Curley's translation is not acceptable not only because the expression "by its own power" (*quantum potest*) is only found in the conclusion of the demonstration and not in the proposition, but also because in the demonstration Spinoza links the expression "by its own power" to the expression "it lies in itself" (*in se est*) via the word *et* (and) and not *sive* (or) (Yovel's translation of the *Ethics*, p. 203, footnote 2). For additional discussion see G.H.R. Parkinson, "Review of Spinoza," in *Studia Spinozana* 2 (1986), pp. 422–423, and Curley's response ("Notes on a Neglected Masterpiece (II): The *Theological-Political Treatise* as a Prolegomenon to the *Ethics*," in *Central Themes in Early Modern Philosophy*, edited by J.A. Cover and Mark Kulstad, Hackett, 1990, pp. 133–134).

38 Benedictus De Spinoza. *Oeuvres Complètes*. Texte nouvellement traduit ou revu, présenté et annoté par Roland Caillios, Madeleine Francès et Robert Misrahi. Paris: La Pléiade, Gallimard 1954, p. 421. In footnote 1 on page 1433 Caillios notes that he is relying on the use Spinoza makes of the term *quantum in se est* in his version of the Cartesian law of inertia in *Descartes' Principles of Philosophy* part II, proposition 14, following Descartes himself in *Principles of Philosophy* part II proposition 37. Indeed, according to Descartes: "Each thing, in so far as it is simple and undivided, always remains in the same state, as far as it can [*quantum in se est*], and never changes except as a result of external causes" (*Philosophical Writings of Descartes*, Vol. 1, pp. 240–241). In Spinoza's version: "Each thing, insofar as it is simple, undivided, and considered in itself alone [*in se solâ*], always perseveres in the same state as far as it can [*quantum in se est*]" (Curley, *Collected Works*, p. 277). However, although Caillios maintains consistency between Spinoza's use of the phrase *quantum in se est* in the definition of the conatus in the *Ethics* and in the formulation of the law of inertia in *Descartes' "Principles of Philosophy,"* he does not maintain consistency between the systematic and unique use Spinoza makes of this phrase in the definitions of the substance and of the conatus in the *Ethics* (I, D3 and III.6). This interpretive choice is problematic not only because it is preferable to maintain consistency in the meaning of terms in the same work, but also, and principally, because *Descartes' "Principles of Philosophy"* is not an independent work of Spinoza's but rather an interpretive one in which he presents Descartes' ideas, not his own, while explicitly stating: "I had written many things in it [*Descartes' "Principles of Philosophy"*] which were the very opposite of what I held" (Curley, Letter 13, p. 207).

39 Benedictus De Spinoza. *Opera – Werke*. Lateinisch und Deutsch. Hersg. Konrad Blumenstock, 2 Bde., Tractatus de Intellectus Emendatione – Ethica, Darmstadt: Wissenschaftliche Buchgesellschaft 1967, p. 273.

40 Klatzkin's Hebrew translation of the *Ethics* (*Torat-Hamidot*) Leipzig: Shtibl, 1923.

41 Yovel's translation of the *Ethics*, p. 203, footnote 1.

42 Benedict De Spinoza, *On the Improvement of the Understanding, The Ethics and Correspondence*. Translated by R.H.M. Elwes, New York: Dover Publications 1951, p. 136.

116 *The second kind of knowledge*

43 Baruch Spinoza, *Ethic*. Translated by W. Hale White, Oxford: Oxford University Press, 1923, p. 114.
44 Parkinson, "Review of Spinoza," pp. 422–423.
45 Della Rocca, "Spinoza's Metaphysical Psychology," p. 193 and footnote 4 on p. 257.
46 Both Dostoevsky and Freud claimed that human life is based on destruction and building, not on building alone. Dostoevsky, for example, remarks in *The Idiot* that the law of self-destruction is as strong in humanity as the law of self-preservation (Fyodor Dostoevsky, *The Idiot*. Translated by Constance Garnett, New York: Modern Library Classics, 2003, p. 340), and he dedicates his *Notes From the Underground* (Translated by Constance Garnett, New York: Barnes and Noble Classics, 2008) to an in-depth and comprehensive investigation of this claim. Freud, in *Beyond the Pleasure Principle*, situates the death drive as opposing the Eros, the former signifying the primeval urge of every living creature for destruction and self-annihilation. "Everything living," Freud claims in complete opposition to Spinoza, "dies for *internal* reasons ... *the aim of all life is death*" (Sigmund Freud, *Beyond the Pleasure Principle*. Translated by James Strachey, New York: W.W. Norton & Company, 1990, p. 38). For an additional discussion see Yovel, *Spinoza and Other Heretics*, pp. 421–423; also see Yaakov Golomb, *The Temptation of Might – From Nietzsche to Freud*. Jerusalem: Magnes Press, 1987 [Heb.], pp. 117–122. In the fourth notebook of the *Blue Octavo Notebooks*, Kafka, while making the point that the enduring continuity of transience is no consolation, remarks that new life blossoming among ruins proves the endurance of death no less than the tenacity of life (Franz Kafka, *Blue Octavo Notebooks*. New York: Exact Change Press, 2004, p. 47).
47 In the framework of the false meaning with which Spinoza imbues the pair of concepts "good" and "evil" he asserts that they are "beings, not of reason, but of imagination [*entia, non rationis, sed imaginationis*]" (Appendix to Part I, *Ethics*, p. 446). Yovel notes in this context that the expression *entia imaginationis* constitutes a kind of "word game that refers to the routine concept *entia rationis* (beings of reason), the usual meaning of which is (also in the Cartesian lexicon): non-realistic beings that exist only in thought" (Yovel's translation of the *Ethics*, p. 121, footnote 4).
48 The two contradictory meanings of the pair of concepts "good" and "evil" are presented side by side in the preface to Part IV of the *Ethics*. For a survey of the positions of various interpreters regarding the exact relation between the two meanings – which signify the relation between the traditional moral conception that Spinoza rejects and the philosophical alternative he suggests in its place, among other things – see Henry E. Allison, *Benedict de Spinoza: An Introduction*. Hartford, CT: Yale University Press, 1987, p. 236, footnote 23. For a comparison between the contradictory meanings with which Spinoza and Maimonides imbue this pair of concepts see Zev Harvey, "Maimonides and Spinoza on the Knowledge of Good and Evil," *Iyyun: The Jerusalem Philosophical Quarterly*, 28 (1978), pp. 167–185 [Heb.].
49 *Potentia sive conatus*, Spinoza posits in this demonstration regarding the action of a thing "either along or with others."
50 For example, man, and only man, delineates the discussion of the concept of good, both in the series of propositions 27–31 as well as 37–42 in the fourth part of the *Ethics*. The first series of propositions focuses on identifying good with true knowledge, and the second series of propositions discusses, among other things, the sociopolitical elements of human good.
51 In the appendix to the first part of the *Ethics*, Spinoza unfurls a broad criticism against this theological claim, which he presents as a metamorphosis of the erroneous attribution of the final causes to God.
52 For example, see Harvey, "Maimonides and Spinoza," p. 177.
53 Without a doubt, in the demonstration to proposition IV.39, Spinoza directs us to the definition before L4 in proposition II.13, in the framework of which this physical principle is determined.

54 Spinoza himself does not explicitly note the principle of the conatus in the demonstration to proposition IV.39; however, it is easy to prove that this principle stands at the foundation of this proposition. The demonstration to proposition IV.39 claims the conatus to be based on proposition IV.38, which itself is based, as is explicitly stated in its demonstration, on proposition IV.26 and IV.27. The latter proposition is based on the first, while the first proposition, IV.26, is based on the principle of the conatus, as follows explicitly from Spinoza's demonstration there, in the framework of which he directs us to propositions III.6 and III.7, where this principle is presented.
55 In the sixth chapter of the first part of *Metaphysical Thoughts*, Spinoza writes:

> *Good and bad are only said in respect to something*: No thing is said to be either *good* or *evil* considered alone, but only in respect to another [thing], to which it is advantageous in acquiring what it loves, or the contrary.
> (Curley, *Collected Works*, p. 313)

Here too Spinoza does not explicitly raise the concept of the conatus, though later on in the passage he clarifies that what is good is that which preserves the being of the one who benefits from that good. Moreover, according to the *Ethics*, what benefits the true knowledge of that which we love, is none other than what benefits the conatus; love is defined as "a Joy, accompanied by the idea of an external cause" ("General Definition of the Affects," VI), Joy is defined as "man's passage from a lesser to a greater perfection" ("General Definition of the Affects," II), and perfection is defined as identical with reality (II, D6), and the striving of each thing to increase its reality is none other than its conatus (according to the demonstrations to propositions III.6 and III.7).
56 In fact, the gap between the good (X) and that which is made better (Y) also collapses for a man who has true knowledge in that in the framework of this knowledge – whether it belongs to the second or third kinds of knowledge – the gap between man and God also collapses. See Sigad, *Philo-Sophia*, pp. 56–86.
57 In the definition of virtue Spinoza posits:

> by virtue and power [*potential*] I understand the same thing, i.e (by IIIP7), virtue, insofar as it is related to man, is the very essence, *or* nature, of man, insofar as he has the power [*potestas*] of bringing about certain things, which can be understood through the laws of his nature alone.
> (IV, D8)

58 Even if the context of the discussion of proposition IV.68 and its demonstration is the false meaning of the pair of concepts "good" and "evil," by treating the two mutually, i.e., in that they are joined concepts, there is no difference between the false meaning Spinoza grants them in the appendix to Part I of the *Ethics*, and the true meaning with which he imbues them in the first two definitions of the fourth part.
59 Indeed, in the second scholium to the proposition I.33, Spinoza adopts theological language from rhetorical considerations, and presents in a general way the relation between God and his decrees as a correlative relation when he asserts, "God was not before his decrees [*sua decretal*], and cannot be after them" (ibid., p. 437). However, starting from the corollary to proposition I.25, it is already completely clear that God's decrees, to continue to use theological language, contain not only infinite modes, such as in propositions I.21–23, but also finite modes.
60 If in the framework of Spinoza's philosophy we faced only the claim that the concepts good and evil are conjoined concepts, without the claim that God and the individual things that follow from him are also conjoined concepts, it would be possible to avoid attributing evil to God. Indeed, it would be possible to claim that his absolute otherness negates the correlate relationship between good and evil that exists in the realm of individual things that follow from God. In other words, it would be possible to claim that while in the realm of the individual things that follow from God the concept

of good is conjoined to the concept of evil, in the divine realm the correlate relation between the concepts of good and evil is abolished, and the singular organizing concept of the divine realm is the concept of good. From here it would also be possible to conclude that Spinoza in fact accepts the traditional portrait of "the good God" while at the same time revising it, as he does to foundational concepts and other conceptions from the theological school of thought. Yet this is not possible because the claim that God and the individual things that follow from him are conjoined concepts forces us, as we will see, to attribute not only good to God, but also evil.
61 We will discuss the temporality of the conatus in the following chapter.
62 We discussed the contradictions between the infinite and the finite and between staticity and dynamicity in Chapters 2 and 4, respectively.

6 Eternity and time
The contradiction and the circularity

The nature of time in Spinoza's philosophy, which presents itself as a philosophy of eternity, raises one of the more severe problems in Spinoza's system. By defining eternity as necessary existence, it follows not only that existence in its entirety is eternal, given that it is necessary, but also that all of the details of existence are eternal as well in that they are necessarily derived from eternal existence. The concept of time, however, is presented as a result of the inadequate knowledge of the logical necessity embedded within existence. Yet, abolishing the veracity of time not only detaches Spinoza's system from human experience, it also threatens to raise the axe on several principles of the system itself, such as the principle of movement and rest and the conatus. How, if at all, is it possible to understand the status of time in Spinoza's philosophy in a way that will not disconnect the system from experience on the one hand, and not bring about its internal collapse on the other?

In order to deal with these difficulties, the present chapter will outline a new conception of the relation between eternity and time in the *Ethics*, which will be supported by a new reading of all of Spinoza's references to this issue. This reading will demonstrate that Spinoza's approach to eternity and time is similar to his approach to the other oppositional elements in his system, such as: staticity and dynamicity, unity/multiplicity, and infiniteness/finiteness. I will therefore aim to show that God, as an absolute concept, includes not only eternity but also time and that the viewpoint of time is absolutely equivalent to the viewpoint of eternity in terms of its truth-value. Moreover, uncovering Spinoza's sub-textual understanding regarding this matter will reveal the relation between eternity and time to be circular; time flows from eternity and eternity flows from time. Spinoza, as will become clear, on the one hand completely separates eternity from time, but on the other hand he also connects them and equates between the two.

The discussion will proceed as follows: the chapter will open by presenting the widely-accepted stance that conceives of Spinoza's philosophy as a philosophy of eternity, and will then present the problems that arise from his apparent banishing of time from the realm of metaphysical truth. Thereafter a solution to these problems will be presented by relying on the circularity embedded in the definition of eternity (I, D8), and from the passages in the *Ethics* from which it follows that time flows from eternity precisely as eternity flows from time. Applying the constructive contradiction that is in God to the relation between eternity and time in Spinoza's philosophy will aid us especially at the end of the chapter when grappling with proposition II.8 and the corollary and scholium that follow it; the latter are not only problematic and difficult in the context of eternity and time in Spinoza's philosophy, but also in the more obscure passages of the *Ethics* as a whole.

Spinoza's philosophy as a philosophy of eternity

It is common to present Spinoza's philosophy as a philosophy of eternity (*aeternitas*). Indeed, from the definition of eternity as necessary existence (V.30, Dem),[1] it follows that all of Spinoza's system is eternal in that its existence is necessary. The substance is eternal in that its existence is its essence (I.7, Dem).[2] The attributes are eternal in that they express the essence of the substance (I.19, and its demonstrations).[3] Both the finite and the infinite modes (II.45 and I.21–23 respectively) are also eternal in that they necessarily follow from the substance (II.44, Cor 2, Dem), and thus their existence, like the existence of the substance, is necessary *or* eternal.[4] In other words, all that exists follows from God and all that follows from God is eternal like God:[5] "For all things follow from God's eternal decree [*aeterno Dei decreto*] with the same necessity as from the essence of a triangle it follows that its three angles are equal to two right angles" (II.49, Cor, Schol, II/136).[6]

Spinoza's philosophy, therefore, is a philosophy of eternity. As such time is conceived of as resulting from human imagination, which expresses confused, fragmented, and inadequate knowledge of the eternal logical necessity embedded in reality in its entirety (II.44, Cor 1, Schol; V.29, Schol).[7]

The problems resulting from abolishing the truth-value of time

Abolishing the truth-value of time in Spinoza's philosophy is perplexing: Spinoza turns his back on a foundational category in human knowledge by claiming that it is merely a result of human imagination. However, time does not characterize *only* the human imagination, but also the rest of the territories of human experience. Therefore, the dismissal of time is in fact the dismissal of experience. However, despite dismissing experience, Spinoza does not avoid turning to it (and this is especially perplexing) in order to reinforce the equivalence between time and the imagination. Spinoza claims that "no one doubts … we also imagine time" (II.44, Cor 1, Schol, II/125), while the complete opposite is in fact true: no one doubts that time sprawls beyond the imagination into existence itself.

Furthermore, Spinoza's denial of time raises the axe on several principles of his system; and as such, at least apparently, this denial leads to the collapse of the system into itself. Spinoza equates time with the principle of motion and rest (II.44, Cor 1, Schol). Therefore, if time belongs to the imagination, the principle of movement and rest also belongs to the imagination. However, from a systematic standpoint, ascribing the principle of movement and rest to the imagination is not possible and cannot be possible. Firstly, because this principle functions as the first axiom in Spinoza's physics, which is presented in a textual enclave in the second part of the *Ethics* (after the corollary to proposition II.13). And secondly, because in the framework of the metaphysical map of Spinoza's system the principle of movement and rest is given a central place as it is the infinite, immediate mode in the attribute of extension (Shirley, Letter 64, p. 298).[8]

Additionally, the concept of the conatus – without which, as we saw previously, it is not possible to understand God or the things that follow from him – becomes completely invalid if Spinoza's philosophy is closed off within eternity. Eternity signifies static, frozen existence closed off within itself (according to the second corollary to proposition I.20,[9] as well as the scholium to proposition V.20), while the conatus signifies dynamic existence that strives to shatter its own boundaries.[10] Moreover, the conatus is a principle of change, and every change takes place in time; Spinoza indeed equates the conatus with duration, which "can be defined by time" (V.23, Dem), even if it is not limited by time in that it is defined as "an indefinite continuation of existing" (II, D5). Eternity, by contrast, is detached completely from both time and duration (I, D8, Exp). Eternity "can neither be defined by time nor have any relation to time" (V.23, Schol, II/296), and correspondingly: "eternity cannot be explained by duration" (V.29, Schol, II/298), nor can it have any relation to duration. Given that Spinoza equates God with eternity on the one hand, and the conatus with duration on the other, God does not and cannot have a conatus. Abolishing the truth-value of time is therefore utterly untenable, not only (a) beyond the boundaries of Spinoza's system because of its undeniable presence in human experience, but also (b) within his system which clearly adopts the axis of time as an axis of existence itself, and not only as an illusory appearance in the deceptive human imagination.

The circular definition of eternity and the metaphysical equivalence between eternity and time

Spinoza already exposes his non-Euclidean approach in his treatment of the issue of eternity and time in the way in which he chooses to define eternity in the first part of the *Ethics*:

> By eternity I understand existence itself, insofar as it is conceived to follow necessarily from the definition alone of the eternal thing.
>
> Exp: For such existence, like the essence of a thing, is conceived as an eternal truth, and on that account cannot be explained by duration or time, even if the duration is conceived to be without beginning or end.
>
> (I, D8 and Exp)

The definition of eternity is scandalous in that it is circular.[11] However, it is not conceivable that Spinoza, who in the *Ethics* clearly demonstrates outstanding analytic abilities, was not aware of this circularity. Moreover, this is not a matter of an incidental comment or an alternative demonstration, but rather it is one of the foundational definitions of Spinoza's philosophy. Spinoza presents a non-circular definition of eternity towards the end of the *Ethics* in the demonstration to proposition V.30 where he claims that "[e]ternity is the very essence of God insofar as this involves necessary existence" (by ID8). Nevertheless, even in the framework of this revised definition that clarifies that eternity is necessary existence, Spinoza again directs us to the circularity of the formal definition of eternity (I, D8). Thus, it is as though he is seeking to prevent us from fully exchanging the circular definition of eternity (I, D8) for its non-circular definition (V.30, Dem). Without the circularity, we are told between the lines via the reference in the definition from the fifth part to the definition from the first part, it would not be possible to grasp eternity. Indeed, a careful study of Spinoza's well-measured phrasings of the relation between eternity and time, reveals that this circularity in the definition of eternity (I, D8) expresses the very core of the following metaphysical circularity: eternity draws up time from within itself, and time draws up eternity from within itself. Thus, eternity in fact flows from within itself. We will now explore the metaphysical underpinnings of time as flowing from eternity.

Time flowing from eternity

Logically, all that is derived from eternity is eternal; because "God is eternal, *or* all God's attributes are eternal" (I.19), the infinite, immediate modes that follow directly from God's infinite attributes also must be eternal. Indeed, in proposition I.21 and its demonstration, Spinoza explicitly claims that the immediate, infinite modes are eternal (*aeterna*).

Yet to the amazement of the reader, in those same lines in proposition I.21 and its demonstration in which Spinoza attributes eternity to the immediate, infinite modes, he also attributes to them the duration (*duratio*) which he had completely detached from eternity (I, D8, Exp). Furthermore, he also posits in this proposition the *or* of equivalence (*sive*) between the eternity of these modes and their constant existence (*semper*). Adjoining the two passages that will be quoted here, the latter of which is a revised version of the first, makes it clear that attributing unrestricted duration (*duratio*) to the infinite modes is absolutely equivalent to the claim that they must always exist (*semper*). In other words, in this proposition, Spinoza links, as he does in other places, the distinct temporal, but un-systematic term "always" (*semper*) with the systematic term "duration" (*duratio*) that connotes unrestricted temporal existence:[12]

> All the things which follow from the absolute nature of any of God's attributes have always [*semper*] had to exist and be infinite, *or* [*sive*] are, through the same attribute, eternal [*aeterna*] and infinite.
>
> (I.21, II/65)

At the end of the demonstration that follows this proposition, when articulating what he took upon himself to demonstrate, Spinoza posits:

> God's idea in thought, or anything else which follows necessarily from the absolute nature of some attribute of God, cannot have a determinate [*determinatam*] duration [*durationem*], but through the same attribute is eternal [*aeternum*].
>
> (I.21, Dem)

Spinoza's refusal in the demonstration to proposition I.21 to attribute determinate (*determinata*) duration (*duratio*) to the infinite, immediate modes indicates that he is ready to attribute unrestricted duration to them, as he in fact does in the proposition itself when he states that they must always (*semper*) exist. Moreover, and this is critical, even if Spinoza had maintained textual consistency and insisted on attributing the infinite, unmediated modes *only* eternity or *only* duration, the contradiction in the systematic status of these modes would not have been solved but would rather simply have been transferred to another place in the system. Indeed, there are only two alternatives:

a These modes are eternal. If so, their existence is necessary (V.30, Dem), and if their existence is necessary, then they are the cause of themselves (I, D1), but if they are the cause of themselves then they are not modes. Only the substance is the cause of itself in that it is "in itself and is conceived through itself" (I, D3), as opposed to the mode as "that which is in another through which it is also conceived" (I, D5). Given that this argument can be applied not only to the infinite, immediate modes, but to all modes, mediated or immediate, infinite or finite, it follows that eternal modes are a conceptual contradiction;[13]

b These modes are not eternal. However, even if the infinite, immediate modes are not eternal but rather only temporal, they cannot derive from the substance because the latter is eternal and therefore all that follows from it must be eternal as well. From all of this it follows that whether the modes are eternal or have duration, their very existence casts a contradiction onto Spinoza's system.

Despite this, and as if to mock us, Spinoza claims that the infinite, immediate modes are both eternal and constant; thus he presents us with a contradiction between two claims, each of which involves a contradiction in and of itself.

As if this double contradiction is not enough, from Letter 35 to Hudde it is clear that the contradiction between eternity and duration spreads to the *natura naturans*, and it is not only the *natura naturata* that is infected by it. From the first section of the letter it is evident that Spinoza refuses to attribute even to the substance itself not only determinate duration, but also duration that is not determinate. When clarifying for his friend and correspondent, Hudde, "what properties must be possessed by a Being that includes necessary existence" (Letter 35, Shirley, p. 203),[14] Spinoza posits:

It [the being that includes necessary existence] is eternal (*aeternum*). For if a determinate duration were ascribed to it, beyond the bounds of its determinate (*determinata*) duration (*duratio*) this Being would be conceived as not existing, or as not involving necessary existence, and this would be in contradiction with its definition.

(Ibid.)

In the *Ethics* as well as in his letters, Spinoza equates eternity with duration, as long as it is not determinate duration. However, if it is not even possible, as we saw in the explanation to the definition of eternity (I, D8), to explain eternity through duration "even if the duration is conceived to be without beginning or end" (ibid.), then it is certainly not possible to equate eternity and duration. Hence it is absolutely clear that Spinoza contradicts himself with regard to the relation between eternity and duration. He disconnects and separates eternity and duration (I, D8, Exp) as well as connects and equates them (I.21 and its demonstration; Letter 35).[15]

Seemingly, in order to rehabilitate the consistency in Spinoza's system of eternity and time one should maintain one or two of the following claims:

a   There is no full correlation between the letters and the *Ethics*; therefore, Spinoza's crystallized position in the *Ethics* regarding the matter of eternity and duration could differ from the position he maintains in Letter 35 to Hudde.[16]
b   One of the two references from the *Ethics* – either that in which Spinoza separates eternity from duration (I, D8, Exp) or that in which he equates them (I.21 and the demonstration there) – is simply a slip of the pen that does not bring his whole system to the point of collapse.[17]

However, whoever chooses to adopt these two claims, or even one of them, will ultimately be proven wrong.[18] Spinoza, during the course of presenting his system, takes great pains to strengthen and reinforce both the separation of eternity and duration, as well as the equivalence between them.[19] The separation between eternity and duration is presented immediately with the raising of the system's curtain (I, D8, Exp), at the moment of the curtain's drawing (V.29 and its demonstration; V.34, Cor, Schol), and during the course of the presentation of the system (II.44, Cor 2, Dem).[20] The equivalence between eternity and duration is repeated and presented in several places in the *Ethics*: in the scholium to proposition I.17, in proposition I.21 and its demonstration, as well as in the demonstrations to propositions II.11 and IV.62.[21]

Moreover, as he had done with the contradiction regarding the essence of the things that follow from God (propositions I.24 and I.25), Spinoza again takes care to link, from a textual standpoint, the two positions that exclude one another. In this case, however, it is not a contradiction between two consistent references, but rather a contradiction that arises and bursts forth from within those very references. We discussed one of these two references, proposition I.21, at the beginning of the present section, and we will discuss the second one presently.

At the opening of proposition II.45, Spinoza, who attributes God's eternal and infinite essence to the existence of the things that follow from God, negates their existence as "duration [*durationem*], i.e., existence insofar as it is conceived abstractly, and as a certain species of quantity" (II.45, Schol, II/127). Contrarily, at the end of this scholium, Spinoza again attributes duration to the things that follow from God. As he writes at the close of the scholium: "the force by which each [thing] perseveres in existing [*existendo perseverat*] follows from the eternal necessity of God's nature. Concerning this, see IP24C" (ibid.). This force, by which each thing perseveres in its existence, as we saw in the previous chapter, is none other than the conatus of all things that is equivalent with the duration in existence of all things, according to propositions III.7 and III.8. Indeed, in the corollary to proposition I.24, to which Spinoza directs us here, it is explicitly stated that God, i.e., eternity, is the *only* cause of the duration (*duratio*) of all the things that follow from him.[22] Spinoza, therefore, completely contradicts himself. At the beginning of the scholium to proposition II.45 he detaches and separates eternity and duration, while at the end of that same scholium he connects and equates them.

Nonetheless, here, as in the previous contradictions that we saw, Spinoza presents himself before his readers and interpreters as walking a straight geometric line. In order to remove all doubt for the reader for whom uncertainty has crept in regarding the consistency of the scholium to proposition II.45, Spinoza takes special pains to present this scholium, in the framework of the scholium to proposition V.29, as a consistent reference based only on the disconnect (and not on the equivalence) between eternity and duration.[23] It is important to again emphasize that the contradiction between eternity and duration is in fact a contradiction between eternity and time. Indeed, even if duration, as we saw earlier, is not limited by time in that it is defined as "an indefinite continuation of existing" (II, D5), it "can be defined by time" (V.23, Dem).

Time flowing from within eternity in proposition II.8 and its corollary

To all of the references that we have already looked at, we should now add proposition II.8 and its corollary, in which the most blatant expression of the claim according to which time flows from eternity can be found. In the proposition itself Spinoza claims:

> The ideas of singular things [*rerum singularium*], *or* of modes, that do not exist [*non existentium*] must be comprehended [*comprehendi*] in God's infinite idea in the same way as the formal essences of the singular things, *or* modes, are contained [*continentur*] in God's attributes.
>
> (II.8, II/90)

In the corollary, Spinoza adds:

> so long as singular things do not exist, except insofar as they are comprehended in God's attributes, their objective being, *or* ideas, do not exist

except insofar as God's infinite idea exists. And when singular things are said to exist, not only insofar as they are comprehended in God's attributes, but insofar also as they are said to have duration, their ideas also involve the existence through which they are said to have duration.

(II.8, Cor)

These propositions broaden the scope of the general principle of the parallelism according to which "[t]he order and connection of ideas is the same as the order and connection of things" (II.7, II/89). In addition, they claim, as though incidentally, that individual things belong to one of the two following phases: the first phase is "non-existence," in the framework of which individual things are included in God's attributes *only* through mediation of the infinite, immediate modes. In this phase, Spinoza explicitly grants to the individual things that do not exist eternity and eternity *only*. All that is included in eternity is eternal, and God's attributes are eternal (I.19); therefore, the individual things that do not exist are nonetheless eternal in that they are included in God's attributes; the second phase is "existence" in the framework of which "singular things are said to exist, not only insofar as they are comprehended in God's attributes," i.e., not only in that eternity is attributed to them, as we saw, "but insofar also as they are said to have duration" (II.8, Cor). Thus, in this phase, Spinoza attributes to the individual things that exist both eternity and duration.

Three central difficulties, which branch out of the contradiction between eternity and time, stem from proposition II.8 and its corollary.

The first difficulty arises from the first phase. This phase, as we saw, is populated by "singular things, *or* [...] modes, that do not exist (*non existentium*)" (II.8). However, there is no place in Spinoza's system (nor could there be) for "singular things, or modes, that do not exist." God does not have stockpiles of unrealized powers dormant in individual things that do not yet exist; indeed: "God's power (*potentia*) is his essence itself" (I.34, II/76)[24] and "God's existence (*existentia*) and his essence are one in the same" (I.20, II/64). In another of Spinoza's formulations, "[w]hatever we conceive to be in God's power (*potestas*), necessarily exists (*est*)" (I.35, II/77). From the sum of Spinoza's assertions in proposition II.8 and its corollary it becomes clear that when he refers to "singular things, or modes, that do not exist (*non existentium*)" (II.8), he does not mean things that do not exist entirely, but rather things whose existence, or essence, is only objective. However, given that this existence is in opposition to the existence of things whose essence is formal – the latter are presented as having more existence than the former because they contain not only existence of eternity but also existence of duration – it is not clear how there could exist things whose existence is only partial in that their essence is only objective. It is not clear what prevents these things from having absolutely full existence, i.e., from having formal essence. In other words, even if Spinoza does not make a distinction between individual things that do not exist completely and between individual things that do exist completely, he does distinguish between individual things that exist more in that their essence is formal, and individual things that exist less and whose essence is only objective. It appears, therefore, at the very least, that Spinoza has no systematic basis for this distinction. In fact, because Spinoza links existence to perfection (II, D6),[25] this difficulty is actually another incarnation of the difficulty that arose from Spinoza's hierarchy of perfections that we discussed in Chapter 3: how, if at all, can we justify from a systematic standpoint the claim that certain things are more perfect than others given that all things follow from God whose perfection is absolute?

The second difficulty relates to the possibility for individual things to transition between the two phases as is claimed in the corollary to II.8. As we saw, because the first phase connotes non-existence and the second existence, when an individual thing moves from the first phase to the second it comes into existence, and when it moves from the second phase to the first it perishes. However, even if beyond the limits of Spinoza's system, in the framework of daily experience, the claim that individual things come into existence and perish is trivial and obvious, in Spinoza's system this claim, at least apparently, is null and void. The first phase, as we saw, connotes eternity, whereas the second phase connotes temporality. Temporality is characterized by duration, which although not limited by time (II, D5), can be defined by time (V.23, Dem). Therefore the transition from the first phase to the second connotes the emergence of individual, temporal things from within eternity, while the transition from the second phase to the first connotes the return of individual, temporal things to the bosom of eternity. However, logically, neither of these things is possible. As we saw in the previous section, a logical chasm separates eternity and time, thus the migration of details between the two realms is not possible. All eternal things are chained by eternity, which decrees upon them static, frozen existence from logical necessity, and all temporal things are chained by time, which moves incessantly and which decrees upon them a dynamic and continual existence of motion and rest.

The third difficulty is the most severe, and it refers to the status of individual things in the second phase. Spinoza claims that when individual things have *only* objective being, they are contained *only* eternally in God's attributes, whereas when they have formal essence they are contained in God's attributes *both* eternally and continuously; i.e., while individual things that have objective being only exist eternally, the individual things that have formal essence are involved both in eternal existence and in an existence of duration (II.8, Cor). It follows that there is an existence, below the surface as it were, of eternal things that do not exist – either because they have not yet come into existence or because they came into existence and perished – and there is an existence, above the surface, of temporal things that contain eternity in addition to duration. However, the status of existing things is scandalous not only because eternity and time become one in the things that exist, but also (and principally) because Spinoza attributes to existing things, i.e., to temporal things, *more* existence than he attributes to eternal things in that he claims temporal things contain both existence of eternity and existence of duration. Thus, when a temporal thing emerges from eternity, by mediation of duration, not only does its existence not diminish, it increases.

128 *The second kind of knowledge*

The same goes for the opposite case: when a certain thing perishes, its existence shrivels up in that it retreats from an existence that had duration *in addition* to eternity to an existence of eternity alone.

Nevertheless, the claim that time has an advantage over eternity is not conceivable. Temporal existence, even that which is continuous, lacks the necessity of eternity. Eternity, to paraphrase Kafka, is not temporality standing still;[26] eternity is existence from another order of magnitude than that of temporality, an existence that contains a necessity that cannot be found in time. Therefore, for Spinoza the opposite is true: eternity has an advantage over time, even over time that has no beginning or end, i.e., even over duration.

Moreover, if, as is claimed in II.8, Cor, sprawling out on the axis of time provides an additional layer of existence, and existence, as has been claimed earlier, is equivalent to perfection (II, D6), it follows necessarily that the more each individual thing perseveres over the course of a long time, the more it is perfect. However, Spinoza himself explicitly dismisses this conclusion outright when he claims that "no singular thing can be called more perfect for having persevered in existing for a longer time" (Preface to IV, p. 546).[27]

Applying the unique position of the constructive contradiction in God to the realm of eternity and time in Spinoza's philosophy, which we will discuss more extensively below, solves the three problems presented here in the following way:

a The constructive contradiction grants true status to temporal as well as eternal things, and thus lays the metaphysical foundation for distinguishing between things whose essence is formal and things whose essence is objective alone.

b The definition of the cause of itself (I, D1) adjoined to the principle of the constructive contradiction leads necessarily to the flowing of time from within eternity, and the opposite, i.e., eternity flowing from within time, exactly as it necessarily leads to the flowing of the finite from the infinite and the flowing of the infinite from the finite.[28] Thus a systematic meaning is granted to the coming into being and the annihilation of individual things in existence.

c The constructive contradiction leads to the claim that along with the advantage of eternity over time, time also must have an advantage over eternity. Indeed, during the discussion of the intellectual love of God in the eighth chapter we will see that just as the temporal is redeemed by the eternal, the eternal is redeemed by the temporal.

The temporal is a kind of secret to which God clings. Given that the temporal begins and ends, the temporal has an advantage over the eternal, as the latter is confined within the necessity of itself. Therefore, just as time is dependent on eternity, eternity is dependent on time. Despite the fact that eternity and time exclude each other, they are ultimately equivalent to one another. Therefore God, in that he is a total concept, must contain them both.

The flowing of eternity from within time

In the two previous sections we saw that Spinoza derives time from eternity; however, as stated, Spinoza is not satisfied only with the claim that time flows from eternity, but also argues the opposite: that eternity flows from time. Deriving the eternal from the temporal is embedded in the following three central junctions of Spinoza's philosophy.

(a) In the opening proposition of the second part of the *Ethics*, when Spinoza seeks to demonstrate "[t]hought is an attribute of God, *or* God is a thinking thing" (II.1, II/86), he derives eternal and infinite existence in its own kind of the attribute of thought not from the substance, which is eternal and absolutely infinite, but from our individual thoughts, which are finite and temporal.[29] These individual thoughts, Spinoza claims in the demonstration to proposition II.1, "are modes that express God's nature in a certain and determinate way (by IP25C)." From here it follows that

> (by ID5) there belongs to God an attribute whose concept all singular thoughts involve, and through which they are also conceived. Therefore, Thought is one of God's infinite attributes, which expresses an eternal and infinite essence of God (see ID6), *or* God is a thinking thing.
> (Ibid.)

In this short demonstration, the contradiction in deriving the infinite from the finite is connected to the contradiction in deriving the eternal from the temporal. In fact, this double contradiction is not unique to the attribute of thought alone, and it extends to the attribute of extension. In the demonstration to the next proposition in the second part of the *Ethics* that claims "[e]xtension is an attribute of God, *or* God is an extended thing" (II.2, II/86), Spinoza posits "the demonstration of this proceeds in the same way as that of the preceding Proposition" (II.2, Dem).[30] Moreover, from the parallelism determined in proposition II.7 it follows that this double contradiction extends, and necessarily so, to the many infinite attributes of God.

(b) The flowing of eternity from within time is also embedded in the demonstration of the next proposition, namely, the third proposition of the second part of the *Ethics*. Here too when Spinoza seeks to demonstrate that "[i]n God there is necessarily an idea, both of his essence and of everything that necessarily follows from his essence" (II.3, II/87), he continues to undermine the central stream of the first part of the *Ethics*; instead of presenting *natura naturans* as the cause of *natura naturata* he presents the latter as the cause of the former. The demonstration to proposition II.3 has the utmost importance for understanding the organizing metaphysical procedure of Spinoza's philosophy in its entirety. Therefore, before tracing the way in which the flow of eternity from time is embedded in this demonstration, I will seek to clarify the precise meaning and intent of the demonstration.

While from proposition I.21 and its demonstration it follows that God's intellect, in that it is an infinite, immediate mode in the attribute of thought, is an effect of the attribute of thought, from the demonstration to proposition II.3 it is clear that the attribute of thought is itself an effect of God's intellect that locates it as that which connotes the essence of God and grasps itself as his idea. Indeed, in this demonstration Spinoza claims that God, in that he "(by P1) can think infinitely many things in infinitely many modes" (according to proposition II.1), i.e., in that he has God's intellect (according to proposition I.16), he has the ability to form an idea of his own essence, an idea of the attribute of thought that connotes God's essence according to definition I, D4. Similarly, God has the ability to form an idea of all that necessarily follows from his essence, i.e., of all that necessarily follows from the attribute of thought, including himself.

It is easy to see that the demonstration to proposition II.3 is completely invalid: it assumes the existence of God's intellect that it is seeking to demonstrate. However, even if there is no demonstration here, there is a definition. God's intellect is here defined as a reflective concept; it establishes itself by establishing God's essence (from the viewpoint of thought) as an essence of which God's intellect itself is a necessary effect in that the intellect itself is the idea of God. God's intellect is none other than the idea of God, as is determined in the demonstration to proposition II.4. As such, God's intellect grants meaning to Spinoza's claim that "God must be called the cause of all things in the same sense in which he is called the cause of himself" (I.25, Schol).

Proposition I.16 grants meaning to God as the cause of itself from the viewpoint of *natura naturans*, while proposition II.3, just as the two preceding propositions, grants meaning to God as the cause of itself from the viewpoint of *natura naturata*. Furthermore, in the demonstration to proposition II.3 Spinoza posits the *or* of equivalence (*sive*) between the procedure of propositions I.16 and II.1. He therefore claims that these two procedures, which from a logical-Euclidean standpoint exclude each other in that they exchange cause for effect and effect for cause, are equivalent in his metaphysics. Indeed, they close and bind, each from its own direction, the basic circularity embedded in reality as the cause of itself (I, D1).

Moreover, the demonstration to proposition II.3 sheds light on the surprising insertion of the intellect in the definition of the attribute in the first part of the *Ethics*. As mentioned earlier, Spinoza defines the attribute as "what the intellect perceives of a substance, as constituting its essence" (I, D4). Spinoza's definition of a thing indicates the cause of that thing.[31] Therefore, in the textual context in which the definition appears, it is not clear to the reader, and justifiably so, why Spinoza inserts the intellect in the definition of the attribute. From the metaphysical map spread out before us in the first part of the *Ethics* it is clear that the intellect is not the cause of the attribute; on the contrary, it is the effect of the attribute (I.21, Dem), and as such it has no place in the definition of the attribute. Even If the intellect perceives the attribute, from among all its perceptions, as constituting the essence of the substance, it is still not justified for the intellect to appear in the definition of the attribute.[32] Furthermore, in light of the uncharacterized appearance of the intellect in the definition of the attribute, the reader wonders if Spinoza means the human intellect or the divine one. In fact, when the intellect appears in the definition of the attribute it is not at all clear why it appears at all. Even worse, it is not at all clear exactly what it is that appears.

The demonstration to proposition II.3 allows us to understand the meaning and intent of the enigmatic appearance of the intellect in the definition of the attribute: the intellect appears in the definition of the attribute because it is the exact cause of the attribute. As part of its self-constitution, the intellect constitutes the attribute in terms of what connotes the essence of the substance, an essence of which the intellect itself is a necessary effect in that the substance is the idea of that essence. Moreover, the uncharacterized appearance of the intellect in the definition of the attribute now removes its garb of vagueness and shows itself to be intentional. Indeed, the double meaning concealed within it is clearly intentional in that it makes it possible to situate within the definition of the attribute both the human intellect when it grasps truth, as well as the divine intellect that necessarily grasps truth (II.11, Cor); this is in accordance with what Spinoza does in the demonstrations to propositions II.1 and II.3, respectively. A crucial maneuver in Spinoza's metaphysics, which unfolds at the opening of the second part of the *Ethics*, is already embedded in the definition of the attribute (I.D4). As such, the definition of the attribute joins the other opening definitions of the *Ethics*, which, as we saw in other contexts, are like miniatures of the system which require special attention in order to be fully understood.[33]

After this brief, though necessary, detour from our path, we will return to the matter at hand. If we take into consideration that Spinoza attributes both eternity and duration to God's intellect (I.21 and its demonstrations) – i.e., unspecified temporality, though temporality nonetheless – while he attributes eternity alone (I, D6) to the attribute of thought (just as he does to the rest of the attributes), the necessary conclusion is that beneath the surface of the demonstration to proposition II.3 – which presents the attribute of thought as derived from God's intellect – eternity flows from within temporality. As a matter of fact, proposition II.3 and its demonstration are the inverse of proposition I.21 and its demonstration since in the latter we see that temporality flows from within eternity, while in proposition II.3 eternity flows from within temporality.

(c) The salvation of man, as we will see below, constitutes an act in the framework of which the eternal flows from the temporal. In the context of the act of true cognition man deviates beyond time to eternity while also remaining caught in time; the action in which man uncovers the eternal necessity embedded in reality takes place on its own along the axis of time. Salvation, therefore, assumes both time and eternity, and it connotes the flowing of eternity from within time. Without time, there is nothing from which to be redeemed, and without eternity, there is nothing to be redeemed to.

In summary, deriving the eternal from the temporal which itself flows from the eternal, closes and binds the circularity embedded in the definition of eternity (I, D8), which determines that eternity flows from within itself. The circularity in the definition of eternity, which closes the definitions of the first part of the *Ethics*, brings us back to the circularity of the cause of itself (I, D1), which opens the list of definitions as well as the *Ethics* itself. Thus, the issue of eternity and

132 *The second kind of knowledge*

time sheds additional light on the centrality and supreme importance of the definition of the cause of itself as a definition that summarizes, on a miniature scale, the entirety of Spinoza's philosophy.

Concealing and revealing the contradiction between eternity and time

The contradiction between eternity and time, just like the other contradictions in Spinoza's metaphysical system, is concealed behind a fortified wall of heavy silence. Again, not only is Spinoza not willing to reveal the meaning of the contradiction, he is even unwilling to explicitly admit its very existence. However, Spinoza does again intentionally leave a small crack in the wall through which it is possible to peer into the heart of his metaphysical system and behold the contradictions embedded in it. As one of the great masters of esoteric writing, Spinoza makes sure this crack in the wall, which he locates in the scholium to proposition II.8, is well hidden. Therefore, only one who does not despair from the contradictions revealed in the system can find those cracks, and he must continue to seek out these hidden secrets while circling the walls of the system again and again.

In the scholium to proposition II.8, Spinoza presents a geometric example through which he seeks to shed light on his metaphysical position as it is expressed in proposition II.8 and in the corollary to which this scholium is attached. In these propositions, as we have seen, Spinoza examines the relations between eternity and time via an examination of the relations between individual things whose existence has objective essence, and individual things whose existence has formal essence. In order to demonstrate, as clearly as possible, the relations of the latter, Spinoza uses an example seemingly borrowed from proposition III.35 in Euclid's *The Elements*, which determines that if AC and GF are the coordinates of a certain circle, and if segmented at point B, the rectangle whose base is AB and whose height is BC is equal in surface area to the rectangle whose base is GB and whose height is BF.

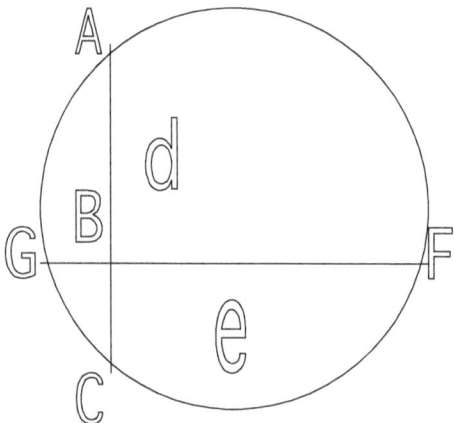

Eternity and time 133

While relying on the feature of these pairs of coordinates of the circle, Spinoza claims that

> in a circle there are contained infinitely many rectangles that are equal to one another. Nevertheless, none of them can be said to exist except insofar as the circle exists, nor also can the idea of any of these rectangles be said to exist except insofar as it is comprehended in the idea of the circle. Now of these infinitely many [rectangles] let two only, viz. [those formed from the segments of lines] D and E, exist. Of course their ideas also exist now, not only insofar as they are only comprehended in the idea of the circle, but also insofar as they involve the existence of those rectangles. By this they are distinguished from the other ideas of other rectangles.
>
> (II.8, Schol, II/91)[34]

Indeed, as least at first glance it seems that Spinoza was able to demonstrate, via the geometric example, his metaphysical distinction between individual things whose existence has objective essence, and those whose existence has formal essence. It is easy to see that the existence of infinite many potential rectangles, which can be created through the possible segments of the infinite many potential coordinates of the circle, is not equivalent to the existence of the two specific rectangles created by a specific segmentation of the coordinates D and E which in fact do exist. While the existence of the first rectangles is absolutely dependent on the existence of the circle, the existence of the latter rectangles is not absolutely dependent on the existence of the circle and they, therefore, exist independently. In the same sense, it is easy to realize that while the ideas of infinite many potential rectangles (which can be created from a possible segmentation of the infinite many potential coordinates of the circle) involve existence only in so far as they are contained in the idea of the circle, the ideas of the rectangles that exist in actuality (which were created through a specific segmentation of the coordinates D and E) involve existence "not only insofar as they are only comprehended in the idea of the circle, but also insofar as they involve the existence of those rectangles" (ibid.). Thus, in sum, it can be claimed that the relation between the first rectangles and the latter rectangles is exactly like the relation between individual things whose existence has objective essence and individual things whose existence has formal essence.

Up until this point there has been a wall of silence and concealment regarding the existence and status of contradiction in the scholium to proposition II.8. Now, to the fissure in the wall, i.e., to Spinoza's revelation through allusion. In the general landscape of thought in the *Ethics*, of which sophistication, complexity and entanglement are the main characteristics, the example in the scholium to proposition II.8 stands out especially in terms of its simplicity and its immediate and full suitability, at least seemingly, to the metaphysical matter that it demonstrates.[35] For this reason, Spinoza's words in the short preface to the scholium are particularly surprising:

134 *The second kind of knowledge*

> If anyone wishes me to explain this further by an example [*exemplum*], I will, of course, not be able to give one which adequately [*adaequatè explicet*] explains what I speak of here, since it is unique [*unicam*]. Still I shall try as far as possible to illustrate [*illustrare*][36] the matter.
>
> (II.8, Schol)

These obscure and vague statements raise two perplexing questions:

a Why is the matter that is determined in proposition II.8 and its corollary "unique"? It seems to be just another branching-out in Spinoza's vast metaphysical system. Even if this particular branch would be especially important, there still seems to be no reason to consider it "unique" within the vast entirety of matters with which Spinoza's system deals.[37]
b Why does Spinoza claim not only that the Euclidean example presented in the scholium to proposition II.8 is not capable of adequately explaining that same special matter that is discussed in the propositions to which this scholium is attached, but that in principle no other example is suitable to this "unique" matter? All that can be done, Spinoza claims, is to try and illustrate (*illustrare*) this unique matter as far as possible.

We must here cling to the Latin text, like Ariadne's thread, in order to escape the labyrinth in which we find ourselves. The proper understanding of the matter before us requires the proper understanding of the term *unicam*, which Spinoza uses in the passage at hand. The exact meaning of this term is unclear here, but is elucidated in another place; therefore, in order to understand it we must again join together the different parts of the *Ethics*, and we must begin by returning to the first part, in which Spinoza posits:

> God is unique [*unicam*].
>
> (I.14, Cor 1, II/56)[38]

Spinoza reserves the term *unicam* for God alone.[39] The metaphysical meaning of this term in the *Ethics* deviates from its literal, narrow and quantitative meaning.[40] God is *sui generis*, a singular and unique kind in its own class.[41] Thus, by using the term *unicam* in the scholium to proposition II.8, Spinoza hints to the reader that the object of the propositions to which he attaches this scholium is none other than God. We should relate this textual finding, from which it follows that the "unique" matter that Spinoza refers to is in fact God, to the fundamental logical finding that arises from the study of the concept of God in the *Ethics*. The logical meaning of God being "unique" is that the law of contradiction is applied to him in a manner opposite to the way in which it is applied to all the things that follow from him. While the logical contradiction destroys all that follows from God, that same logical contradiction is that which constructs God.[42] Now, after having cracked the codeword *unicam* and finding the general logical key to Spinoza's system, we can solve the two problems that have arisen.

a Given that proposition II.8 and its corollary present us with the contradiction between eternity and time, Spinoza is precise when he claims that the matter that these propositions treat is unique, i.e., God. For God is the exact meaning of this contradiction in that his totality is the source of the contradictions of depth in Spinoza's system, and God's totality is the final meaning of the contradiction between eternity and time. If God contains a thing and its opposite, he must be both eternal and temporal. Thus, in actuality the *unicam* in the scholium to proposition II.8 does not refer to the contradiction between eternity and time since this contradiction is not the only contradiction in Spinoza's metaphysics, nor is there anything unique about it from a logical viewpoint. The object of the *unicam* in our scholium is God, who is systematically unique and singular, and for whom the contradiction between eternity and time constitutes an additional and necessary layer of his complete logical otherness.[43]

b It is now possible also to clarify why neither the Euclidean example that Spinoza chooses, nor any other example, can adequately explain (*adaequatè explicet*) the "unique" matter in proposition II.8 and its corollary. We will begin with the specific example that Spinoza presents, and we will then turn more generally to other possible examples. The Euclidean example that Spinoza presents is not suitable for the matter that it is demonstrating because it lacks, and necessarily so, the logical contradiction in the unique metaphysical matter to which it refers. Indeed, there is no contradiction between the first Euclidean phase, which indicates coordinates whose essence is objective, and the second Euclidean phase, which indicates coordinates whose essence is formal. By contrast, as we saw earlier, between the first metaphysical phase, which indicates individual things that have objective essence, and the second metaphysical phase, which indicates individual things that have formal essence, there exists the logical contradiction between eternity and time, i.e., the contradiction between necessary existence and unnecessary existence.

Moreover, and this is critical, in the scholium to proposition II.8 Spinoza does not merely claim that the specific example presented there does not adequately explain the matter being treated, but rather that *no other example* is capable of properly explaining the issue. Given that the matter to which Spinoza refers here is God, we are faced with a meta-systematic claim with far-reaching consequences, the importance of which goes beyond the context of the issue of eternity and time in the framework of which the claim is made. Any example of God, in that it is an example, cannot be God. God, and only God, contains the constructive logical contradiction in that he is different in principle from all that follows from him. Therefore, all that follows from God, including all that is contained in Spinoza's own speculative system dedicated to a Euclidean investigation of God *or* nature, is not suitable to God except to serve as an illustration *or* an inadequate explanation of God. Here again we see the transcendental trend emerge in Spinoza's philosophy; between the lines Spinoza presents his system as a speculative tower the top of which will never reach the heavens, and necessarily so.

Notes

1 For reasons that will be presented below, I prefer here to rely on V.30 and not I.D8.
2 In the formulation that refers to God as being the only substance (I.14, Cor 1): "God's existence and his essence are one and the same [*idem sunt*]" (I.20). Therefore, "eternity," as Spinoza asserts in another place, "pertains to the nature of substance" (I.19, Dem).
3 In fact, the eternity of the attributes appears explicitly in the definition of God as "a substance consisting of an infinity of attributes, of which each one expresses an eternal and infinite essence" (I.D6).
4 Spinoza positions the *or* (*sive*) of equivalence between eternity and necessity in the demonstration to proposition IV.62 when he claims: "Whatever the Mind conceives under the guidance of reason, it conceives under the same species of eternity, *or* necessity (by IIP.44.C2)." In another place, Spinoza, while relying on existence being an infinite and necessary existence, claims "infinity and necessity of existence, *or* (what is the same, by D.8) eternity" (I.23, Dem).
5 "(by I.16) this necessity of things is the very necessity of God's eternal nature," Spinoza claims in the demonstration to Cor. 2 of proposition II.44, which posits: "It is of the nature of Reason to perceive things under a certain species of eternity [*sub quadam aeternitatis specie*]." This is the first appearance in the *Ethics* of this famous expression.
6 Knowledge of the eternal laws and order of nature belong to the second kind of knowledge, in the framework of which Spinoza claims:

> He who rightly knows that all things follow from the necessity of the divine nature, and happen according to the eternal laws and rules of nature, will surely find nothing worthy of Hate, Mockery, or Disdain, nor anyone whom he will pity. Instead he will strive, as far as human virtue allows, to act well, as they say, and rejoice [*bene agree*].
>
> (IV.50, Schol)

Emotion also joins this knowledge in the framework of the third kind of knowledge, which is itself eternal like its object: "The intellectual Love of God, which arises from the third kind of knowledge, is eternal" (V.33). Moreover, as Spinoza asserts later on: "no Love except intellectual Love is eternal" (V.34, Cor).
7 Bennett sees the removal of time from the territory of metaphysical truth in Spinoza's philosophy as part of the latter's general attempt to conduct a philosophy that fundamentally lacks space for the first person. In Bennett's words:

> Spinoza resolutely resists doing philosophy in a first-person way. He is as far as possible from Descartes' stance in the *Meditations*: "Here I am, with my own inner states; where, intellectually, do I go from here?" Where Descartes and Leibniz are both sure that the mind or soul is absolutely simple and indivisible, Spinoza insists, as he ought to, that "a human mind is not simple, but composed of a great many ideas" (2p15).... It is therefore not surprising that in the *Ethics* there is no hint of the special aspect of tenses, and of past-present-future, which engage the first-person singular attitude of mind.
>
> (*A Study of Spinoza's Ethics*, pp. 195–196)

8 At this point I would like to concur with Donagan's apt claim:

> Since Spinoza held the immediate infinite and eternal mode of extension to be motion and rest, he must have conceived at least one eternal mode as being in time. The concept of timeless existence may be intelligible; that of timeless motion is not.
>
> ("Spinoza's Proof," p. 246)

Despite this, for reasons that will become clear below, I reject Donagan's sweeping claim that Spinoza never denies identifying eternity with necessary existence in all time. See

Alan Donagan, "Spinoza's Proof of Immortality," in Green (ed.), *Spinoza: A Collection of Critical Essays*, Garden City: Anchor Books, 1973, pp. 241–258. For a discussion of the meager amount of information Spinoza provides regarding the equivalence and role of the infinite immediate modes in his system, see Curley, *Behind the Geometrical Method*, pp. 34–36, and Allison, *Benedict de Spinoza*, pp. 68–71.

9 Bennett treats this proposition, which claims that "God, *or* all of God's attributes, are immutable," as he does other places in the *Ethics* in which a Parmenidean tendency is embedded, namely, as necessarily derived from Spinoza's conception of eternity. And he does so without any treatment of the principle of the conatus. Bennett writes: "Such remarks do not force us to conclude that Spinoza thought change to be unreal, and I am reluctant to attribute to him anything so manifestly false" ("Spinoza's Metaphysics," p. 78). Indeed, as we saw in Chapter 4, alongside the strict Parmenidean portrait of reality, Spinoza also presents a Heraclidean portrait of reality in the *Ethics*, in the framework of which existence is understood to be a being of infinite many parts caught in an infinitely flowing stream.

10 Nonetheless, as we saw in the previous chapter, for Spinoza the dynamic state of the conatus is identical to its static state.

11 This definition is "provocatively unhelpful" as Mason rightfully states (*The God of Spinoza*, p. 38). Even a fledgling philosopher like Meno, who never finished his philosophical training, admits to Socrates that a circular definition is invalid. See Plato, *Meno*, 79e-d. Also see I.M. Crombie, "Socratic Definition," in Day (ed.), *Plato's Meno in Focus*. London: Routledge, 1994, pp. 172–207. Thus, one cannot rely exclusively on the definition of eternity in Part I (I.D8), as many of Spinoza's interpreters have done, without revising it via the non-circular alternative definition that Spinoza suggests in Part V (V.30, Dem). See Donagan, "Spinoza's Proof of Immortality," p. 244; Hampshire, *Spinoza*, pp. 171–173; Kneale, "Eternity and Sempiternity," in *Spinoza: A Collection of Critical Essays*, edited by Marjorie Grene. New York: Anchor Books, 1973, pp. 236–240; Bennett, *A Study of Spinoza's Ethics*, p. 204 and "Spinoza's Metaphysics," pp. 76–78; Allison, *Benedict de Spinoza*, p. 66; and Scruton, *Spinoza*, p. 7 and on.

12 Spinoza adjoins the term *semper* with the term *duratio* at the end of the preface of the fourth part of the *Ethics* when he states:

> the duration [*duration*] of things cannot be determined from their essence, since the essence of things involves no certain and determinate time of existing. But any thing whatever, whether it is more perfect or less, will always (*semper*) be able to persevere in existing by the same force by which it begins to exist.
>
> (p. 546)

In the demonstration to proposition III.8 as well Spinoza adjoins these two terms when he claims that neither the conatus nor the "thing's duration" (*rei durationem*), which are identical to each other, refer to definite time, but "[o]n the contrary, since (by P4) it will always (*Semper*) continue to exist" (ibid.). Despite this, Spinoza uses the term *semper* in the literal sense that signifies determined temporary existence, and not the systematic meaning of *duratio*. See, for example, propositions 35, 42, 48 and 72 in Part IV. In any case, adjoining the term *semper* to the systematic term *aeternitas* in proposition I.21, like in additional places that will be discussed below, casts a contradiction in the system because it inserts the element of time into that of eternity, whether we equate the term *semper* with *duratio*, or whether we take its literal, non-systematic meaning. In this context Curley claims: "The word 'always' (*Semper*) suggests temporality, omnitemporality, to be sure, but temporality nonetheless" (*Spinoza's Metaphysics*, p. 107).

13 See Curley, *Spinoza's Metaphysics*, p. 107. Here, we in fact return, from a different direction, to the contradiction between the definition of the substance (I.D3) and the definition of the mode (I.D5), which we discussed in the previous chapter.

138 *The second kind of knowledge*

14 It is reasonable to assume that Spinoza's friendship with Hudde was not only based on common philosophical interests, optics, and mathematics; as Nadler claims:

> A friendly acquaintance with Hudde had the potential of being a long-term practical value, as Spinoza was constantly on the lookout for some protection against the orthodox preachers from the political elite, to which Hudde surely belonged. It may have been for just this reason that he cultivated their relationship.
>
> (*Spinoza*, p. 223)

Indeed, in those days Hudde's political power grew; in 1667 he was appointed as member of the Amsterdam city council, and in 1672 he began the first of several terms as one of the senior burgemeesters of the city. On the importance Spinoza attributed to the protection of those in positions of political power see Curley, Letter 6, p. 173.

15 The double-characterization, both eternal and having duration, that Spinoza grants immediate, infinite modes in proposition I.21 and its demonstration, just as in the first paragraph of Letter 35, expressly refutes the interpretive position that attributes them eternity alone, as well as the interpretive stance that attributes them as having duration alone. The former position can be found Genevieve Lloyd, *Spinoza and the Ethics*. London: Routledge, 1996, p. 42, while the latter position can be found in Yovel's introduction to his translation of the *Ethics*, in which he states:

> This characterization [of duration] is in principle applied to all the modes, finite and infinite. Even an infinite mode, such as the law of nature, which cannot be annihilated, is not eternal in the sense in which it is defined [by Spinoza], but rather exists forever in the realm of duration.
>
> (Ibid., p. 25, footnote 8)

Nevertheless, even if we include the laws of nature as infinite, mediated modes as Yovel suggests (ibid., p. 24), we cannot negate eternity from these modes. Indeed, in proposition I.22 Spinoza explicitly claims that the infinite, mediated modes necessarily exist, and if they necessarily exist they are eternal since eternity is none other than necessary existence as stated in the demonstration to proposition V.30. Moreover, as we will see immediately by relying on propositions I.28, II.8, Cor, and II.45, Spinoza attributes eternity not only to the infinite modes, be they immediate or mediated, but also to the finite modes.

16 This letter was written in April of 1666.

17 In fact, if the disconnect between eternity and duration (I.D8, Exp) is understood as loose penmanship on Spinoza's part, there is no need to reject Letter 35. On the contrary, proof can be found there for the equivalence Spinoza asserts (I.21 and its demonstration) between eternity and duration.

18 For example, Curley treats the characterization of the infinite, immediate modes as eternal (*aeterna*) in proposition I.21 as a slight stumble on Spinoza's part that is repaired later on in the same proposition, which characterizes the modes as also always existing (Curley translates *semper* as "always"). Curley writes in footnote 53 on page 429 of his translation of the *Ethics*:

> It is sometimes suggested that it is inappropriate for Spinoza to characterize any mode (even an infinite one) as eternal, and so the use of temporal language here has been taken to show that the infinite modes exist at all times, but not (strictly speaking) eternally.

At this point, Curley is following Wolfson, who also sought, in his interpretation of proposition I.21, to rescue Spinoza from his own words. For that purpose Wolfson is not hesitant to suggest an ad-hoc definition to the term eternity in this proposition, which equates eternity with duration, and through which Wolfson clearly claims that when Spinoza asserts in proposition I.21 that the immediate modes are eternal (*aeterna*), he means that they have duration (*durationem*). Wolfson writes:

> By the term eternal in its application to modes ... it cannot mean necessary existence per se or the identity of essence and existence, for the modes have no necessary existence per se and their existence is not identical with their essence.... "Eternal" in this case means only to be immutable, or to exist forever, as Spinoza directly expresses himself in Proposition XXI, or to have indeterminate existence or duration, as he indirectly expresses himself in the Demonstration of Proposition XXI where he describes the opposite of it to have "determinate existence or duration."
>
> (*The Philosophy of Spinoza*, Vol. 1, p. 376)

These interpretations are not convincing because they do not adhere to the text they are analyzing. In the framework of Curley's interpretation an unacceptable attempt is made to blur one expression in the text (*aeterna*) by means of another (*semper*); while in the text itself, in proposition I.21, the *or* of equivalence (*sive*) is posited between the two expressions which, from a systematic perspective, as we saw earlier, mutually exclude one another. In Wolfson's case, it is even more problematic from an interpretive standpoint since an attempt is made to distort the strict, unbending definition Spinoza posits for the term "eternity" (I.D8 and V.30, Dem), and to put in its place a definition of eternity unique and local to proposition I.21, which equates eternity with duration. However, Spinoza himself explicitly claims in the explanation to the definition of eternity (I.D8) that it "cannot be explained by duration," and that explaining eternity through duration, as he claims elsewhere, is a confusion that characterizes "the common opinion of men" (V.34, Cor, Schol), and is philosophically untenable. Moreover, these interpretations are refutable from within other places in the *Ethics*, as will be shown below.

19 In fact, the disagreement between Plato and Aristotle regarding the meaning of eternity echoes in this contradiction. As Wolfson claims:

> The term eternity started on its career in the history of philosophy with two meanings.... To Plato eternity is the antithesis of time and it means the exclusion of any kind of temporal relations. To Aristotle eternity is only endless time.
>
> (The Philosophy of Spinoza, Vol. 1, p. 358)

For a discussion of the different historical instances of this disagreement in philosophical as well as the theological contexts, and for an examination of the possible logical relations between the two meanings of eternity, see Kneale, "Eternity and Sempiternity," pp. 227–235.

20 In the second corollary to proposition II.44, Spinoza claims that "to perceive things under a certain species of eternity [*sub quadam aeternitatis specie*]" means to understand them "without any relation to time." However, if eternity does not relate to time it also cannot relate to duration, for duration, as we saw earlier, relates to time (V.23, Dem).

21 Precluding the demonstration to proposition I.25 in which Spinoza uses the term *duratio*, in the other relevant places he uses the term *semper*, which, as we saw earlier, he adjoins to the term *duratio*.

22 In addition, as we saw in the previous chapter, the corollary to proposition I.24 contradicts the adjoining of proposition III.8 and II.D5. The corollary claims that the essence of things does not contain duration, while III.8 and II.D5 together claim that the essence of things does indeed contain duration in that duration is identical to the conatus, and the conatus is the essence of things.

23 Wilson, who analyzes the scholium to proposition II.45 with particular attention, notes that at the end of the scholium, when Spinoza is referring to "the force by which each thing perseveres in existing" he refers to the conatus of things. However, she does not take note of the contradiction between eternity and duration created in the wake of this assertion. See Margaret D. Wilson, "Spinoza's Theory of Knowledge," in Garrett (ed.), *The Cambridge Companion to Spinoza*. Cambridge: Cambridge University Press, 1996, pp. 121–123. Indeed, Wilson neither takes heed of the identification of the conatus with duration, nor the contradiction between duration and eternity.

Therefore, she does not note that while in the second corollary to proposition II.44 reason is presented as that which perceives things only from some standpoint of eternity, in the scholium to proposition II.45 it follows that reason perceives things not only from some standpoint of eternity but also from some standpoint of time. Wilson indeed points out, and rightfully so, that among all of Spinoza's references to true knowledge from some standpoint of eternity, the scholium to proposition II.45 deserves particular attention (ibid., p. 122), though she disregards the main issue in this scholium – i.e., the contradiction between eternity and duration.

24 Hampshire rightfully presents this proposition, among others, as opposing Leibniz's concept of possible worlds. It follows from this proposition, as Hampshire posits, that: "The possible cannot be wider than the actual, in the sense that the actual world is one of a number of possible worlds, as Leibniz was to hold; the actual world is the only possible world" (*Spinoza*, p. 54). In another place Hampshire adds: "We acknowledge, not (as Leibniz suggested) that all is for the best in the best of all possible worlds, but that all must be as it is in the only possible world" (ibid., p. 167).

25 In this definition Spinoza indeed uses the term "reality" (*realitas*), though this term is identical for him with the terms "being" (*esse*) and "existence" (*existentia*). For example, see I.10, Schol.

26 Kafka, *The Blue Octavo Notebooks*, p. 46.

27 This metaphysical claim is echoed in Spinoza's theological-political critique of the vocation of the Hebrews in the TTP. Indeed, the chasm that Spinoza leaves between the duration of a political entity and its perfection enables him to claim that

> [t]he Hebrew people, accordingly, was chosen by God above others not for its understanding or for its qualities of mind, but owing to the form of its society and the good fortune, over so many years, with which it shaped and preserved its state.
> (TTP, III, p. 46 [47])

28 In the following section I will expand the scope of this important claim that is embedded in, as I will attempt to show, the official definition of the attribute (I.D4) and the unofficial definition of God's intellect (II.D3).

29 Indeed, from a literal standpoint, this demonstration is only referring to singular thoughts (*singulares cogitationes*) in general, though in terms of the matter at hand it is entirely clear that the intent is to singular human thoughts as is explicitly stated in the scholium there.

30 This claim is problematic because the attribute of extension is not achieved by extension, but by thought. Therefore, at least seemingly, here the attribute of thought precedes the attribute of extension. In the framework of the intellectual love of God too, as we will discuss at length below, this troubling priority of the attribute of thought opposes the parallelism of the system (II.7).

31 "[T]he true definition of each thing neither involves nor expresses anything except the nature of the thing defined," Spinoza asserts in the second scholium to proposition I.8, while "nothing belongs to the nature of anything," he posits in the preface to Part IV, "except what follows from the necessity of the nature of the efficient cause" (ibid., p. 545). For additional discussion of this see Chapter 2.

32 Moreover, not only does Spinoza not bother to precede the definition of the attribute with that of the intellect, but also after the definition of the attribute he does not bother to define the intellect systematically and in an official way. However, despite that "God's intellect," as well as "God's idea," which are equivalent, are not given definitions in the first part of the *Ethics*, they repeatedly appear. For example see I.16; I.17, Schol; I.21, Dem; I.33, Schol 2.

33 In this context see, for example, the discussion of the definition of God in the introduction to the current part of the book, as well as the discussion regarding the relation between the definition of the substance and the definitions of the mode and attribute in Chapter 4.

Eternity and time 141

34 In the original diagram Spinoza attaches to this scholium the letters appear only on the side of the coordinates *d* and *e*. The additional letters were intended to make prominent the Euclidean proposition that is seemingly embedded here. See Curley, *Collected Works*, p. 452, footnote 15.
35 Compare with the confusing and obscured example from within the system in the demonstration to proposition I.21. For a summarizing discussion of the different positions in the interpretive debate on this demonstration see Curley, *Collected Works*, p. 429, footnote 54.
36 Curley notes here in his translation:

> The NS translator renders *illustrare* (here translated by "illustrate"): "explain with an example." Akkerman finds this an unhappy choice given the opening sentence of the scholium, and suggest "clarify." I would take what follows as an example which explains the matter imperfectly, i.e., an analogy. In any case, Gebhardt's assumption that a phrase has been omitted from the Latin text is clearly wrong.
>
> (*Spinoza Opera*, p. 452, footnote 14)

37 We should not accept Yovel's claim (his translation of the *Ethics*, p. 134, footnote 2) that the one and only issue to which Spinoza directs us here is that of the eternity of the mind in his system (proposition V.21 and on). Indeed, Spinoza's claim in proposition II.8 and its corollary refers to singular things (*rerum singularium*) in general, and is not limited to the mind of man alone.
38 Also see I.8, Schol 2. Already in *Descartes' "Principles of Philosophy"* 1.11, Dem, Spinoza claims: "it follows necessarily from the mere fact that some thing involves necessary existence from itself (as God does) that it is unique [*unicam*]."
39 The phrase *primum et unicum* that Spinoza uses in the corollary to proposition IV.22, when he claims that the conatus "is the first and only foundation of virtue," also refers to God in that the definition of God (I.D6) is couched in the definition of the conatus (III.6), as we saw earlier.
40 In Letter 50 to Jelles Spinoza posits: "he who calls God one or single [*deum unum, vel unicum*]," in the numerical sense, i.e., "only in respect of [his] existence, not of [his] essence," has no true idea of God, or is speaking of him very improperly." Indeed,

> we do not conceive things under the category of numbers unless they are included in a common class. For example, he who holds in his hand a penny and a dollar will not think of the number two unless he can apply a common name to this penny and dollar, that is, pieces of money or coins. For then he can say that he has two pieces of money or two coins, because he calls both the penny and the dollar a piece of money or a coin. Hence it is clear that a thing cannot be called one or single unless another thing has been conceived which, as I have said, agrees with it. Now since the existence of God is his very essence, and since we can form no universal idea of his essence, it is certain that he who calls God one or single has no true idea of God, or is speaking of him very improperly.
>
> (Shirley, Letter 50, pp. 259–260, slightly rephrased)

In *The Foundations of Arithmetic*, Frege finds confirmation for his own position in Letter 50. However, despite that he seconds Spinoza's claim that "we do not conceive things under the category of numbers unless they are included in a common class," Frege claims that Spinoza errs in claiming:

> a concept can only be acquired by direct abstraction from a number of objects. We can, on the contrary, arrive at a concept equally well by starting from defining characteristics; and in such a case it is possible for nothing to fall under it.

If this did not happen, we should never be able to deny existence, and so the assertion of existence too would lose all content.

(Gottlob Frege, The Foundations of Arithmetic: A Logico-Mathematical Enquiry into the Concept of Numbers. Translated by J.L. Austin, Oxford: Basil Blackwell, 1980, p. 62)

However, Frege himself is mistaken here in the position that he attributes to Spinoza. For when Spinoza asserts: "we can form no universal idea of [God's] essence [*aeque eius essentia universalem non possimus formare ideam*]" (Letter 50, p. 260), he negates only the universal concept of God based on a kind and type, not the possibility to create an adequate idea of God. Moreover, Spinoza himself creates the concept of the substance, which he couches in his concept of God, by means of definitive characteristics and not by means of direct abstraction from a certain number of objects. See Mason, *The God of Spinoza*, pp. 39–40; Bennett, *A Study of Spinoza's Ethics*, pp. 196–198.

41 The word 'one' in Hebrew (*ehad*), which serves the description of God in the verse "Hear O Israel the Lord is God the Lord is One" (Deuteronomy 6:4), also has double meaning: both quantitative and qualitative. Its quantitative meaning appears, for example, in the verse "Have we not all one father?" (Malachi 2:10), and its qualitative meaning appears in the verse "And who is like Thy people, like Israel, a nation one in the earth" (Samuel 2, 7:23). In Maimonides' words: "This God is one. He is not two or more, but one, unified in a manner which [surpasses] any unity that is found in the world" (*Mishneh Torah*, Book of Knowledge, Hilchot Yesod haTorah, Chapter 1, Halacha 7, translated by Isadore Twersky in *A Maimonides Reader*. Springfield, NJ: Behrman House Publishers, 1972). This foundational insight of monotheism repeats itself in the writings of other Jewish philosophers after Spinoza. Cohen opens the first chapter of *Religion of Reason* claiming: "It is God's uniqueness, rather than his oneness, that we posit as the essential content of monotheism" (Hermann Cohen, *Religion of Reason: Out of the Sources of Judaism*, translated by Simon Kaplan. New York: Frederick Ungar Publishing, 1972, p. 35). Buber, in *Kingship of God*, dismisses outright Lagrange's claim according to which Jewish monotheism "stands on the same level as the report of a junior officer attached to the commissariat who reports the existence of only one exemplar of any object" (Martin Buber, *Kingship of God*. Translated by Richard Scheimann, New York: Humanity Books, 1990, p. 109). Levinas follows suit declaring decisively: "monotheism is not the arithmetic of the divine" (Emmanuel Levinas, "Monotheism and Language" in *Difficult Freedom: Essays on Judaism*. Translated by Seán Hand. Baltimore: Johns Hopkins University Press, 1997, p. 178). For the different developments, creations, and incarnations of the concept of the unity of God in Israelite faith see Yehezkel Kaufmann, *History of the Israelite Faith*. Tel Aviv: Dvir, 1955, Vol. 2, pp. 221–254.

42 See Sigad, "God as Final Cause," p. 398.

43 In fact, the principle of constructive contradiction that we uncovered in examining earlier issues in Spinoza's metaphysics should have required that we conclude the equivalence between eternity and time even if we did not have the references from which we extracted this equivalence. Indeed, this equivalence necessarily stems from the organizing logic of the system.

Part III
The contradiction in the concept of God in the third kind of knowledge

Introduction

In light of Spinoza's silence regarding the logical contradictions in his system, his correspondence with Blijenbergh gains particular importance. Indeed, Blijenbergh, a grain merchant interested in philosophy, thrusts one of the ubiquitous logical contradictions in Spinoza's system on him, and urgently demands that Spinoza critically account for it. Spinoza, as we will see in the next chapter, does not loosen his lips, as it were, in this exchange of letters, but instead links, again and again, the contradiction in the concept of God to the intellectual love of God; thereby hinting that only in the context of the intellectual love of God, which belongs to the realm of the third kind of knowledge, can we find the final solution to the meaning of the contradiction in the concept of God within his system.

However, as we will see in Chapter 8, a fundamental examination of the intellectual love of God in the third kind of knowledge demonstrates that this concept contains the most destructive contradiction nesting in Spinoza's system. Within its framework, at least apparently, Spinoza not only attributes distinct human affection to God, but also alters God's knowledge from true to false; he even nullifies God's infiniteness and freedom in that God is made to be an effect of an external cause. The closing propositions of the *Ethics* and their demonstrations and scholia, during the course of which Spinoza surprisingly brings up the idea of the intellectual love of God, have therefore frustrated interpreters of the *Ethics* for 300 years. Despite this, Spinoza insists – and this insistence only increases our fervor to clarify things – that with the matter of the intellectual love of God his system approaches its apex. Indeed, as we will see, couched in this love is the final meaning – which Spinoza presents as a distinctly religious meaning – of the contradiction that permeates every corner of his system. Thus, it can be claimed that society, reason, and salvation are the spheres in which the meaning of the logical contradiction in the concept of God, in the three kinds of knowledge respectively, are embedded.

7 The philosopher and the grain merchant
On contradiction and its concealment in the Spinoza–Blijenbergh letters

In the winter of 1644, Spinoza, who just a year prior had published his book on Cartesian philosophy, receives a letter concerning philosophical matters from a man unknown to him by the name of Willem van Blijenbergh (1632–96). This letter, which we will discuss presently, is the first in a four-round exchange of letters – each one of which contained a question from Blijenbergh and a response from Spinoza – that took place until June of 1665.[1] A fundamental examination of this correspondence, as I will seek to demonstrate in the present chapter, can aid us in uncovering the basic, logical, though well-hidden infrastructure of Spinoza's thought. As such, these early letters can shed light, which was later hidden, on the status and meaning of the logical contradictions in Spinoza's mature philosophical system, in particular as expressed in the *Ethics*.

The first round: initial acquaintance and the start of discussion

The first round of letters was dedicated to an initial acquaintance between the two as well as raising the philosophical matter with which the entire correspondence would deal. In his first letter, Blijenbergh presents himself to Spinoza as a respected merchant who in his spare time is "driven only by a desire for pure truth" (Curley, Letter 18, p. 355) through which he seeks to obtain "peace of mind" (ibid.); he is also one who "among all truths and sciences, takes pleasure in none more than in those of *Metaphysics*" (ibid.).

In his metaphysical-existential research, Blijenbergh testifies, he read with interest and several times Spinoza's new book, *Principles of Cartesian Philosophy* and its appendix *Containing Metaphysical Thoughts*. This book left a great impression on him that he describes in the introduction to his letter, though it also raised a grave philosophical problem that Blijenbergh attributes to the amateurish character of his metaphysical explorations, setting him far behind Spinoza, the sharp-minded philosopher who dedicates all of his time to philosophical inquiry (ibid.).[2] Though this problem arises in Spinoza's book on Cartesian philosophy, it goes beyond it as well. Blijenbergh brings up anew an ancient theological paradox: given that God is the source of not only the existence of all things, but also the manner of the action of all that exists, including the actions of man's mind, "either there is no evil in the Soul's motion or will, or else ... God himself does that evil immediately" (ibid., p. 356).[3] This theological paradox forces the faithful to choose between what are for them two problematic possibilities. The first possibility denies the existence of evil in the world, and subsequently exempts man from his obligations to his neighbor and to God and leads to the establishment of a society in which each person does what is right in their eyes. The second possibility, which hangs the collar of evil around the neck of God, completely contradicts the definition of God as absolutely good.

Spinoza opens his response by declaring his earnest willingness not only to answer Blijenbergh's question, but also to create a bond of genuine friendship. Moreover, Spinoza grants supreme philosophical importance to the friendship with Blijenbergh that he is seeking to establish, writing: "To me, of the things outside my power, I esteem none more than being allowed the honor of entering into a pact of friendship with people who sincerely love the truth" (ibid., p. 357).[4] Later on Spinoza will re-articulate Blijenbergh's difficulty:

> it *seems* clearly to follow, both from God's providence, which does not *differ* from his will, and from his concurrence and continuous creation of things, either that there are no sins and no evil, or that God does those sins and that evil.
>
> (Ibid., p. 358)

However, instead of answering Blijenbergh's question, at least as well as he could, Spinoza, under the pretext of a sophisticated philosophical response, adopts and demonstrates the two contradictory possibilities without deciding between them.

In his response Spinoza pairs the concepts "good" and "evil" to the concepts "perfection" and "imperfection," respectively. Therefore, Spinoza equates the conception that determines there is no evil in the world with the conception that attributes complete perfection to all the details of existence (the conception of non-hierarchical perfections) and the conception which claims that evil persists in the world and that its source is God, with the conception of a hierarchy of perfections. The latter claims that all things that follow from God are different from each other in terms of their perfection, and thereby constitute in existence a hierarchy of perfections.[5]

In the first part of his reply to Blijenbergh Spinoza rejects outright the existence of evil and sin in the world, and claims that "when we say that we sin against god, we are speaking inaccurately, or in a human way, as we do when we say that men anger god" (ibid.). For only from the viewpoint of the imagination, which fabricates general ideas of things for itself, is it possible to attribute imperfection to one detail or another while relying on the comparison between the thing and the general idea of the thing. However, from the viewpoint of God – who "does not know things abstractly, and does not make such general definitions" (ibid., p. 359), but instead creates all the details of existence from his complete perfection – "whatever there is, considered in itself, without relation to any other thing, involves perfection, which always extends, in each thing, as far as the thing's essence does" (ibid., p. 358).

Spinoza could have ended his response here. "By this," he states right after presenting the previous argument, "the problem is completely solved" (ibid., p. 359). This solution, however, is only satisfactory from a logical viewpoint, and not from a theological or moral viewpoint. While the non-hierarchical conception of perfections completely fortifies the logical consistency between God's perfection and the perfection of the things that follow from him, this conception cannot be in line with the idea of repentance that is one of the foundations of religious faith,[6] nor can it be in line with the claim that the righteous have advantage over the wicked, which is one of the basic insights of moral law. Therefore, Spinoza, who is aware of these limitations, decides that "to make the path smooth and to remove every objection," (ibid.) he will answer the following two questions that he himself poses:

> (1) Why does Scripture say that god wants the godless to repent ... when he had decided the opposite? (2) From what I say, it seems to follow that the godless, with their pride, greed, despair, etc., serve god as well as the pious do, with their legitimate self-esteem, patience, love, etc., because they also follow god's will.
>
> (Ibid., pp. 359–360)

The spirit of the TTP, on which he was working at that time, can be found in Spinoza's response to the first question.[7] The goal of Scripture, Spinoza claims, is to drive the multitude that is "not capable of understanding high matters" (ibid., p. 360) to moral action. Therefore, Scripture uses baseless metaphysical concepts, such as that which describes God as a king of flesh and blood who yearns for the repentance of his subjects, and this should not bother the "[p]hilosophers, and with them all those who are above the law [*qui sunt supra Legem*], i.e., who follow virtue not as a law, but from love, because it is the best thing" (ibid.).[8] Spinoza's answer to the second question is surprising not only in the style in which it is formulated, but also in its content:

> As for the second difficulty, it is indeed true that the godless express God's will in their fashion. But they are not on that account to be compared with the pious. For the more perfection a thing has, the more it has of godliness, and the more it expresses God's perfection. So since the pious have inestimably more perfection that the godless, their virtue cannot be compared with that of the godless. They lack the love of God which comes from knowledge of God and through which alone we are said, according to our human understanding, to be servants of God. Indeed, since they do not know God, they are nothing but a tool in the hand of the master, that serves unknowingly, and is consumed in serving. The pious, on the other hand, serve knowingly, and become more perfect by serving.
>
> (Ibid., p. 360)

148 *The third kind of knowledge*

In a heavily metaphorical-theological language, which is not appropriate for philosophy by way of geometry, Spinoza compares the pious and the wicked to tools in the hands of God. The pious, who serve God knowingly and through love based on knowledge of God, are like instruments that become more enhanced through use. The wicked, on the other hand, who serve God unknowingly and without love for God in their hearts, are like instruments that become worn out and consumed through the use made of them.[9] However, beyond the stylistic change in Spinoza's language, there lies a change in content that has far-reaching consequences for his position.[10] The conception of static perfection, which attributes complete perfection to all the details of existence, is replaced here with the conception of dynamic perfection, which claims that humans ascend and descend on the hierarchical ladder of perfections in accordance with the place in their minds held by the intellectual love of God.

Spinoza, who has exchanged the conception of non-hierarchical perfections for the conception of a hierarchy of perfections, has indeed, rejected the possibility according to which "the godless, with their pride, greed, despair, etc., serve god as well as the pious do with their legitimate self-esteem, patience, love, etc." (ibid., pp. 359–360); however, he again raises the previous problem that was solved by the conception of non-hierarchical perfections. How can it be that from a God absolutely perfect there follow things lacking perfection? Or, in other words, how can God, absolutely good by definition, do "those sins and that evil" (ibid., p. 358)? Hence, instead of unraveling the entanglement in which Blijenbergh was caught, Spinoza finds himself, even if he denies it, caught in it as well. The problem again arises: either there is no evil in the world and therefore no advantage of the pious over the wicked, or there is evil in the world but God carries the responsibility for its existence. Although Spinoza confesses to Blijenbergh at the close of the letter his difficulty in expressing his thoughts in Dutch,[11] and implores him "if you still find some difficulty, I ask you to let me know it" (ibid., p. 361), he ultimately presents the problem that Blijenbergh raised as the solution to that very problem.

The second round: the crisis of uncovering the contradiction and its concealment

"For though the wish for friendship arises quickly," Aristotle states in the *Nicomachean Ethics*, "friendship does not."[12] Indeed, already in the second round of letters, the enthusiasm to establish an earnest friendship in the shared search for the truth had cooled to the extent it seemed the correspondence was likely to come to a sudden end. Blijenbergh's letter (Letter 20), which opens this round of exchange, sprawls out over 15 pages of the *opera posthuma*, making it the longest letter in the collection. According to Blijenbergh he completed writing the letter only when he realized he had run out of paper (Letter 20, Curley, p. 374). However, this letter is not only quite long but also more cumbersome and difficult to follow. It is packed with banal points, redundancies, and associative digressions from the main subject. Therefore, it is easy to misinterpret this exhausting letter and to conclude that it is simply an outburst of meaningless chatter.[13] Yet in actuality, as I will attempt to show, in this letter Blijenbergh engages in an unprecedented frontal attack on the very core of Spinoza's system. Blijenbergh himself, as it seems, does not completely understand the scope and far-reaching implications of his criticism, and certainly does not present this criticism in an organized and clear manner. Furthermore, as we shall see, examining this criticism as well as Spinoza's response to it has great importance for understanding the status of logical contradiction in Spinoza's philosophical system.

At the opening of his letter, just before hurling criticism at Spinoza's first response, Blijenbergh presents the method of investigation guiding him and "according to which I [Blijenbergh] always try to philosophize" (ibid., p. 361). It then becomes evident that in addition to his obligation to reason, which in his previous letter received total exclusivity, Blijenbergh is also taking upon himself the obligation to revelation as understood in Scripture. By the first obligation Blijenbergh seeks to be a "lover of truth," and by the second obligation he seeks to be a "Christian philosopher" (ibid.). Moreover, like others adopting the double faith theory who preceded him,[14] Blijenbergh claims that there is "agreement" between the "word of God" and "the soundest conceptions of my mind" (ibid.). However, in the case of a clash between revelation and reason, Blijenbergh prefers the former over the latter. Blijenbergh also testifies that God's

> word has so much authority with me that I suspect the conceptions I imagine to be clear, rather than put them above and against the truth I think I find prescribed to me in that book ... since now I suspect myself.
>
> (Ibid., p. 362)[15]

Therefore, according to Blijenbergh's methodology, every matter should be treated by two separate inquiries: the first rational, and the second theological. Afterwards, a comparison should be made of the conclusions of the two inquiries. In the event that they correspond, the rational inquiry receives total divine guarantee of its truth. On the other hand, in the event that the conclusions do not correspond, those of theological inquiry should take precedent over those of rational inquiry. In addition, we should attempt to locate the errors of rational inquiry in order to make them correspond to theological inquiry. Blijenbergh bases his preference for revelation over reason on the gaping chasm between the "absolutely perfect" God who ensures the truth-value of theological inquiry, and "our clearest knowledge" that "still involves some imperfection" and the conclusions of which, he claims, expose only that which "I, with my finite intellect, can conceive" (ibid.).

However, despite the preference Blijenbergh grants to revelation over reason, he seeks to fully exhaust rational examination before turning to judge its conclusions in the court of revelation. Indeed, in accordance with his methodology, Blijenbergh conducts two separate discussions in the present letter (Letter 20) of the response he received from Spinoza (Letter 19). The first discussion is carried out from the viewpoint of reason (pp. 362–369), while the second from the viewpoint of revelation (pp. 369–375). The conclusions of the two discussions are the same. From the viewpoints of both reason and revelation, from considerations that will be presented here, Spinoza's reply to the problem raised by Blijenbergh should be dismissed outright. Blijenbergh's first criticism of Spinoza's response, which is conducted from the viewpoint of reason, opens with gentle language: "I would have to grant a great many things (as I do, too) and admire your penetrating conceptions" (ibid., p. 362). However, in the following paragraph such polite words make way for poignant criticism that attributes a logical contradiction to Spinoza's position.[16] The grain merchant who devotes his free time to philosophical study succeeds, after a not-insignificant wallowing in a jumble of futile examinations and claims, in striking at the heart of the matter when he hurls at the philosopher, who in those days already had gained a reputation that went beyond the limited circle of friends and correspondents,[17] the following words:

> It seems to me to involve a contradiction, if we are so dependent on God that we can do neither more nor less that we have been given essence for, i.e., than God has willed, and yet we can become worse through imprudence or better through prudence.
>
> (Ibid., p. 368)

Blijenbergh rightfully claims that Spinoza contradicts himself when on the one hand he maintains the concept of non-hierarchical perfections, while on the other hand he maintains the opposing concept, namely that of a hierarchy of perfections. At this point, Blijenbergh, who is not prepared to take into account any statement "that would posit a contradiction in God" (ibid., p. 365), and, in addition, who thinks that God's perfection serves as a guarantee that there is nothing superior to it so much that "the creature that proceeds from [God] can involve no contradiction" (ibid., p. 371), should have judged Spinoza to be a philosopher who does not understand his own arguments.[18] However, Blijenbergh's low self-confidence in all matters related to logical investigation prevented him from celebrating his victory over Spinoza. A suspicion lurks within Blijenbergh, as he testified at the opening of the letter stating, "now I suspect myself" (ibid., p. 362), that the deficiency is his own, not the philosopher's in whose writings he finds "great solidarity" (Letter 18, p. 354). At the last moment, after Blijenbergh has already drawn his sword, instead of dealing a severe blow to his correspondent he retreats, hesitating, and in the end almost apologizes for seeking to accuse Spinoza in such a grave manner:

> I fear that here I must not properly understand your meaning, for your conceptions seem to me too penetrating for you to commit such a grave error.
>
> (Ibid., p. 367, parenthesized in the original)

In addition, he writes:

> But though this, on your view, involves some absurdity, to admit, for that reason, all the absurdities mentioned above seems very dangerous to me. Who knows whether, if we spent much meditation on it, we would not find an expedient to reconcile this in some measure?
>
> (Ibid., p. 164)[19]

Blijenbergh is torn in light of Spinoza's philosophical position. Indeed, he finds this position, just as our own analysis did, to be one organized in a strict geometric order, yet plagued with grave logical contradictions. Therefore, Blijenbergh is not alone in demanding that Spinoza disentangle him from the perplexity in which he is caught after uncovering the contradiction in Spinoza's philosophical position. We too, the perplexed readers of the *Ethics*, well-versed in the contradictions of Spinoza's system, are caught in the same tension and are waiting for an explicit answer, clear and satisfactory, to come from Spinoza.

However, as noted, in addition to the logical front, Blijenbergh also seeks to subdue Spinoza on the theological one. On the theological front, Blijenbergh's hesitation dissipates as his self-confidence returns and he firmly rejects Spinoza's claim of the existence of metaphysical errors in the Scriptures (Letter 19, p. 360). If "done in the way you maintain," Blijenbergh again points to Spinoza's logical sin, "it would involve a contradiction in God" (ibid., p. 372). Indeed, an all-powerful god, absolutely perfect, who deceives his believers when he reveals himself to them, is a contradiction in terms.[20] Blijenbergh could have been satisfied here with Spinoza's defeat on the theological front as according to the methodology he adopted for himself, the conclusions of logical inquiry are completely subordinate to the conclusions of theological inquiry. However, in Letter 20, Blijenbergh's victory over Spinoza is two-fold, at least in his own eyes. He presents himself as one who has succeeded in defeating his correspondent on both the logical and the theological fronts (ibid., p. 372). Therefore, it can be assumed that as Blijenbergh set down his quill, after signing his name at the end of his long-winded letter, an expression of self-satisfaction spread over his face.

In response to his critiques, Spinoza sends Blijenbergh a letter containing a completely different approach from the previous one. While in his first letter to Blijenbergh (Letter 19) Spinoza dipped his quill in honey, in the second letter (Letter 21) he presents a bouquet of thorns. Blijenbergh himself accurately described the response letter from Spinoza as "interlarded here and there with touchy reproofs," (Letter 22, p. 382), which do not "sound very friendly" (ibid.). Indeed, as we will see, in this letter Spinoza, in a radical and often harsh way, adopts the strategy according to which the best defense is a good offense.

At the beginning of his letter, Spinoza does not conceal his disappointment with Blijenbergh for deceiving him when he declared in his first letter (Letter 18) complete obligation to reason. However now, Spinoza claims, given that it has become clear that Blijenbergh's first obligation is not to reason but to

152 *The third kind of knowledge*

revelation as it is presented in the theological interpretations of Scripture, there is no reason to continue corresponding. "I see," Spinoza writes," that we disagree not only about the things ultimately to be derived from first principles, but also about the first principles themselves. So I hardly believe that we can instruct one another with our letters" (Letter 21, p. 375). Yet in addition to presenting himself as the antipode of his correspondent, Spinoza attempts to prove that even if Blijenbergh declares himself to be, either through naivety or by pretending innocence, one who prefers the divine over the human, it is actually the opposite that is true. In fact, Spinoza states to Blijenbergh, behind the preference you grant to revelation over reason there hides a preference for human interpretation, "which you, or Theologians known to you, attribute to sacred Scripture" (ibid.) over the divine wisdom that is hidden in each of us.[21] Blijenbergh, who requested that Spinoza see him as a "lover of truth" on the one hand, and a "Christian philosopher" on the other, is perceived by Spinoza to be the hybridization of two things: a dissembling philosopher and a dissembling theologian. While as a philosopher he should have preferred the general to the particular, and as a theologian the divine to the human, Blijenbergh in fact prefers the particular to the general and the human to the divine.

Despite that Spinoza could have been content with this last grave accusation in order to undermine Blijenbergh's position, he chooses to fully exploit the lack of self-confidence of the grain merchant who sees him as a sharp-minded philosopher, by issuing a bundle of personal accusations, each one more severe than the previous.[22] During the course of the letter, as if throwing salt on the wound, Spinoza attributes to Blijenbergh the following five deficiencies:

1   Grave difficulties in reading comprehension (ibid., p. 375).[23]
2   The tendency to come to the point of confusing "things that concern the intellect with [those which concern] the imagination" (ibid., p. 379).
3   Lack of command of the basic rules of logic (ibid.).[24]
4   Associative thought that introduces irrelevant matters into the discussion (ibid., pp. 381–382).[25]
5   Low moral motivation based on fear of punishment rather than love of God (ibid., p. 380).[26]

However, even if Spinoza gives his addressee the sense that neither he nor his letter are worthy of a response,[27] in an act of mercy, perhaps misplaced, he offers, in between the blows that he deals to Blijenbergh, "a brief explanation of what is necessary to grasp more clearly the meaning of my preceding letter" (ibid., p. 377).

Despite this, instead of shedding light on his previous letter, Spinoza goes on to further obfuscate his position regarding the existence and meaning of the contradiction in the issue of the perfection of things that follow from God, which stands at the center of Blijenbergh's criticism. In his second letter (Letter 21), just as in the first one (Letter 19), Spinoza alternately presents both the conception of a hierarchy of perfections (ibid., p. 376)[28] and the conception of non-hierarchical perfections,[29] while completely ignoring the contradiction between the two. Spinoza goes even further when in one paragraph, in two consecutive sentences, he links the two mutually exclusive conceptions (ibid., p. 379).[30] Yet this does not prevent him from signing his letter to Blijenbergh with the following decisive and unequivocal claim:

> So in the things I have affirmed, there is no contradiction at all, whereas on the other side, many are found.
>
> (Ibid., p. 381)

Spinoza accuses Blijenbergh of the very logical inconsistency of which the latter had accused him.[31] However, while Blijenbergh treats Spinoza as a sharp-minded and perceptive philosopher who at the most stumbled this one time, Spinoza point out to his correspondent that he gives him the opposite impression: a morally doubtful character who is intellectually inadequate, and whose entanglement in a maze of circularity and contradiction is not at all surprising.

The third round: temporary reconciliation and meeting

Blijenbergh most impressively deals with Spinoza's frontal attack; the policy of self-restraint that he adopts in his response (Letter 22) enables him to elegantly thwart Spinoza's attempt to divert the discussion from the contradiction in his philosophical position to a futile argument regarding the moral and intellectual level of his correspondent. Moreover, putting aside his pride, Blijenbergh implores Spinoza's stoic tendencies, and begs to be forgiven for unintentionally offending him in his previous letter (Letter 20).[32] However, it is only then, after implementing every possible means to ensure that Spinoza will not cease the correspondence, that Blijenbergh raises again, without showing any signs of fatigue or anger, the contradiction he had exposed in Spinoza's position regarding the perfection of things that follow from God in his first letter (Letter 18):

> I am confident that there is an error concealed here, either yours or mine. For the only rule I can find in your writings according to which a thing is called more or less perfect is that it has more or less essence. But ... if this alone is the rule of perfection ... everything contains just as much essence as God gives it, which always involves perfection, whatever it is. I confess that I cannot perceive that clearly.
>
> (Letter 22, p. 385)

Again Blijenbergh oscillates between accusing himself and accusing his addressee regarding the actual or imagined existence of the contradiction in the matter of the perfection of things that follow from God.[33] However, this time, a suspicion has already begun to grow in Blijenbergh's mind that perhaps Spinoza is intentionally abstaining from writing openly and explicitly about his position on this issue. Thus, in addition to a response letter from Spinoza through which Blijenbergh "can understand your meaning somewhat better," he requests that when he arrives in Leiden the two meet and "discuss these matters in person somewhat more fully" (ibid., p. 144). This time, Blijenbergh hopes, Spinoza will not succeed in evading him and he will be forced to reveal the meaning of the contradiction, or at least to admit to its existence. That which was concealed in a letter to an anonymous person, Blijenbergh wagers, will be revealed in a personal, face-to-face meeting in a friendly context.

It appears that Blijenbergh achieved his goal. Indeed, in order to prove to his correspondent that he neither has nor had any intent to insult him by disapproving of his position, Spinoza was compelled not only to continue the exchange of letters – despite that it was already clear to him this exchange would benefit neither himself nor Blijenbergh – but also to inform Blijenbergh he would be "very welcome" when coming to visit (Letter 23, p. 390). Nevertheless, Blijenbergh's difficulty was not solved – neither in Spinoza's response nor in the meeting with him, which will be discussed below. Indeed, the response that Spinoza sends (Letter 23) is simply a shorter, though somewhat gentler version of his previous letter (Letter 21), and it contains no new arguments. Spinoza again enumerates Blijenbergh's deficiencies,[34] again contradicts himself regarding the perfection of the things that follow from God,[35] and again claims that there is no contradiction in his arguments, while stating that Blijenbergh's letter "presupposes a contradiction" (ibid.). Moreover, in order to rid himself of Blijenbergh, at least for the present, Spinoza hints to him that the full answer to his difficulty can be found "in my Ethics (*mea Ethica*) (which I have not yet published)" (ibid., p. 389).[36] Thus, although Blijenbergh is granted a letter from Spinoza, he is not granted an answer.

The final round and parting ways

Spinoza met with Blijenbegh during the month of March in 1665. We do not know what exactly took place during the course of this meeting. It is reasonable to assume Spinoza treated his guest precisely as he treated his correspondent, for Blijenbergh left the meeting in the same manner in which he had entered it. Nonetheless, rather than give up on himself or his correspondent following the failure of their meeting, Blijenbergh picks up his quill and writes an additional letter to Spinoza. In this letter (Letter 24), after an abundance of pretexts – his being short of time during the meeting, his deficient memory,[37] and his lack of intellectual prowess – Blijenbergh returns to spread before his addressee a wealth of difficulties troubling him, the last of them being none other than the existence and status of contradiction in Spinoza's conception of perfections (Letter 24, pp. 390–391). Moreover, if the solution to this problem is to be found in your *Ethics*, writes Blijenbergh, "I ask you as a friend to answer me somewhat more fully, and especially to state some of your principal definitions, postulates, and axioms, on which your *Ethics*, and especially this question, rest" (ibid., p. 392). "I entreat you this time at least to satisfy my request," he writes to

Spinoza, completely aware of the task he is assigning, since "[w]ithout a solution to this problem I shall never be able to grasp your meaning correctly" (ibid.).

Yet this time Spinoza decided to put an end to the miserable correspondence, and did not respond, even superficially, to Blijenbergh's request. In his next and final letter to Blijenbergh (Letter 27), Spinoza politely but unambiguously informs him that because he was prevented, in the framework of their correspondence, from presenting "a great part of *Ethics*, which, as everyone knows, must be founded on metaphysics and physics" (Letter 27, p. 394), and because a proper understanding of the *Ethics* is a necessary condition for settling Blijenbergh's difficulties, Spinoza was left with no choice but to cease corresponding, in the hope that Blijenbergh would still retain his "good will toward me" (ibid., p. 395).[38]

The reference to the intellectual love of God as the ultimate meaning of the contradiction

Throughout the course of the correspondence, excluding his final letter of parting, Spinoza marches in two opposite directions. On the one hand, he utterly denies the existence of any logical contradiction in his philosophical position; yet, on the other hand, he continues to blatantly contradict himself in each of the letters he sends to Blijenbergh. Thus, in fact, in his letters to Blijenbergh Spinoza simultaneously reveals and conceals the contradiction regarding the perfection of things that follow from God. Moreover, as someone well-versed in esoteric writing, Spinoza takes care to conceal and reveal, concurrently, not only the very existence of the contradiction in his philosophical position, but also the meaning of this contradiction. Therefore, on the one hand Spinoza dismisses outright Blijenbergh's difficulty by claiming that it is merely an imagined difficulty stemming from the latter's deficient qualifications in terms of logic. However, on the other hand Spinoza hints to Blijenbergh between the lines, letter after letter, that the solution to his problem (which, from a logical standpoint, is completely valid) is unattainable for him because he does not have in his heart a love of God that is based on knowledge of God.[39]

Nevertheless, Spinoza's hints fall on Blijenbergh's deaf ears. In fact, Spinoza is turning to us, as if looking beyond his immediate addressee, and teaching us that only in the framework of the intellectual love of God, which belongs to the third kind of knowledge, does the contradiction in the matter of the perfection of the things that follow from God receive its absolute solution. The contradiction in the matter of the things that follow from God is merely a particular case of the general and fundamental logical contradiction that permeates the entirety of the second kind of knowledge. Therefore, in the reference to the third kind of knowledge there lies a promise that along with the contradiction regarding perfection, all the other logical contradictions belonging to the second kind of knowledge will be resolved. In the following and final chapter, we will turn to a critical examination of the third kind of knowledge while focusing on the intellectual

156 *The third kind of knowledge*

love of God at its center. The link that Spinoza embeds in his letters to Blijenbergh between the status of contradiction in his system and the intellectual love of God is crucial. In the *Ethics* itself Spinoza remains almost completely silent in all things regarding the unique logical infrastructure of the concept of God, thereby leaving his readers with the task of reconstructing it; yet in his early letters to Blijenbergh, when he repeatedly adjoins the logical contradiction presented by his correspondent to the intellectual love of God, he is still willing to reveal that in the shrouded heart of his philosophical system, in the place in which the natural light is cast on the concept of the absolute, God is revealed as different in essence from a logical standpoint. Spinoza did not fear leaving the key to his philosophical castle in the hands of the grain merchant, for it was clear – and he was indeed correct in this – that Blijenbergh would make no use of it.

Notes

1 In addition to the eight letters that have come down to us, the exchange contains two letters that seemingly lack any philosophical content in which Blijenbergh urges Spinoza to respond to his letters, after some delay on the latter's part. See Curley, Letter 23, pp. 387–388; Letter 27, pp. 394–395.
2 "[Y]ou have already ascended to a high level in metaphysics, where I am a beginner," Blijenbergh writes to Spinoza in Letter 22 (p. 382).
3 Shmueli suggests ancient theological versions of this paradox, which generally came up in discussions regarding Adam's sin (Baruch Spinoza, *The Letters*. Translated into Hebrew by Ephraim Shmueli. Jerusalem: Mossad Bialik, 1963 [Heb.], p. 309).
4 Later on in the *Ethics*, Spinoza will claim, from systematic considerations: "There is no singular thing in Nature that is more useful to man than a man who lives according to the guidance of reason" (IV.35, Cor 1).
5 In Chapter 3 we discussed at length these two concepts of perfection and the way in which they are anchored in Spinoza's metaphysics.
6 Spinoza, who posits that the idea of repentance is one of the foundations of faith of the revised religion in the TTP, claims that because "there is no one who does not sin," without faith in "God [who] forgives men's sins … all would despair of their salvation" (XIV, p. 183 [178]).
7 See Letter 30 to Oldenburg, Shirley, p. 185. Following the correspondence with Blijenbergh, according to Curley, Spinoza came to the conclusion that

> the time was not yet ripe for the *Ethics*, that another work was required which would help to further prepare the way for the *Ethics* by freeing people from the reliance on Scripture as a guide to the truth about speculative matters.
> (Curley, *Collected Works*, p. 350)

8 Compare to what Spinoza writes in the TTP, IV, pp. 57–58 [58–59].
9 Spinoza's allegory of the instruments echoes both the allegory of the potter's house in Jeremiah 18, as well as Isaiah's theological-dialectical conception according to which the evil enemies of Israel, who consciously act against God, are none other than the servants of God. Indeed, by means of these enemies the god punishes his rebellious people (Isaiah 10:5 and on). However, despite them being God's instruments, the wicked, as Isaiah asserts elsewhere, "all shall wax old as a garment, the moth shall eat them up" (Isaiah 50:9). In the TTP Spinoza himself, relying on the "ancient proverb" in Samuel I, 24:13, claims that "God uses the pious as the instruments of his own piety, and the impious as the agents and executors of his wrath" (TTP, II, p. 29 [31]).
10 Nadler and Feuer, who analyze this correspondence, do not take note of this important

change to which the following three rounds of letters all relate. See Nadler, *Spinoza*, pp. 213–218; Feuer, *Rise of Liberalism*, pp. 250–251.

11 The letters to Blijenbergh were originally written in Dutch and translated to Latin only later on. In Letter 19, discussed here, Spinoza writes to Blijenbergh: "I wish that I could write you in the language in which I was raised [de taal, waarmee ik opgebrocht ben]. Perhaps I could express my thoughts better" (ibid., p. 361). It is not clear exactly what language (de taal) Spinoza means here: Portuguese, Spanish, or Hebrew? Nadler chooses the first option, Curley the second, while Miran chooses the third. See Nadler, *Spinoza*, pp. 46–47; Curley, *Collected Works*, p. 362, footnote 5; Reuven Miran, afterword to his Hebrew translation of Roger Scruton's *Spinoza*, Tel Aviv: Yediot Ahronot, 2001, pp. 83–88. On Spinoza's special interest in the Hebrew language, see Gideon Katz, "In the Eye of the Translator: Spinoza in the Mirror of the *Ethics*' Hebrew Translators," *Journal of Jewish Thought and Philosophy*, 15 (2) 2007, pp. 39–63.

12 Aristotle, *Nicomachean Ethics*, translated and edited by Roger Crisp. Cambridge: Cambridge University Press, 2000, Book 8, Chapter 3, p. 147 (1156b). See Ilana Sigad, "Aristotle: On Friendship," *Bamikhlala*, 16–17 (2005), pp. 17–24 [Heb.].

13 Nadler notes that it is apparent from Blijenbergh's questions in his letters "that he was a man of narrow intellectual horizons. His letters are long, prolix, and tedious" (Nadler, *Spinoza*, p. 215). Roth does not spare Blijenbergh in his criticism, and he too accuses the latter, in the context of the third round of letters, of heaping upon Spinoza "a farrago of unintelligent questions." Roth claims that by contrast, in his responses to Blijenbergh "Spinoza replies with one of the clearest statements of his principles possible" (Leon Roth, *Spinoza*. New York: Hyperion Press, 1980, p. 189). If the analysis to be presented here is correct then there is an amusing chain of misunderstanding: Nadler and Roth do not understand Blijenbergh, Blijenbergh does not understand Spinoza, while Spinoza gazes down on the tumult from above, pretending not to understand Blijenbergh. Curley suggests a more careful and measured assessment of this exchange:

> Van Blijenbergh is a tedious fellow, obscure, repetitious, and slow to see the point.... But he is not an utter fool ... the basic questions he raises are important.... While we may sympathize with Spinoza for losing his patience with van Blijenbergh, we cannot help wishing that he had been as forthcoming and instructive in his answers to some of these questions as he was to others.
> (*Collected Works*, p. 349)

Nevertheless, Curley too, as I will show below, does not succeed in coming to the full meaning and scope of Blijenbergh's criticism here, nor of Spinoza's sophisticated answer to this criticism.

14 For a discussion of different monotheistic versions of the double faith theory, see Harry Austry Wolfson, "The Double Faith Theory in Clement, Saadia, Averroes and St. Thomas, and Its Origin in Aristotle and the Stoics," *The Jewish Quarterly Review, New Series* 33, no. 2 (October 1942), pp. 213–264.

15 In 1663, the same year that Spinoza's *Descartes' 'Principles of Philosophy'* was published, Blijenbergh published his *Theory and Religion defended against the views of Atheists, wherein it is shown by natural and clear arguments that God has implanted and revealed a Religion, that God wants to be worshipped in accordance with it, and that the Christian Religion not only agrees with the Religion revealed by God but also with the Reason which is implanted in us*. Spinoza, of course, did not know of the existence of this work; if he had known of its existence or of Blijenbergh's preference for revelation over reason, it is quite doubtful Spinoza would have conducted any correspondence at all with Blijenbergh. See Curley, *Collected Works*, p. 349. Also see Nadler, *Spinoza*, pp. 213–214.

16 Blijenbergh attributes contradiction to Spinoza throughout his entire letter. Some examples:

1. "For that there is no evil, and that there is privation of a better state, seems to me to be a contradiction" (Curley, Letter 20, p. 363).
2. "For that would posit a contradiction in God" (ibid., p. 365).
3. "Indeed, doesn't it seem to posit a contradiction in God, that he should give us an order to restrain our will within the limits of our intellect, and not give us enough essence or perfection that we can put it into effect?" (ibid., p. 366).
4. "It seems to me to involve a contradiction" (ibid., p. 368).
5. "But though this, on your view, involves some absurdity" (ibid., p. 369).
6. "if it was done in the way you maintain, it would involve a Contradiction in God" (ibid., p. 372).
7. "for that would be a contradiction in God" (ibid.).

17 See Klever, "Spinoza's Fame in 1667," *Studia Spinozana*, 5 (1989), pp. 359–363.
18 According to Blijenbergh, God's perfection ensures, in addition to internal agreement of the intellect, "that there must be an agreement between our intellect and the things that must be known" (ibid., p. 371).
19 Compare to Oldenburg: "I approve very much of your geometric style of proof, but at the same time I blame my own obtuseness that I do not follow so easily the things you teach so exactly" (Curley, Letter 3, p. 168).
20 In the Prophets as well, Blijenbergh claims, it is not possible to falsely accuse the faithful for their being led astray: "it is not credible that the most perfect God would allow that his word, given to the prophets to explain to the people, should be given to the prophets in another sense than God willed" (Curley, Letter 20, p. 372).
21 The critique of Scripture that Spinoza develops in the TTP enables him to present a more radical version of this argument, which attributes human corruption not only to biblical exegeses, but also to Scripture itself. Opposing Rabbi Jehuda Al-Fakhar: "Assuredly, I am utterly amazed that men should want to subject reason, the greatest gift and the divine light, to dead letters which may well have been adulterated with malicious intent" (TTP, XV, p. 188 [182], translation slightly modified). For additional discussion of this claim and the translation of this passage see the introduction to the present book.
22 While Blijenbergh confesses to Spinoza that due to his lack of self-confidence he seeks validation for the conclusions of his logical inquiries from Scripture (Curley, Letter 20, pp. 361–362), Spinoza reveals that, for him, the situation is the opposite: "But as for myself, I confess, clearly and without circumlocution," Spinoza writes to Blijenbergh, "that I do not understand Sacred Scripture, though I have spent several years on it" (Curley, Letter 21, p. 376). On the other hand, Spinoza firmly asserts:

> And I am well aware that, when I have found a solid demonstration, I cannot fall into such thoughts that I can ever doubt it. So I am completely satisfied with what the intellect shows me, and entertain no suspicion that I have been deceived in that or that Sacred Scripture can contradict it (even though I do not investigate it). For the truth does not contradict the truth.
>
> (Ibid., p. 376)

For discussion of the relation between reason and revelation in this letter as well as its relation to the TTP, see Strauss, *Persecution*, pp. 175–176.

23 "I am, sincerely, very grateful to you," writes Spinoza in bitter irony, "for revealing to me in time your manner of philosophizing. But I do not thank you for attributing to me the things you want to draw from my letter" (Curley, Letter 21, p. 376).
24 Likewise, in his following letter to Blijenbergh (Letter 23), Spinoza reveals, "sometimes I doubt whether the conclusion you draw does not differ from the proposition that you undertake to prove" (Curley, Letter 23, p. 389, parenthesized in the original).

The philosopher and the grain merchant 159

25 Hence Spinoza sees himself exempt from dealing with questions and notes from Blijenbergh's letter "none of [which], I say, concerns the present Problem" (Curley, Letter 21, p. 382).

26 Spinoza is once again using an ironic tone. In the same passage in which he writes to Blijenbergh, "I hope this is not you [one who abstains from knavery only from dread of punishment]" (Curley, Letter 21, p. 380), he demonstrates from Blijenbergh's own words that the latter is in fact counted among those who serve God only from fear and not from love. Later on, in the TTP, Spinoza will claim: "Truly he who gives other men what is due to them because he fears the gallows, is acting at the behest of another man and under a threat of suffering harm, and cannot be called just" (TTP, IV, p. 58 [59]).

27 "I had intended to end this letter here," Spinoza writes at the end of the first third of his letter, "so as not to be more troublesome to you in matters which serve only for joking and laughter, but are of no use (as is clear from the very devoted addition at the end of your letter)" (Curley, Letter 21, p. 377).

28 "I have said quite clearly," Spinoza writes to Blijenbergh at the start of his letter, "that the pious honor God, and by continually knowing him, become more perfect, and that they love God" (Curley, Letter 21, p. 376).

29 In Chapter 3 we discussed at length this section of the letter, in which Spinoza bases his conception of non-hierarchical perfection on the distinction between the terms "negation" (*negatio*) and "privation" (*privatio*) and provides the example of the blind man.

30 At the beginning Spinoza rejects outright the claim that things in existence, "insofar as they depend on God ... are ... imperfect," and asserts that the opposite is correct: "for that reason [that they depend on God], and to that extent, they are perfect" (Curley, Letter 21, p. 379). Given that the dependence of all the things in existence on God is absolute, so then the perfection of all things is absolute (ibid., p. 378; also see *Ethics*, I.26, I.27, and II, D6). However, immediately in the following sentence, without any notice or forewarning, Spinoza exchanges the conception of non-hierarchical perfections for the conception of a hierarchy of perfections, and claims that "we best understand this dependence and necessary operation through God's decree, when we attend not to logs and plants, but to the most intelligible and perfect created things" (ibid., pp. 379–380. Also see *Ethics*, II.13, Schol). In his following letter (22) Blijenbergh asks

> [w]hether intellectual substances depend on God in a different way than lifeless ones do? ... don't they both require God's decrees for their motion in general, and for such and such motions in particular? Consequently, insofar as they are dependent, are they not dependent in one and the same way?
>
> (Curley, Letter 22, p. 386)

31 In addition to the accusation of logical inconsistency, Spinoza attributes to Blijenbergh the nihilistic position that Blijenbergh attributed to him. You, not I, Spinoza hurls at him, "defend the impious, because, in accordance with God's decree, they do whatever they can, and serve God as much as the pious do" (Curley, Letter, 21, p. 376). Spinoza employs a similar tactic in the *Ethics* as well when he claims, in opposition to the theologians who negate the extension of God, that "the weapon they aim at us, they really turn against themselves" (I.15, Schol, p. 423 [II/58]).

32 "Even if your conceptions were true," Blijenbergh addresses Spinoza in gentle language, "I should not assent to them so long as I still have any reason for obscurity or doubt, even if those doubts arise not from what you maintain, but from the imperfection of my intellect ... do not think ill of me.... I want to discover the truth" (Curley, Letter 22, p. 383).

33 Also see Curley, Letter 20, pp. 367 and 369.

160 *The third kind of knowledge*

34 In fact, Spinoza, in a general outline, enumerates again the five defects that he presented to Blijenbergh in his previous letter (21):

 1 An erroneous reading of the response that was sent to him (p. 387).
 2 Anthropomorphizing the concept of God and his attributes based on the imagination and not reason (p. 388).
 3 Grave logical failures (p. 389).
 4 An accumulation of irrelevant problems (p. 390).
 5 Low moral motivation that lacks love of God (p. 390).

35 Spinoza claims without embellishment that

> if we consider the acts alone [of the thief and the just man], and in such a way, it may well be that both are equally perfect. If you then ask, "Whether the thief and the just man are not equally perfect and blessed?" then I answer: "no."
> (Curley, Letter 23, p. 389)

36 Blijenbergh indeed had in his possession drafts of the *Ethics*, which was still in its early stages. However, even if he had had the final and complete version, he would not have found a solution to the contradiction between the conception of hierarchical perfections and the non-hierarchical conception, but instead (and worse yet) a systematic formulation of this contradiction, internal to Spinoza's metaphysics. For a discussion of this see Chapter 3. On this point, Spinoza succeeds in deceiving not only Blijenbergh who did not know the *Ethics*, but Curley as well, translator and interpreter of his work, who, following Spinoza, claims that

> [s]ome of his [Blijenbergh's] difficulties arise from the fact that in the beginning he knows Spinoza only through a work which is primarily an exposition of the thought of Descartes. Although there are many hints in that work of Spinoza's own position, it is much easier to see their implications if you know the *Ethics*, or the *Short Treatise*.
> (*Collected Works*, p. 349)

37 "[I]mmediately on leaving you," Blijenbergh confesses to Spinoza,

> I collected all my thoughts in order to be able to retain what I had heard. So in the next place I came to, I tried to put your opinions on paper myself. But I found then that in fact I had retained not even a fourth of what was discussed.
> (Curley, Letter 24, p. 391)

38 Nine years later, in 1674, Blijenbergh dashed Spinoza's hopes when he published a lengthy lampoon against the TTP. After Spinoza's death, in 1682, Blijenbergh published a similar composition critiquing the *Ethics*. See Curley, *Collected Works*, p. 349. Also see Wiep Van Bunge, "On the Early Dutch Receptions of the Tractatus Theologico-Politicus," *Studia Spinozana*, 5 (1989), pp. 225–251.

39 While in his first letter to Blijenbergh (18) Spinoza claims that in general "[the godless] lack the love of God which comes from knowledge of God" (ibid., p. 360), in the second and third letters (21 and 23) he claims that Blijenbergh's own way to truth and blessedness is obstructed because he does not have intellectual love for God. See ibid., pp. 375, 377, and 387. Only in the final letter (27), in which Spinoza informs Blijenbergh of his decision to cease correspondence, does he refrain from bringing up this matter.

8 The intellectual love of God and the contradiction between the internal and external causes in God

At the opening of the second part of the *Ethics*, having presented the metaphysical map of his system, Spinoza promises to "lead us, by the hand, as it were, to the knowledge of the human Mind and its highest blessedness (*beatitude*)" (Preface to Part II, p. 446). Many propositions come after this promise, along with their corollaries, demonstrations and scholia. However, as we stand at the gates of the fifth and final part of the *Ethics*, we not only realize that this promise has not been kept, but also that it is not possible for Spinoza to keep it. The epistemological conclusion to which we have been led up until the fifth part is that excluding the concept of God and the concept of the conatus, which were presented by Spinoza as true in that they are common concepts, we do not know a thing. However, even God and the conatus – which finds its expression in God's intellect in the attribute of thought and in the principle of movement and rest in the attribute of extension – do not, as common concepts, grant us proper knowledge of individual things in general, and the mind of man in particular. Indeed, while common concepts do provide us with general truths about individual things, they do not provide us with exhaustive knowledge of these things; as finite creatures not capable of tracing infinite chains of logical derivations, we are therefore lost in utter cognitive darkness (II.29, Cor, II/114).

In the framework of his moral doctrine, Spinoza leverages, with a brilliant series of philosophical moves, the knowledge of lack-of-knowledge into an escape, even if only partial, from our misery and from the enslavement of our affections.[1] However important and sophisticated the moral maneuvering that enables us, through a Sisyphean self-overcoming, "to act well ... and rejoice" (IV.50, Cor, Schol, II/247), it does not grant us "our salvation, *or* blessedness (*nostra salus seu beatitude*)" (V.36, Dem, Schol, II/302).[2] Even if our happiness (*felicitas*) is to be found in our moral virtue (according to IV.18, Schol),[3] it becomes clear that our moral virtue alone, necessary and important though it is, will not bring about our salvation (*salus*).[4]

Moreover, not only morals but also reason, at least until now, has not led us to our goal, to say the least. For even though we have held out our hands to reason and attempted to follow it with careful and measured steps in a straight geometric line while maintaining strict consistency, we have become entangled in circularity over and over as a flood of logical contradictions have washed over us from every

162 *The third kind of knowledge*

direction. Even if it is possible to attain knowledge without salvation, Spinoza asserts decisively, there is no salvation without knowledge (V.28, II/297). Yet, it is precisely now, as the curtain is raised on the final act of the *Ethics*, the part directly dedicated to our salvation, that the state of our knowledge is worse than ever. From where, we wonder as we grope in the darkness, will the light of blessedness and salvation that Spinoza promises shine down on us?

The third kind of knowledge: laying the groundwork

The intellectual love of God (*amor dei intellectualis*) is positioned at the zenith of Spinoza's system, for in it is contained our highest blessedness (*beatitudo*) and our salvation (*salus*), three concepts that are one in Spinoza's system.[5] Given that our deficient knowledge stems from both our dearth of knowledge about existence and from the logical sandbank on which we have run aground, we anticipate that if, as promised to us, a radical change in our condition will take place, it will happen both through a significant enrichment of our knowledge of existence, as well as through the presentation of a full logical solution to the series of contradictions sprawling out behind us. However, despite the fact that the intellectual love of God engenders, as we shall see, a cognitive leap requiring a special kind of knowledge – the third kind of knowledge – it will not provide us with even one iota of information about existence. Additionally, instead of reducing the number of contradictions on our plate, the intellectual love of God will only create a further contradiction, this time one of existential depth and especially unusual textual presence. Despite this, Spinoza vigorously reasserts that only in the intellectual love of God can we find our redemption. What, then, is this knowledge of the third kind that will bear us, through the intellectual love of God, to our highest blessedness and salvation? Spinoza does not hasten to answer, and when he does find it fit to respond, which he does twice in slightly different ways, his answer is bluntly laconic:

> The third kind of knowledge proceeds from an adequate idea of certain attributes of God to an adequate knowledge of the essence of things.
> (V.25, Dem, II/296; II.40, Schol 2, II/122)[6]

Instead of a lyrical, uplifting description, we encounter a heavy, technical and punctilious formulation. Furthermore, Spinoza presents us with this textual crumb (II.40, Schol 2) while we still lack the systematic tools through which we can understand its meaning. Only in the second appearance of this formula (V.25, Dem) are we able to understand it, and this only by joining the parts of the *Ethics* together. In the third part of the *Ethics* we learned that the conatus is the essence of all things (III.7, and the demonstration there). Moreover, we saw earlier that as a common notion (III.9), which must appear "equally in the part and in the whole" (II.38), the conatus connotes not only the essence of the finite modes, but also the essence of the infinite modes, both the mediated and immediate ones, that follow directly from the substance (see Chapter 5).

The intellectual love of God 163

Knowledge of the third kind, therefore, perceives *uno intuito*, at first glance and without any deduction, the derivation of the immediate and infinite mode whose essence is the essence of individual things from the attribute of God that is appropriate to it. "[T]he more we understand things in this way," Spinoza posits just after presenting the third kind of knowledge in the demonstration to proposition V.25, "the more we understand God (by V.24)." Proposition V.24, it is important to note, explicitly states that we are dealing with understanding singular or particular things (according to the demonstration that directs us to the corollary of proposition I.25).

Through the mediation of the infinite modes God is embedded in the finite modes in the framework of his different attributes. From here it follows that if we focus our knowledge on this transition of "an adequate idea of certain attributes of God to an adequate knowledge of the essence of things" (V.25, Dem), we will better understand both God and the things that follow from him (V.24). This, however, does not explain why Spinoza makes a distinction in order of magnitude between this knowledge and the rest of the true knowledge at our disposal, and even allocate for it an exclusive kind of knowledge, namely the third? What is in this knowledge that makes it "the greatest striving" and "greatest virtue" of the mind? (V.25). Why does Spinoza claim that in this knowledge is found "the greatest satisfaction of Mind there can be" (V.27, II/297)? And how, from this knowledge does "there necessarily [arise] an intellectual love of God" (V.32, Cor, II/300), identified with, as we saw earlier, our highest blessedness and salvation? We will attempt to answer these and other related questions in the following sections.

The reappearance of the contradictions from the second kind of knowledge in the third kind of knowledge

The third kind of knowledge is eternal, and thus the mind cannot attain it "except insofar as it [the mind] is eternal" (V.31, Dem, II/300). "To conceive things," including the mind, "under a species of eternity, therefore, is to conceive things insofar as they are conceived through God's essence" (V.30, Dem). Indeed, when Spinoza comes to demonstrate that "in God there is necessarily an idea that expresses the essence of this or that human Body, under a species of eternity" (V.22, II/295), he relies on a renewed formulation of the third kind of knowledge aimed at providing a more precise understanding of it:

> God is the cause, not only of the existence of this or that human Body, but also of its essence (by IP25), which therefore must be conceived through the very essence of God (by IA4), by a certain eternal necessity (by IP16), and this concept must be in God (by IIP3), q.e.d.
>
> (V.22, Dem)

All of the references in this new formulation of the third kind of knowledge, which Spinoza makes use of here to prove the eternity of the human mind, are to issues in which we located contradictions in the second kind of knowledge. The first reference (I.25) takes us back to the contradiction regarding the essence of the things that follow from God, presented as both containing and lacking existence.[7] The second reference (I, A4) is to the axiom of causality that engenders several contradictions in the second kind of knowledge, such as, for example, the contradiction between the infinite and the finite and the contradiction regarding the perfection of the things that follow from God, which is presented as both full and partial. The third reference (I.16) brings us back to the contradiction between static unity and dynamic multiplicity. The fourth and final reference (II.3) brings us back to the contradiction between eternity and time. Moreover, as we will see in the following, each one of these contradictions is circular in that the contradicting concepts are derived from each other.

This textual flood of circular contradictions is not coincidental but rather necessary and intended. Knowledge of the third kind, as we have seen, focuses on the direct derivation of the infinite, immediate mode – whose essence is the essence of individual things – from the attribute of God that is appropriate to it. Thus, as we will see, this knowledge necessarily annexes to itself all of the contradictions of the second kind of knowledge, while completely changing their meaning through presenting them in the new and totally different context of the intellectual love of God. Therefore, a proper understanding of what is taking place in the framework of the third kind of knowledge requires: (a) tracing the exact way in which the contradictions from the second kind of knowledge are embedded in the third kind of knowledge; and (b) an exact examination of the way in which the intellectual love of God transforms the logical contradictions from the second kind of knowledge from an obstacle to a bridge leading to blessedness and salvation. In the present section we will discuss the first issue (a) while following the order in which we presented the contradictions in the previous part of the book; in the sections that follow we will discuss the second issue (b).

(1) The first contradiction: the contradiction between the infinite and the finite

Spinoza leads us, as though by hand, from the appearance of the contradiction between the finite and the infinite in the third kind of knowledge (V.24 and its demonstration)[8] to the appearance of this contradiction in the second kind of knowledge (corollary to proposition I.25), which is also the first time this contradiction appears in the *Ethics*. Moreover, as we shall see below, in the framework of the intellectual love of God, which is the necessary result of the third kind of knowledge (V.32, Cor), Spinoza will use this contradiction to reinforce a circularity in which the contradictory elements, the finite and the infinite, are derived from each other. In one passage he will assert that man is the cause of the love of God (V.31), and in another place he will assert that God is the cause of the love of man (V.32), until he ultimately equates man and God even while maintaining the distinction between them (V.36). The very same circularity is embedded in the path of the third kind of knowledge. For sometimes this knowledge begins with the finite and ends with the infinite (V.24), while other times it begins with the infinite and ends with the finite (V.25, Dem). This circularity, like the contradiction in which it is grounded, receives prominence in the text through the adjoining of references that emphasize it.

The equivalence between the cause of a thing and its essence (III.56, Dem), which we discussed in the second chapter, enables Spinoza to present the contradiction between the infinite and the finite from a different angle. In the second part of the *Ethics* Spinoza posited that the body is the essence of the mind (II.13), and thus, despite the problematic nature of this claim, the equivalence in the order of magnitude between a thing and its essence is maintained.[9] Yet, in the fifth and final part of the *Ethics*, when Spinoza claims that God, through his intellect, is the essence of the human mind (V.22), he completely annuls the equivalence in the order of magnitude between the thing and its essence and takes us back to the first part of the *Ethics* in which God is presented as the essence of all the things that follow from him, both the infinite and finite (I.25, and its corollary). Nonetheless, as we shall see, in the framework of the third kind of knowledge, Spinoza will attempt to infuse existential meaning in the formal claim according to which the infinite is the essence of the finite and the finite is the essence of the infinite, a claim which had already appeared in the second kind of knowledge.

(2–5) Four additional contradictions: (2) cause and effect – equivalence or difference (the contradiction between immanence and transcendence) (3) the essence of things that follow from God – involves or lacks existence (4) the perfection of the things that follow from God – complete or partial (5) the status of existence – static unity or dynamic multiplicity

The spotlight of the knowledge of the third kind is directed towards the metaphysical chain that links *natura naturans* to *natura naturata*, for it perceives *uno intuito* the ensuing, from within the appropriate attribute of God, of the infinite, immediate mode, whose essence is the essence of individual things. Thus, all of the contradictions from each territory within Spinoza's philosophy flow into the third kind of knowledge, in the framework of which we become aware of the circularity according to which the contradicting elements are derived from one another. While this circular movement has no end, as we shall see, it does have purpose.

As we saw in the previous chapters, the derivation of the *natura naturata* from the *natura naturans* connotes the derivation of dynamic multiplicity from within static unity (Chapter 4), as well as the derivation of things whose perfection is only partial from within a thing whose perfection is absolute (Chapter 3). In addition, the flowing of the *natura naturata* from the *natura naturans* also connotes the derivation of things whose essence does not contain existence from existence itself, whose essence by definition contains existence (ibid.). As such the flowing of the *natura naturata* from the *natura naturans* signifies – and this necessarily follows from each one of the previous derivations as well as from all of them together – the absolute otherness of God from all that follows from him; this of course, completely contradicts the application of Spinoza's axiom of causality to God (Chapter 2).

These four contradictions join the contradiction between the infinite and the finite in the ascent from the second to the third kind of knowledge. While all these contradictions will not be solved in the third kind of knowledge from a logical point of view, they will find a new metaphysical position or status. This will enable Spinoza to present them not as obstacles to salvation, but as clearing the path leading to salvation both human and divine, which are to be found in the very same place on Spinoza's metaphysical map.

(6) The conatus and the contradictions embedded within it

All five of the contradictions embedded in the principle of the conatus (see Chapter 5) are transferred from the second to the third kind of knowledge. We just now discussed the transfer of two of the five: the contradiction between staticity and dynamicity and the contradiction between the infinite and the finite. Therefore, we will only discuss here the three additional contradictions: the contradiction between efficient cause and final cause; the contradiction between the definition of the conatus and the dichotomy between the substance and the mode as is determined in the definitions of the first part of the *Ethics*; and finally, the contradiction between good and evil in God.

The contradiction between the efficient cause and the final cause is positioned right at the heart of the third kind of knowledge, whose entire significance, as will be seen shortly, is but to perceive *uno intuito* the derivation of the final cause from the efficient cause and vice versa. On the one hand, the *natura naturans* is an efficient cause and the *natura naturata* is a final cause. Therefore, deriving the *natura naturata* from within the *natura naturans* connotes the derivation of the final cause from within the efficient cause; but on the other hand the opposite is also true.

In what follows, we will begin with the identification of the *natura naturans* and the *natura naturata* with the efficient cause and the final cause, respectively. Afterwards we will demonstrate the opposite, i.e., the identification of the *natura naturans* with the final cause and the identification of the *natura naturata* with the efficient cause.

Regarding *natura naturans*, Spinoza asserts, right when he first presents it in the *Ethics*, that one must understand the substance *or* all of its attributes, i.e., "God, insofar as he is considered as a free cause" (I.29, Schol). God is considered a free cause in that he is the cause of himself (I.17, Cor 2 and its demonstration),[10] and he is the cause of himself in that he is the cause of all the things that follow from him (I.25, Schol), and he is the cause of all the things that follow from him in that he is an efficient cause (I.14, Cor 1). It obviously follows from this that *natura naturans* is an efficient cause.

Natura naturata, by contrast, is a final cause. The conatus is a common concept (III.9), and thus it connotes "Those things which are common to all, and which are equally in the part and in the whole," and which "can only be conceived adequately" (II.38). However, as a common notion the conatus must signify not only what is common to all the things in *natura naturata* but also what is common to them and the *natura naturata* in its entirety in that the latter itself is "one Individual [*individuum*], whose parts, i.e., all bodies, vary in infinite ways, without any change of the whole Individual" (II.13, L7, Schol). Furthermore, the conatus is equated with the appetite (*appetitus*) (III.9, Schol), the appetite is equated with the end (*finem*) (IV, D7), and the end, as we saw in chapter 5, relates to the nature and essence of each thing as the cause of some effect (according to I.36); therefore *natura naturata* in its entirety *must* be a final cause.[11]

However, the opposite is also true, i.e., the *natura naturans* is also a final cause and the *natura naturata* is also an efficient cause. Proposition 36 in the first part denotes not only final causality, as we saw in the chapter 5, but also, and principally, the efficient causality that permeates the entirety of the *Ethics*; this is according to I.16, Cor 1, which states that "God is the efficient cause of all things which can fall under an infinite intellect." Therefore, the causality in the *natura naturata* is also an efficient causality. On the other hand, the *natura naturans* is also a final cause. From Spinoza's axiom of causality (I, A4) it must follow, given that the final cause derives from the efficient cause, that the efficient cause must contain within it the final cause. Indeed, as we learned in Chapter 5, through both internal systematic considerations and textual evidence from the *Ethics* and the TTP, God too (in terms of *natura naturans*), and not only what follows from him (in terms of *natura naturata*) is a final cause, i.e., God as well as that which follows from him has a conatus. Therefore, Spinoza intentionally couches the definition of God in the definition of the conatus (I, D6), in which he also integrates the definition of the substance (I, D3) when he asserts that "Each thing, as far as it is in itself [*in se est*], strives to persevere in its being" (III.6, II/146, my translation, see Chapter 5 for a discussion).

Knowledge of the third kind guides us to perceive *uno intuito* the derivation of the *natura naturata* from within the *natura naturans*, which, as noted, connotes the derivation of the final cause from within the efficient cause and vice versa. As we will see, this contradiction, in which the different elements contradict each other while also deriving from each other, will also receive redemptive meaning when it appears in the framework of a unique occurrence in which knowledge and emotion merge.

In fact, the third kind of knowledge only emphasizes and makes more prominent what has already become evident to us in the second kind: the status of the concept of the conatus as a common notion contradicts the dichotomy that was determined in the definitions of the first part of the *Ethics* between the substance, which is "in itself" (I, D3), and the mode that is "in another" (I, D5). Indeed, in the third kind of knowledge, the conception of the conatus as a notion common to God and to individual things, becomes an experience through which the individual things are also understood to be in themselves.

Moreover, knowledge of the third kind, in that it perceives the unity of oppositions between the *natura naturans* and the *natura naturata*, also perceives that the conatus of finite things that follow from God and the conatus of God are simultaneously identical and converse. They are identical in that the striving of all finite things in existence to be more than what they are is none other than the striving of existence in its entirety to burst beyond its own bounds; they are opposite because while God's conatus only increases in that nothing external contradicts him, the conatus of individual things that follow from God, including even the conatus of the man who has reached the third kind of knowledge, constantly oscillates between increasing, weakening, and persevering, until in the end it is totally subdued by external forces whose power is infinitely greater (IV, A1).

It follows from here that not only in the second kind of knowledge but in the third kind as well, God appears at once as both good and evil. Indeed, the incessant strengthening and increase of God's conatus is unified, in the framework of the unity of opposites in the third kind of knowledge, with the incessant fading and dying out of the conatuses of the individual things that constitute God. Hence, in the third kind of knowledge, at the apex of salvation, the moral division between good and evil collapses, thereby bringing us to another and entirely new way of being in existence, which we will discuss at length below.

(7) The contradiction between eternity and time

In the famous opening lines of the *Treatise on the Emendation of the Intellect* the young Spinoza reveals to us, in a rare autobiographical glimpse,[12] that after he discovered the emptiness of things that normal life has to offer, he went out to seek something else:

> something which, once found and acquired, would continuously [*continuâ*] give me the greatest joy, to eternity [*aeternum*].
> (Treatise on the Emendation of the Intellect, [1], p. 7, [II/5])

Apparently, the mature Spinoza dismisses forcefully as an oxymoron the very thing he had yearned for in his youth. With the raising of the curtain in the *Ethics*, Spinoza completely disconnects eternity from time and all that refers to it (I, D8, Exp). He also seemingly maintains this detachment not only in the second kind of knowledge but also in the third kind of knowledge, as we will see below. Indeed, Spinoza returns to emphasize at the conclusion of the *Ethics* that "eternity can neither be defined by time nor have any relation to time" (V.23, Schol). Therefore, because the greatest joy is eternal, just like the kind of knowledge in which it appears, it would seem Spinoza should not have described it as "continuously [*continuâ*] ... the greatest joy."

Yet, positioning eternalness and temporariness on the same plane is not a stumble of youthful indiscretion that does not reappear in Spinoza's later, more mature philosophy. On the contrary, as we saw in Chapter 6, the contradiction between eternity and time is a fundamental and intentional contradiction in the second kind of knowledge, and as we will see, it continues to exist in the third kind of knowledge as well. Although in the context of the third kind of knowledge Spinoza returns and ratifies the total detachment that he posited between eternity and time, he also is once again connecting and equating the two. In terms of their appearance in the text, he presents these two contradictory positions one after the other. Indeed, when he turns to present his position on the issue of the eternity of the mind, which in its theological iteration stood at the center of a heated debate that stirred the emotions of the Jewish community in which he grew up,[13] Spinoza writes the following:

> and eternity can neither be defined by time nor have any relation to time – still, we feel and know by experience [*sentimus experimurque*] that we are eternal. For the Mind feels those things that it conceives in understanding no less than those it has in the memory. For the eyes of the mind, by which it sees and observes things, are the demonstrations themselves.
> (V.23, Schol, II/296)

The first two sentences in the passage contradict each other. The first sentence severs eternity from time, while the second sentence connects the two in that it asserts that we feel and know eternity by experience, an empirical phenomenon that is by nature temporal.[14] In addition, the passage is in contradiction with the fifth axiom of the first part of the *Ethics* that claims: "Things that have nothing in common with one another also cannot be understood through one another, *or* the concept of the one does not involve the concept of the other." Eternity is an entirely necessary existence (V.30, Dem), but "the essence of man does not involve necessary existence" (II, A1), and therefore the essence of man is not eternal and cannot be eternal.[15]

In the demonstration to proposition V.23 (the scholium of which we have just discussed), Spinoza uses the technique of directing us to references that contradict the proposition at hand in order to make even more prominent the contradiction between eternity and time in the third kind of knowledge. In this demonstration, Spinoza claims that the essence of the mind is eternal and infinite by necessity, since it is identical to God's intellect, which derives from the attribute of thought.[16] However, during the course of the demonstration to proposition V.23 he directs us to proposition II.13, which claims that the essence of the mind is "the Body, *or* a certain mode of Extension which actually exists." Yet existing in actuality is a temporal existence, as we saw in the corollary to proposition II.8 to which Spinoza also directs us here. Therefore, the claim according to which the essence of the mind is the body, is equivalent to the claim according to which the essence of the mind is temporal and finite. Thus the essence of the mind is presented here as both eternal and infinite (V.23, Dem), as well as both temporal and finite (II.13).

In fact, Spinoza distinguishes, even if only implicitly, between a thing's eternal and infinite essence and its second, temporary and finite essence. In the case of the human mind, for example, the first essence is God's intellect, an infinite mode, and the second is the human body, a finite mode. These two essences contradict each other, and Spinoza emphasizes this contradiction in his own way when in the apparently innocent textual proof to V.23, which demonstrates the eternal essence of the mind, he directs us to the second, limited essence (II.13) of the human mind.

An additional hint, at least apparently, to the existence of this contradiction between the eternal essence and temporal essence of the mind can be found in the paradoxical declaration that opens the discussion of the eternalness of the mind and in which it is determined to be temporal. "So it is time now," Spinoza states in what is seen by some as an unfortunate slip of the pen[17] in the scholium to proposition V.20, "to pass to those things which pertain to the Mind's duration without relation to the body."[18]

If we return now to the scholium to proposition V.23 we will find that the contradiction between the temporal nature of the experience of the third kind of knowledge and its eternal content, correlates completely with the contradiction inherent to the metaphysical occurrence perceived in the framework of this knowledge. Indeed, knowledge of the third kind *uno intuito* and without any process of deduction perceives the metaphysical occurrence through which the infinite, immediate mode – whose essence is the essence of individual things – is directly derived from the attribute of God that is appropriate to it. As we saw in Chapter 6, this derivation also connotes, as part of the derivation of the *natura naturata* from the *natura naturans*, the derivation of time from eternity.

Therefore, even if in terms of their definitions eternity and time exclude one another, they are identical in so far as they are derived from one another. Indeed, in the third kind of knowledge, we find equivalence as well as difference between eternity and time both in he who perceives as well as in that which is perceived. Moreover, in the third kind of knowledge the circle closes; for he who perceives – eternity flows from time, and for that which is perceived – time flows from eternity. Thus, in fact, eternity flows from within itself, just as is claimed in eternity's circular definition (I, D8) that perplexed us due to its non-Euclidean character when we first encountered it at the opening of the *Ethics*.

The contradiction between eternity and time and its circularity already appear in the second kind of knowledge, but only in the third kind of knowledge do they lead, as we will see, to that greatest joy and highest blessedness. Yet, we can already confidently claim that the young Spinoza was indeed precise when, in the opening of the *Treatise on the Emendation of the Intellect*, he chose to present the greatest joy as both eternal and temporal with one stroke of the pen. And so, to paraphrase Spinoza, it is time now to pass to those things which pertain to that greatest of all joys and the intellectual love of God upon which it depends.

The intellectual love of God: initial discussion

Not only do the contradictions from the second kind of knowledge reappear in the context of the third kind of knowledge, but there also appears a new and surprising contradiction. The essence of this contradiction, which will be discussed at length, is the blatant anthropomorphizing of God that arises from the claim according to which "God loves himself with an infinite intellectual love" (V.35, II/302), and as such also "loves men" (V.36, Cor, II/302). Systematically, however, love is a human affect that does not and cannot refer to God, for "God is without passions" (V.17, II/291), and he "loves no one, and hates no one" (V.17, Cor). We will open the discussion of this contradiction by clarifying Spinoza's concept of love and the way in which it functions in the *Ethics*. Spinoza defines love in the following way:

> Love is a Joy, accompanied by the idea of an external cause.
> ("General Definition of the Affects," VI, p. 533 [II/192]).[19]

The following is the definition of joy:

> Joy is a man's passage from a lesser to a greater perfection.
> ("General Definition of the Affects," II, p. 531 [II/191]).

Joy is man's ultimate goal. Indeed, increasing perfection is an increase of reality (II, D6), and increasing reality is the conatus, the final cause that constitutes the essence of man (III.7, Dem) as we saw in Chapter 5. Therefore, if we wish to choose "a correct principle of living [*rectam vivendi rationem*]," Spinoza teaches us in the scholium to proposition V.10, "in ordering our thoughts and images, we must always (by IVP63C and IIIP59) attend to those things which are good in each thing so that in this way we are always determined to acting from an affect of Joy."[20] Joy is the outcome of an action through which man expands his own bounds. However, only when true knowledge has been obtained can we be sure that we are acting and not acted upon by external causes (III.3).

Given that all true knowledge is linked to the idea of God, all true knowledge brings about love of God. Therefore Spinoza claims that

> He who understands himself and his affects clearly and distinctly rejoices (by IIIP53), and this Joy is accompanied by the idea of God (by P14). Hence (by "General Definition of the Affects," IV), he loves God, and (by the same reasoning) does so the more, the more he understands himself and his affects, q.e.d.
> (V.15, Dem, II/290)

By definition, there is no love that is not dependent on something. Yet while regular love, as that which is dependent on individual things, is the root of human misery, the love of God, that is utterly and completely dependent on the absolute, offers man an alternative way of life in which salvation substitutes for misery.

> Next, it should be noted that sickness of the mind and misfortunes take their origin especially from too much Love toward a thing which is liable to

many variations and which we can never fully possess. For no one is disturbed or anxious concerning anything unless he loves it, nor do wrongs, suspicions, and enmities arise except from Love for a thing which no one can really fully possess.

From what we have said, we easily conceived what clear and distinct knowledge – and especially that third kind of knowledge (see IIP47S), whose foundation is the knowledge of God itself – can accomplish against the affects. Insofar as the affects are passions, if clear and distinct knowledge does not absolutely remove them (see P3 and P4S), at least it brings it about that they constitute the smallest part of the Mind (see P14). And then it begets a Love toward a thing immutable and eternal (see P15), which we really fully possess (see IIP45), and which therefore cannot be tainted by any of the vices which are in ordinary Love, but can always [*semper*] be greater and greater (by P15), and occupy the greatest part [*lateque*] of the Mind (by P16), and affect it extensively.

(V.20, Schol)

The intellectual love of God provides an answer to the problem of the lack of stability in human life, and the quest for joy and happiness that occupies Spinoza throughout his philosophical project.[21] The source of the mind's oscillation (*animi fluctuatio*) is in the clash between opposing affects caused by man's deficient knowledge of himself and of existence around him (III.17, Schol).[22] In the absence of rational stabilizers, Spinoza claims "that we are driven about in many ways by external causes, and that, like waves on the sea, driven by contrary winds, we toss about, not knowing our outcome and fate (*fatum*)" (III.59, Schol). However, because "an affect cannot be restrained or taken away except by an affect opposite to, and stronger than, the affect to be restrained" (IV.7, II/214), true knowledge cannot restrain an affect unless it were itself to become one (IV.14).[23]

The strength of an affect is a result of the number of things stimulating it as well as of the frequency of its appearance (V.11). The mind can relate each thing to God (V.14) in a way that will bring it to a love of God based on knowledge of him (V.15), and therefore, by means of a recurring exercise, "This Love towards God must engage the Mind most (*maxime*)" (V.16, II/290). "[T]his love [of God] is the most constant of all the affects" (V.20, Schol), and as such it has the power to stabilize the mind in a maximal way. Even if intellectual love of God cannot completely conquer the mind while totally subduing the affects opposing it, it can reduce to the minimum the sustenance of the affects that are not guided by reason, and minimize as much as possible the damage they cause (V.20, Schol; V.38).

As we saw earlier (V.20, Schol), the object of the love of God is totally different from the object of normal love, and therefore its internal dynamic and its effect on the mind are totally different as well. The love of God is the love of an eternal, static thing that is not evasive like the changing, temporary things to which regular love is directed. Therefore, while the love of God only becomes stronger the longer it continues in that it is guided by true knowledge, normal love weakens because it is mistaken and distorted from the start. As opposed to regular love, the intellectual love of God "cannot be tainted by an affect of Envy or Jealousy" (V.20), but "instead, the more men we imagine to be joined to God by the same bond of Love, the more it is encouraged" (ibid.). For this love is based on true knowledge that only it can be truly good for us; true good has a cooperative nature, thus not only can everyone enjoy it at once, but everyone who walks on the good path aspires to see as many people as possible walking with him (V.20, Dem).[24]

From all this it follows that "love towards the eternal and infinite thing," as Spinoza posits in the *Treatise on the Emendation of the Intellect*, "feeds the mind with a joy entirely exempt from sadness" ([10], p. 9 [II/7]), while regular love saddens the mind and takes away its joy.[25] Moreover, at least apparently, whoever loves God will be required to give up that which in the framework of normal love is the utmost striving, namely, that this love be requited (III.33). The love of God, however, is one-sided by nature:

> He who loves God cannot strive that God should love him in return.
>
> (V.19, II/292)

Spinoza's demonstration here is through negation. God does not love (nor does he hate) humans (V.17, Cor) in that he has no part in the affects (V.17), for the affects express inadequate ideas whereas, with God, all ideas are adequate (V.17, Dem).[26] Therefore, whoever aspires for God to love him, aspires for the destruction of the idea of God that causes him joy (according to III.19), which would be absurd and in opposition with man's essence, which is to increase his joy as much as possible (according to III.28).

The intellectual love of God as a philosophical problem within Spinoza's system

Everything claimed in the previous section regarding the man that loves God intellectually is of utmost importance from a systematic standpoint, demanding from a psychological standpoint, and particularly deep from a religious standpoint. However, at the very close of the *Ethics*, Spinoza completely reverses the meaning of all that was put forth regarding this issue:

> God loves himself with an infinite intellectual love.
>
> (V.35)

God is presented here as a man, and not just any man but a rational narcissist perpetually caught in a state of love that is a distinct human affect (according to "General Definition of the Affects," II; VI; and propositions V.17; V.17 Cor; and V.34, Cor).[27] Immediately, in the following proposition and its corollary, without a recess by which we might recover from the blatant anthropomorphizing of "a being absolutely infinite, i.e., a substance consisting of an infinity of attributes, of which each one expresses an eternal and infinite essence" (I, D6), Spinoza lands an additional blow that completely contradicts his explicit claim that God loves "no one" (V.17, Cor), not even those men who love him intellectually with all their might (V.19):

> insofar as God loves himself, he loves men, and consequently ... God's love of men and the Mind's intellectual love of God are one and the same.
>
> (V.36, Cor, II/302)

Spinoza presents this contradiction (which will be discussed at length) in such a blatant and glaring way that we cannot deny its existence. From what is being asserted here it is entirely clear that Spinoza is not only interested in casting a contradiction on God, but also in closing out the *Ethics* while waving with both hands at this contradiction. This obvious emphasis is a kind of rebuke to whomever at this point has not noticed, or avoided looking directly at, the pile of contradictions in God, which have been heaped up piece by piece.[28]

Spinoza takes care to ensure that it will not be possible to finish reading the *Ethics* without the concept of God appearing – at least one time in a clear, explicit and transparent form – as a contradictory concept. Moreover, as we will see in the following – and this is the main point – the exact meaning that the intellectual love of God casts upon the contradiction in God transforms the intellectual love of God from the system's dark riddle to the great light of the highest blessedness and to the final answer that the system provides for man's existential yearning for salvation. Examining this issue requires us to deal with the final and most severe wave of contradictions in the *Ethics*, which are created by the image of the loving god.

Attributing love to God contains the following three contradictions:

1. By definition love is a type of joy (according to "General Definition of the Affects," VI) and joy is a "passage from a lesser to a greater perfection" ("General Definition of the Affects," II). However, the perfection of God cannot increase (V.17, Dem) not only because God does not change (I.20, Cor 2) but also, and in principle, because he is "absolutely perfect" (I.11, Schol). Therefore, fundamentally God cannot rejoice nor can he love.[29]
2. "Love is a Joy, accompanied by the idea of an external cause" ("General Definition of the Affects," VI), but beyond God there is nothing (I.15), and therefore there is nothing that God can love. Moreover, God cannot even love himself, since love, by definition, depends on an external cause. Despite this, when Spinoza asserts that God loves himself, he directs us to the external cause in the definition of love from the third part of the *Ethics* ("General Definition of the Affects," VI).[30]
3. Love is, by definition, an affect, and therefore it cannot correspond to true knowledge that is pure action (III, D2; III.3; "General Definition of the Affects," II). Love is dependent on an external cause while intellectual

knowledge is the effect of an internal cause. Therefore, systematically, true knowledge will never be able to lead to love, whether man's love of God (V.15) or God's love of man (V.36, Cor), and not even to God's love of himself (V.35). Intellectual love is a contradiction in terms.

The first contradiction is not as grave as the latter two. Indeed, this first contradiction is merely a variation of two contradictions we dealt with in the previous chapters: the contradiction between static and dynamic states (Chapter 4), and the contradiction between the conception of a hierarchy of perfections and the conception of non-hierarchical perfections (Chapter 6). Therefore, it is easy to count this contradiction with the contradictions that build the concept of God in Spinoza's system. Indeed, as we have seen, in this system, God appears as simultaneously a static being that has absolute perfection and a dynamic being in an infinite process of becoming more perfect. By contrast, at least apparently, the second and third contradictions destroy, down to its very foundations, Spinoza's concept of God. Indeed, the second contradiction completely negates God's infiniteness in that it presents something outside of him, and it negates God's freedom in that it makes him dependent on that same external thing. The third contradiction transforms God's knowledge from true to false. For God's love is an affect that prevents him from being able to know true knowledge, which by nature requires pure action.

At this point, not only does Spinoza *not* help us, but he continues to contradict and destroy the concept of God when for no apparent reason, he joins Scripture (*sacris*) in equating the intellectual love of God with the glory (*gloria*) of God.[31] "And this love, *or* blessedness," Spinoza states in the scholium to the corollary of proposition V.36, "is called Glory in the Sacred Scriptures – and not without reason." Here, just as regarding God's love, Spinoza himself directs us without hesitation, to the distinct, systematic, human definition of this term: "Love of esteem [*gloria*] is a Joy accompanied by the idea of some action of ours which we imagine that others praise" ("General Definition of the Affects," XXX; see Curley p. 635 for an explanation of his English translation of *gloria*). Indeed, unlike ambition (*ambitio*, "General Definition of the Affects," XLIV), "Love of esteem [*gloria*] is not contrary to reason, but can arise from it" (IV.58, II/253), since the joy that the rational man arouses in whomever praises him only encourages and increases his joy (III.53, Cor, and its demonstration).[32] However, despite there being no dependence here on an external cause, there still is a benefit from one. Rational glory, therefore, can appear only in man and not in God, since there is nothing outside of God he could benefit from.

Spinoza carefully makes the last contradiction prominent, like he did with other contradictions we saw in Chapter 2, by means of joining together two contradictory claims. In the scholium to the corollary of proposition V.36 he identifies God's love and glory with God's self-esteem, and while the first two terms posit an external cause to God's joy, the latter term posits an internal cause to it. Indeed, similar to "love," "self-esteem" (*acquiescentia in se ipso*) is by definition ("General Definition of the Affects," XXV) a distinct human affect. Yet as opposed to love, self-esteem is at least "Joy accompanied by the idea of an internal cause" (III.30, Schol, II/164).[33] Therefore, self-esteem can be attributed not only to man but also to God.

Moreover, if we take into consideration that Spinoza posits the *or* of equivalence (*sive*) between love of himself (*amor sui*) and self-esteem ("General Definition of the Affects," XLVIII, Exp),[34] and that in addition he explicitly claims that only "self-esteem which does arise from reason is the greatest there can be" (IV.52), the necessary conclusion is that if God loves himself in that he derives joy from understanding himself in his infinite intellect, his self-esteem is the maximal that is possible. God cannot in principle come to be arrogant, i.e., exaggerate his self-praise ("General Definition of the Affects," XLVIII). Indeed, in the scholium to the corollary of proposition V.36, as if in order to prove to us that he has not forgotten the concept of self-esteem, Spinoza equates God's love of himself with his self-esteem. Yet at the same time, as if to demonstrate he once again refuses to walk in a straight geometric line, Spinoza equates that same self-esteem with God's esteem (*gloria*) when he takes the trouble to refer us to the definition ("General Definition of the Affects," XXX) of esteem, which again makes God dependent on something external to him. Thus it is entirely clear that Spinoza knowingly chooses here to contradict himself. Indeed, instead of attributing to God self-esteem alone and thereby maintaining the consistency of his system while legitimately expanding the bounds of the notion of self-esteem in order to enable it to refer to God and not just man, Spinoza chooses to attribute to God both self-esteem (joy from an internal cause) and love and esteem (joy from an external cause). As such, at least apparently, he contradicts and destroys the concept of God, which is the most significant and foundational concept in his system.

From all of this it follows that in concluding the *Ethics*, in the very place in which Spinoza declares he is bringing his system to its zenith, with one wave of the hand he destroys all that he put great effort into building throughout the length of the entire work.[35] This extreme and perplexing conclusion has turned the issue of the intellectual love of God into the nightmare of Spinoza's interpreters. There are even some who impose a sort of informal embargo on the subject of the intellectual love of God, and call for discussing Spinoza's philosophy without attending to this strange outburst at the end of the *Ethics*, which seemingly lacks all systematic meaning.[36]

Solving the problem of the intellectual love of God: on the contradiction between the internal cause and the external cause in God as a redemptive and constructive contradiction

The interpretive capitulation mentioned at the end of the last section is understandable and even forgivable, though as it is not necessary it is not ultimately justified. To claim that Spinoza ends his book with an outrageous mistake would be to claim that Spinoza does not understand his own system; this is totally baseless. On the contrary, in all that Spinoza writes – and certainly in the TTP and the *Ethics* – he demonstrates supreme caution and extensive sophistication. Moreover, in all that Spinoza writes – especially the criticism of Scripture in the TTP and the Euclidean structure of the *Ethics* – it is clear without a shadow of doubt that he was endowed with phenomenal memory as well as exceptional analytical ability. We have no basis to assume that when Spinoza wrote the last pages of the *Ethics*, he wrote them in total loss of his power of memory and deduction. Moreover, as we shall see shortly, and this is the main point, we also have no need to rely on this dubious assumption. Therefore, as long as not proven otherwise, we should assume that Spinoza wrote the finale of his magnum opus intentionally; i.e., that the intellectual love of God that posits an external cause to God, even if it contains a contradiction, does so intentionally. As we shall see, this is not a contradiction that destroys the concept of God, but rather one that constructs it.

However, before we continue, it is important to emphasize that the idea of the constructive contradiction is not one that appears in the text itself. This is an idea that we as readers deploy in order to complete the text from without, and thereby we take part in its writing. Yet, even if the idea of the constructive contradiction does not appear in the text it is embedded within it, or at least it does not contradict it. Thus we have the right, even the obligation, to make use of it in order to save the text through a meticulous reading of its entirety, while linking all of its different parts together.

When tackling the intellectual love of God, just as at the other central junctions in Spinoza's philosophy, we are required to return to the foundational definition of his philosophy, the definition of the "cause of itself" that opens the *Ethics* (I, D1). However, this time, in order to find our way out of the maze, we must adjoin to this definition the first proposition in the book that posits: "A substance is prior in nature to its affections" (I.1). In Chapter 2 we already discussed at length the transcendental position couched in this proposition and the contradiction between it and the immanent position that can also be found in the *Ethics* (see, for example, I.33, Schol 2). In addition, we learned that Spinoza identifies the cause of itself with the substance (I.7, Dem) and the substance with God (I, D6). Therefore, all that remains for us to do is to connect the dots. If God is the cause of himself and is both immanent and transcendent, he is certainly not only the internal cause of himself, as is seen in proposition I.18 that states, "God is the immanent, not the transitive, cause of all things," but also the external cause of himself, as can be seen in proposition V.35, which states that "God loves himself with an infinite intellectual Love," while love is defined as "a Joy, accompanied by the idea of an external cause" ("General Definition of the Affects," VI).

Indeed, "Whatever is, is in God" (I.15), and beyond God there is nothing. Yet from here it does not follow that God has no external cause, but just that if God has an external cause, as is necessary from proposition V.35, God himself is that external cause as well. Moreover, only because God is his own external cause does he precede all that follows from him, as in proposition I.1. Thus, propositions I.1 and V.35 in fact strengthen and reinforce each other, while, by means of the external cause, they reformulate the definition of the cause of itself (I, D1) upon which Spinoza's entire philosophical system is based.

The contradiction between God being the internal cause of himself and his being the external cause of himself is a constructive contradiction, equivalent to the contradiction between God being immanent and his being transcendent. God's absoluteness is realized in that he is simultaneously identical to the world that follows from him while also being completely other than it. God's uniqueness, God's being a *sui generis*, reaches its apex here; the most distinctly destructive contradiction of the things that follow from God comes to play the role of a constructive contradiction in God. While all the things that follow from God are contradicted and destroyed by an external cause (III.4),[37] God is *built* by an external cause (according to V.35). He bases his love for himself on that external cause through which he breaks the bounds of himself and increases his being *or* his perfection (according to the definition of love, joy, and perfection, "General Definition of the Affects," VI; II; and II, D6, respectively).

Moreover, since there is no real difference between God's intellectual love of himself and man's intellectual love of God (V.36),[38] the contradiction between the internal and external cause must appear as a constructive contradiction not only for God but also for the man who has obtained knowledge of the third kind. Indeed, Spinoza presents the cause of human knowledge of the third kind in one place as an internal cause – in that he equates it with the human mind (V.31) – and in another place as an external cause – in that he equates it with the idea of God (V.32); doing so while taking care, from a textual standpoint, to link the mutually exclusive claims.

God is a *sui generis*, and as such God's knowledge must also be *sui generis*. Therefore, God's knowledge is completely distinct from all other forms of knowledge, both in terms of its internal structure and in terms of the change that it causes in the mind of one who knows it. The knowledge of all things that follow from God is a pure action devoid of any passion (III.3). As such, even if knowledge of God is meant to lead to the greatest self-esteem (*acquiescentia in se ipso*) (IV.52), it is not meant to arouse love. The joy involved in the knowledge of the things that follow from God is a joy whose cause is internal and not external. By contrast, God's knowledge is based, as is God himself, on a constructive contradiction, and as such it is an action and an affect at the same time.

Similarly, the cause of knowledge of the third kind, and of the joy couched within it, is internal (V.31) and external (V.32) at the same time. Therefore, not only does it bring the one who knows it to "the greatest satisfaction of Mind there can be" (V.27, II/297), but it also arouses in him love that "must engage the Mind most" (V.16), II/290). Love, therefore, is an affect, and as such it is linked to inadequate knowledge, apart from the case of intellectual love of God. Hence, while there exists an inverse relation between the knowledge of things that follow from God and the love of those things, a direct relation exists between the knowledge of God and the love of God (V.20, Schol). Knowledge of the absolute necessarily leads to love of the absolute. This is the systematic and unique meaning that Spinoza grants to "philo-sophia," which, since its inception in Ancient Greece, integrates the emotional and rational, the love and wisdom that are engraved in its very name.

Hence it is absolutely clear that it is not necessary to adopt the common interpretation according to which Spinoza concludes the *Ethics* with an outrageous systematic error. The opposite is true: the *Ethics* ends with the drawing of the necessary and final conclusions of the first definition and the first proposition to appear in it (I, A1; I.1). Moreover, when his system soars to its height, Spinoza demonstrates deep responsibility towards his readers which stems from a sober and poignant understanding of the phenomenology of religion. On the one hand, in the issue of the intellectual love of God it becomes clear to man that he takes part in the general, dialectical relations between the *natura naturans* and the *natura naturata*, relations through which it becomes evident that the *natura naturata* is not just a platform on which the *natura naturans* leaves its mark, but that it too leaves its mark on the *natura naturans*. Without the *natura naturata* in general, and man in particular, God would be an infinite being in a barren wasteland devoid of joy or love. However man, just like the *natura naturata* in its entirety, not only grants God joy and love, but also finiteness, temporality, multiplicity, a dynamic state, an end, and the process of becoming more perfect. Therefore, all of the contradictions of the second kind of knowledge become, in the third kind of knowledge, redemptive contradictions in that they lead man to dialectically identify with God, not only from a speculative viewpoint, but also from an emotional viewpoint.

On the other hand, by means of that same concept of love ("General Definition of the Affects," VI), which enables him to claim man makes God dependent on him, Spinoza makes sure to maintain an essential division between man and God, and to prevent both the anthropomorphizing of God and the deification of man. Man can love God only because God is the external cause of his joy. God's love, therefore, is dependent on his being other, alien, and completely transcendent. The transcendentalism of God is therefore neither negated nor reduced, not even at the apex of the intellectual love of God. Man, Spinoza cautions his readers, will never achieve formal, simple unity with God. Even in his greatest and most exceptional moments (V.42, Schol), man's identification with God will remain dialectical. This identification will always exist within a dichotomy.

Spinoza reveals himself here not only to be well-versed in matters of religiosity but also in matters of love. Indeed, love, as we perceive it in a less metaphorical way, instills in us not only happiness and satisfaction but also a sense of alienation and distancing in that it makes us dependent on a thing that is other than us, something that fundamentally evades us in that it is different from us. Therefore, if Spinoza had been satisfied only in the concept of self-esteem for the description of the apex of the religious experience (V.27), he would have negated God's otherness and led us back to the claim that God is the immanent essence of all things (I.18). He would then have been cooling the flame of love ignited by the contact and friction of two totally different things. Spinoza understood well that the Eros of love is constructed from a dialectical identification with the beloved, and therefore he claims that even the highest knowledge of

God cannot be complete. Hence it follows that the intellectual love of God will necessarily contain the magic sense of distance within the momentum of achievement. This is the nature of love, this is the nature of God, and this is the nature of the love of God. The contradiction between immanence and transcendence, therefore, constructs not only the concept of God but also the bridge of the intellectual love that connects man and God while ensuring that man remains man and God remains God. Even when Spinoza reached the peak of the metaphysical Olympus of his system, he did not forget the imperative that was engraved on his seal: CAUTE!

Notes

1 For a comprehensive discussion of this issue, which is beyond the scope of the present discussion, see Sigad, *Philo-Sophia*, pp. 56–74.
2 The equivalence Spinoza posits here between blessedness (*beatitudo*) and salvation (*salus*) relies on the definition of the highest blessedness as "satisfaction of the mind that stems from the intuitive knowledge of God" (Appendix to Part IV, Clause IV, p. 588). Indeed, most of the appearances of the highest blessedness in the *Ethics* are in line with this definition, which completely annexes highest blessedness to the third kind of knowledge (V.42, Dem). Nonetheless, sometimes Spinoza uses this concept in a looser sense from which it arises, at least seemingly, that highest blessedness can serve one who is still within the second kind of knowledge. See, for example, II.49, Cor, Schol, and IV.21.
3 Adjoining happiness to true knowledge requires it be ranked accordingly. Indeed, even if not openly, Spinoza distinguishes between happiness (*felicitas*), which belongs to the second kind of knowledge (scholium to proposition IV.18), and the highest blessedness (*beatitudo*), which belongs to the third kind of knowledge and which he identifies with the highest happiness (*summa felicitas*) (scholium to the corollary of proposition II.49, p. 490). However, Spinoza does not maintain this distinction when he posits equivalence between happiness (*felicitas*) and blessedness (*beatitudo*) in the fourth clause of the appendix to Part IV.
4 Moral excellence is achieved by restraining the affects, but "no one enjoys blessedness," Spinoza states in the demonstration to the final proposition of the *Ethics* (V.42), "because he has restrained the affects."
5 The equivalence between the first two concepts is determined in the demonstration to proposition V.42, and the equivalence between the latter two concepts is determined in the scholium to the corollary of proposition V.36.
6 In the second scholium to proposition II.40 a slight addition appears: "an adequate idea of the formal essence of certain attributes of God."
7 The citations of this reference, like the three following references, will be presented in the sub-sections below.
8 Proposition V.24 refers to the third kind of knowledge, as follows from the demonstration to proposition V.25, which we discussed in the previous section.
9 Also see III.3, Dem. Claiming the body as the essence of the mind raises a problem the discussion of which deviates from our present one. It follows from the equivalence between a thing's essence and its cause that if the body is the essence of the mind, it is also necessarily the cause of the mind, and vice versa. However, the existence of causal relations between the body and the mind is completely opposed to the parallelism of the system (II.7) as well as to Spinoza's firm claim according to which: "The modes of each attribute have God for their cause only insofar as he is considered under the attribute of which they are modes, and not insofar as he is considered under

any other attribute" (II.6). In fact, this contradiction is a manifestation of the general dialectical relations of equivalence through difference that Spinoza posits between thought and extension (II.7, Cor, Schol).

10 Indeed, in the demonstration to the second corollary of proposition I.17 there is no explicit reference to the definition of the "cause of itself" (I.D1), but in terms of subject matter it leads us back to the "cause of itself." For a free cause, as is claimed in this demonstration, can signify only that which "exists only from the necessity of [its] nature," i.e., only that which according to its nature and definition is the cause of itself.

11 See Sigad, "God as Final Cause."

12 Here, I tend to accept Hampshire's (*Spinoza*, pp. 25–26) and Klever's ("Spinoza's Life," p. 21) position, and not Ben-Shlomo's who claims that there is no autobiographical content at the start of the *Treatise on the Emendation of the Intellect*. See Ben-Shlomo's introduction to his Hebrew translation, pp. 7–8.

13 The eternity of the mind belongs to the third kind of knowledge despite that it can also be achieved in the framework of the second kind of knowledge, as claimed in the demonstration to proposition V.38. The question as to if, and to what degree, the Mishnaic claim that "all of Israel has a part in the world to come" (Sanhedrin 10:1) includes the conversos was at the center of a theological-political controversy that stirred up the emotions of the Jewish community of Amsterdam in the 1630s. It touched on the fate of relatives of community members who still lived as conversos in Iberia. Altmann discusses this controversy at length and also presents a critical edition of several texts that were written during its course. See Altmann, "Eternality of Punishment: A Theological Controversy within the Amsterdam Rabbinate in the Thirties of the Seventeenth Century," in *Proceedings of the American Academy for Jewish Research*, 40 (1972), pp. 1–88. See also Steven Nadler, *Spinoza's Heresy: Immortality and the Jewish Mind*. Oxford: Oxford University Press, 2001, pp. 157–181; Steven Nadler, *Spinoza: A Life*, pp. 51–55; Biderman and Kasher, "Why Was Baruch de Spinoza Excommunicated?"

14 Yovel's attempts at softening the contradiction here between temporal experience and its eternal content by presenting it as a logical experience that belongs to "a logical world and is thus timeless" (Yovel's translation of the *Ethics*, p. 386, footnote 2). However, in a later footnote to a passage where Spinoza directs us back to this issue, Yovel admits to the existence of

> a paradox that exists in the idea of using eternity within time, which is a foundation of Spinoza's thought in the last part of the *Ethics*. The paradox is in that we are meant to pass in our lives to a timeless state, or to arrive to it as a result of the process of time, and to realize it in this life and in this world.
>   (p. 397, footnote 2, attached to Spinoza's demonstration to proposition V.38 which contains a reference to proposition V.23)

15 For a comprehensive presentation of the last contradiction see Martha Kneale, "Eternity and Sempiternity," p. 236.

16 Spinoza explicates this claim in the preceding proposition that we already discussed, V.22. In fact, God's intellect, just like every other infinite, immediate mode, is both eternal and temporal, as follows from proposition I.21. However, Spinoza chooses here to maintain the eternity of God's intellect which stems from the attribute of thought that constitutes its direct cause.

17 A similarly problematic formulation can be found in proposition V.23, which claims: "The human Mind cannot be absolutely destroyed with the Body, but something of it remains [*remanet*] which is eternal." The verb *remanere* signifies duration on the axis of time. As opposed to interpreters such as Pollock and Hampshire who claim that Spinoza's style here is metaphorical, Kneale attributes the contradiction to the change that took place in Spinoza's stance during the course of writing the *Ethics*. See

Kneale, "Eternity and Sempiternity," pp. 237. She writes: "during the writing of the *Ethics*, which continued for a number of years, he [Spinoza] changed his mind about the relation between eternity and duration" (ibid., p. 238). According to Kneale, the early Spinoza of *Metaphysical Thoughts* and the first four parts of the *Ethics* maintained the Platonic disconnect between eternity and time, whereas the later Spinoza of the fifth part of the *Ethics* exchanged the Platonic position for an Aristotelian one according to which everything that is eternal also has duration, i.e., sprawls out on the axis of time. These two interpretations (Kneale's on the one hand and Hampshire's and Pollock's on the other) are problematic. It is preferable to assume that Spinoza intended all that he wrote, and that all that he wrote and presented to us as a single unit expresses his final, united and crystallized position. Moreover, the identification of eternity with duration does not only appear in the fifth part of the *Ethics*, but can already be found in the first part (I.21). Finally, as we saw in Chapter 6, while at the start of the scholium to proposition II.45 Spinoza detaches and separates eternity and time, at the end of the same scholium he connects and equates them. Should we also claim that here Spinoza changed his position during the course of writing? For additional discussion of Kneale's stance see Donagan, "Spinoza's Proof of Immortality." For additional references see Curley, *Collected Works*, pp. 606–607, footnote 13.

18 The end of the proposition, as well as the scholium to proposition V.38, raises an additional problem that digresses from our present discussion. The existence of an eternal or temporal mind without any relation to its body completely shatters the parallelism of the system (II.7). Moreover, the body – just as its idea, the mind – must appear not only in the medium of time but also in the medium of eternity. Indeed, later on Spinoza refers explicitly to the eternity of the body. In proposition V.29, for example, he claims: "Whatever the Mind understands under a species of eternity, it understands not from the fact that it conceives the Body's present actual existence, but from the fact that it conceives the Body's essence under a species of eternity." Also see V.30. Thus if the first essence of the human mind is the human body, and its second essence is the intellect of God, then the first essence of the human body is the human mind and its second essence is movement and rest, the infinite, immediate mode in the attribute of extension.

19 In the polemical explanation Spinoza attaches here he claims: "This definition explains the essence of Love clearly enough. But the definition of those authors who define *Love* as *a will of the lover to join himself to the thing loved* express a property of Love, not its essence." Among those authors to whom Spinoza might be referring here we can count Descartes (*Passions of the Soul*, Part II, Paragraph 79 in *The Philosophical Writings of Descartes*, Vol. I, pp. 386–387), Hasdai Crescas (*The Light of the Lord*, Mekor Press, 1970 [Heb.], Article B, Law VI, Chapter 1), Judah Leon Abravanel (*Dialogues of Love*, translated by F. Friedeber. London: Soncino Press, 1937, First Dialogue, p. 49). Even Spinoza himself in his youth, in the *Short Treatise on God, Man, and His Well-Being*, claims that "Love, then, is nothing but enjoying a thing and being united with it" (Part II, Chapter V, Clause 1). See Ben-Shlomo's Hebrew translation of the *Short Treatise* p. 282, footnote 138. See also Dorman's introduction to his Hebrew translation of *Dialogues of Love*, Jerusalem: Mosad Bialik, 1983, pp. 165–171. Also see Wolfson, *Philosophy of Spinoza* Vol. 2, pp. 274–288. In this context, as in others, the interpretive controversies regarding Spinoza's sources are informative but futile. As Rice notes:

> Spinoza's mandate of the destruction of earlier drafts and notes of his own completed works, indicates that he took pains to prevent scholarly chases through the history of philosophy in pursuit of sources. He appears to have been largely successful in this endeavor.
> (Lee C. Rice, "Love of God in Spinoza," in Ravven and Goodman (eds), *Jewish Themes in Spinoza's Philosophy*. Albany: State University of New York Press, 2002, p. 101)

20 In situating joy as the bridge between man and God, just like negating the alienation of the human body and the conception of God as saturating existence in its entirety, Spinoza anticipates characteristics of religious conceptions that would be at the center of Hasidism one hundred years later. "Although from the point of view of history Spinoza has no important influence on Jewry," Buber writes, "he yet belongs essentially to this historical cycle" (Martin Buber, "Spinoza, Shabbtai Zvi, and the Ba'al Shem Tov," in *Hasidism*, translated by Greta Hort. New York: Philosophical Library, 1948, p. 95). Also see Ron Margolin, *The Human Temple: Religious Interiorization and the Structuring of Inner Life in Early Hasidism*. Jerusalem: Magnes Press, 2005 [Heb.], pp. 3–6; pp. 447–450 in Yuval Jobani, "A Critique of Ron Margolin's Book *The Human Temple: Religious Interiorization and the Structuring of Inner Life in Early Hasidism*," *Iyyun: The Jerusalem Philosophical Quarterly* 55 (2006), pp. 445–453 [Heb.].

21 Among other things, it should be noted in this context that at the beginning of the *Treatise on the Emendation of the Intellect* Spinoza declares that he is seeking to give up "a good by its nature uncertain ... for one uncertain not by its nature ... but only in respect to its attainment," (ibid., Clause 6) which would grant him the new way of life he was organizing for himself through reason. See Yovel, *Spinoza and Other Heretics*, Vol. 1, p. 226, footnote 1. See also Ben-Shlomo in the introduction to the *Short Treatise*, p. 69. The problem of the vacillation of the mind and lack of spiritual and political stability is also how Spinoza begins the introduction to the TTP (pp. 3–5 [5–7]).

22 "*Vacillation of mind*," Spinoza posits, "*arises from two contrary affects* ... [it is] related to the affect as doubt is to the imagination (see II.44S); nor do vacillation of mind and doubt differ from one another except in degree" (ibid.).

23 Spinoza's claim that "[n]o affect can be restrained by the true knowledge of good and evil insofar as it is true, but only insofar as it is considered as an affect" (IV.14) echoes Parmeno's claim, in Terence's play *The Eunuch*, that one can't use reason to control a situation devoid of reason (Terence, *The Eunuch*. Translated by A.J. Brothers: Warminster, England: Aris and Phillips Ltd., 2000, p. 59). This systematic philosophical formulation of an epigram from a comedy play, especially one written by Terence, is not surprising. This is firstly because, as Yovel notes: "Spinoza took an interest in the theater, in which he saw (like some of his friends, notably L. Meyer) a vivid study – through art rather than science – of the psychology of the emotions" (Yermiyahu Yovel, "Incomplete Rationality in Spinoza's *Ethics*: Three Basic Forms," in *Spinoza on Reason and the 'Free Man,'* edited by Yirmiyahu Yovel and Gideon Segal. New York: Little Room Publishers, 2004, pp. 20–21); and secondly, because Spinoza knew Terence's plays intimately, especially *The Eunuch*, from his Latin studies in the Van den Enden school. Klever notes:

> Spinoza's Latinity shows much familiarity with the Latin of Terence. We know from other sources that this Latin comedy writer had an important place in Van den Enden's educational method. Under his leadership, the pupils played the *Andria* and the *Eunuchus* in the Town Theater of Amsterdam several times during the first months of 1657 and 1658. Many of Spinoza's crypto-citations of Terence may be traced back to certain roles of the comedies which, therefore, could have been played by Spinoza himself, one of the older pupils.
>
> ("Spinoza's Life and Works," p. 21)

In this context Bedjai supposes that Spinoza also acted in a play that Van den Enden himself wrote, in which the vacillation of the mind was the main subject. See Yovel, *Spinoza and Other Heretics*, Vol. 1, p. 226, footnote 1.

24 "To me," Spinoza writes to Blijenbergh in the letter we discussed in the previous chapter,

> of the things outside my power, I esteem none more than being allowed the honor of entering into a pact of friendship with people who sincerely love the truth; for I

believe that of things outside our power we can love none tranquilly, except such people. Because the love they bear to one another is based on the love each has for the knowledge of the truth, it is as impossible to destroy it as not to embrace the truth once it has been perceived.

(Curley, Letter 19, p. 357)

25 Experience, too, teaches that normal love leaves behind misery. However this misery, along with the lesson that should have been learned from it, are completely blurred by the mechanism of repression, which ensures that "[w]hen the Mind imagines those things that diminish or restrain the Body's power of acting, it strives, as far as it can, to recollect those things that exclude their existence" (III.13). Therefore, everyday life is conducted through constant movement between new love and the misery it leaves behind. As Spinoza notes in another context: "one who has been badly received by a lover thinks of nothing but the inconstancy and deceptiveness of women, and their other, often sung vices. All these he immediately forgets as soon as his lover receives him again" (V.10, Schol).
26 Spinoza returns here to the ancient conception of divine "apathy." See Rudolf Otto, *The Idea of the Holy*. Translated by John W. Harvey. Oxford: Oxford University Press, 1958, pp. 95–96.
27 Love is a type of joy (according to "General Definition of the Affects," VI), while joy is defined more explicitly as "man's passage from a lesser to a greater perfection" ("General Definition of the Affects," II).
28 Herder, for example, wrote in this vein to Jacobi: "Since I started to philosophize, I became more and more convinced in the truth of Lessing's words that in fact only Spinoza's philosophy compares to itself without contradiction [*ganz eins sei*]" (Ernst Baur, *Johan Gottfried Herder – Leben und Werk*. Stuttgart: Kohlhammer, 1960, pp. 106–107). On this position see also the introduction to the present book.
29 From similar considerations Spinoza claims that God does not become sad nor does he hate anything (V.17 and the corollary there).
30 In the demonstration to proposition V.35 Spinoza directs us to the corollary to proposition V.32, and there he directs us to the definition of love from Part III ("General Definition of the Affects," VI).
31 Harvey, relying on the TTP (69–71 [70–72]) and on Maimonides' interpretation in the *Guide of the Perplexed* (Part III, Chapter 51), suggests that Spinoza hints here to Isaiah 58:8, "Then shall thy light break forth as the morning, and thy healing shall spring forth speedily; and thy righteousness shall go before thee, the glory of the Lord shall be thy reward." According to Harvey, Spinoza follows Maimonides' philosophical interpretation of the verse, which claims that the eternity of the mind, i.e., the reward of God's glory that is none other than God's intellect, is achieved by moral excellence. However, even if this verse is in line with the position Spinoza puts forth in the TTP, it is not in line with his position in the *Ethics*. Indeed, in the *Ethics*, as we saw at the beginning of the present chapter, it is claimed that even if moral excellence is the necessary condition for salvation and the highest blessedness, it is not a sufficient condition for achieving those things. Therefore, one cannot assume that Spinoza intended to refer to this verse, as it does not give expression to the amoral character of the third kind of knowledge upon which intellectual love and the glory of God are based. See Zev Harvey, "The Biblical Term "Cavod" in Spinoza's *Ethics*," *Iyyun* 48 (1999), pp. 447–449 [Heb.]. Yovel presents other verses that different interpreters have suggested; see Yovel's translation of the *Ethics*, p. 396, footnote 1.
32 See Spinoza's treatment of the two meanings of esteem during the course of his discussion dismantling negative affects and turning them into positive affects in the scholium to proposition V.10.

33 For a discussion of the difference between the Latin version and the Dutch version see Yovel's translation of the *Ethics*, p. 255, footnote 1.
34 In this explanation Spinoza adjoins "love of oneself" (*amour sui*) and "self-love" (*philautia*).
35 Facing the intellectual love of God recalls in some sense A.D. Gordon's description in *Man and Nature* of the cognizant "I" that

> sees in the world and in life endless oppositions and contradictions, and sees himself, to the degree that he seeks to solve the contradictions, caught in dire straits from one contradiction to a deeper and worse contradiction, until finally he collides with the abysmal, foundational contradiction that contains all contradictions.
> (A.D. Gordon, *Writings*, Volumes 1–3, edited by H. Bergmann and A. Shohat. Tel Aviv: HaSifriyah HaTziyonit, 1957 [Heb.], Vol. 2, p. 62)

36 During the course of several meetings I had with Jonathan Israel at Princeton in 2009–2010 he repeatedly disapproved in this same way of the end of the *Ethics*. Pollock still tries to blur the contradictions in the final sections of the text that conclude the *Ethics* by claiming that here Spinoza attempts to cast "a sort of poetical glow over the formality of his exposition" (Frederick Pollock, *Spinoza, his Life and Philosophy*. London: Brown Reprint Library, 1880, p. 308), i.e., by a naïve or dissembling concealment of the content through the form. Hampshire finds it sufficient to express reserved discomfort from the fact that this section of the text forces the reader to deviate "beyond the limits of literal understanding" (*Spinoza*, p. 176). On the other hand, Bennett writes:

> Most of the faults in the *Ethics* occur while Spinoza is tackling real problems and are traceable to specific sources in the foundations of his thought. That makes his failures worth studying. But the final one-twentieth of the work, from 5p23 to the end, contains a failure of a different order – an unmitigated and seemingly unmotivated disaster.
> (*A Study of Spinoza's Ethics*, p. 357)

Later on Bennett describes the concluding section of the *Ethics* as follows: "it is rubbish which causes others to write rubbish" (ibid., p. 374). Bennett calls for liberation from any inhibition stemming from the canonical status of Spinoza's philosophy in the history of philosophy, and to admit the truth: "we should say openly that Spinoza is talking nonsense and that there is no reason for us to put up with it" (ibid., p. 373), and like the child in *The Emperor's New Clothes*, he loudly declares: "After three centuries of failure to profit from it [the second half of Part V], the time has come to admit that this part of the *Ethics* has nothing to teach us and is pretty certainly worthless" (ibid., p. 372). Devoted to this unofficial boycott of the conclusion of the *Ethics*, in an article entitled "Spinoza's Metaphysics" that Bennett wrote for *The Cambridge Companion to Spinoza*, he completely ignores this final section of the *Ethics* as though it did not exist. See Bennett, "Spinoza's Metaphysics." According to Yovel, Bennett's interpretation defeats itself. Indeed,

> one dismisses this dimension of Spinoza's thought only at the risk of losing much of its philosophical meaning. Without the third kind of knowledge, Spinoza would be as crippled throughout as Plato would be without the Ideas. In both cases we shall be unable to form an adequate notion of the *rest* of the system without considering where it is meant (and construed) to lead.
> (Yovel, Spinoza and Other Heretics, p. 155)

Yovel also claims that "this flaw [of Bennett's] could have been avoided if Spinoza's aims about religion, the transformation of religious language and religious emotions, and ultimately his search for an alternative way to salvation, had been taken into

186 *The third kind of knowledge*

account" (ibid., p. 229, footnote 2). Nonetheless, whatever the importance of Spinoza's personal-historical background, it does not aid us in dealing with the logical contradictions and the grave systematic problems that spring up before us at the conclusion of the *Ethics*. Sigad suggests another interpretive possibility:

> analysis of proposition 35 in the fifth part shows that Spinoza is breaking beyond the bounds of his system and attributes love to God himself, which is human according to its definition and cannot refer to God at all. Spinoza does this, it seems, because he did not want to make God dependent on human action, though in trying to avoid this he damaged God's perfection and the definitions of God and of love as well.
>
> (Sigad, *Philo-Sofia*, p. 84)

Contrarily, Allison and Scruton do not even pay attention to the gravity of the contradictions embedded in the conclusion of the *Ethics*. Allison is satisfied by presenting them as seeming contradictions that only have rhetorical purpose; he claims, "By expressing himself in this convoluted and paradoxical manner, Spinoza is, in effect, saying to the theologians that this is the only way one can understand their central contention that God loves mankind" (*Benedict de Spinoza*, p. 174). Scruton claims the *Ethics* to be "what is perhaps the most enigmatic book of philosophy that has ever been written" (Scruton, *Spinoza*, p. 73), though during the course of his discussion of the conclusion of the *Ethics* there is not even a single reference to any problematic elements in the issue of the intellectual love of God; see ibid., pp. 55–60.

37 We should here also note the only axiom of Part IV of the *Ethics*, which claims: "There is no singular thing in nature than which there is not another more powerful and stronger. Whatever one is given, there is another more powerful by which the first can be destroyed." For a discussion see Chapter 5.

38 One should read the end of the sentence, which states, "the Mind's intellectual Love of God is part [*pars*] of the infinite Love by which God loves himself" as subordinate to the beginning of the proposition, which states,

> The Mind's intellectual Love of God is the very Love of God by which God loves himself, not insofar as he is infinite, but insofar as he can be explained by the human Mind's essence, considered under a species of eternity.

Additionally, this is subordinate to the conception of "common notions" (*notiones communes*) that signify what is common to all things and equal in the part and in the whole (II.37). For a discussion of the dialectic relations between the whole and its parts, see Chapter 4.

Afterword

Spinoza's concept of God, this study has argued, is constructed from within a contradiction in each of the three kinds of knowledge. These contradictions and their meaning are concealed punctiliously by Spinoza, not only in the first kind of knowledge that he discusses in the TTP, but also in the second and third kinds of knowledge to which he dedicates the *Ethics*. However, while in the TTP he adopts a double writing method in order to conceal the contradiction, in the *Ethics* he succeeds (and this is much more difficult) in concealing the contradiction in the framework of the Euclidean writing method, while elegantly evading the transparency this method seemingly obliges him to adopt. In this afterword, I would like to explore the meaning and intent of concealing the contradictions in each kind of knowledge. This explanation is hypothetical, and necessarily so. Indeed, concealing the contradiction naturally leads Spinoza not only to conceal the meaning of the contradiction but also to conceal the meaning of the concealment; in fact, in this matter Spinoza's silence is deafening.

Just as in each of the three kinds of knowledge the contradiction in the concept of God arises from a different point of view – social, rational, and redemptive, respectively – the explanation for the concealment must also change according to each kind of knowledge. Earlier we dealt extensively with the social motivations that led Spinoza to conceal the contradiction in the conception of God in the first kind of knowledge. In the TTP, as we saw in Chapter 1, Spinoza addresses the potential philosopher as well as the political ruler. Therefore, in order to ensure that the contradictory interests of these two addressees will not damage social stability, Spinoza is forced to conceal the contradiction between the reduction of the religious to the moral (which he essentially directs to the potential philosopher in the first part of the TTP) and the reduction of the religious to the political (which he essentially directs to the political ruler in the second part of the TTP). Moreover, and this is the main point, concealing the contradiction enables Spinoza to successfully instill in the multitude, who are dependent on *revised religion* more than any other audience, double loyalty to two authorities that stand in opposition to one another; moral authority on the one hand and political authority on the other. This contradiction, as he shows via a meticulous analysis of the ancient Hebrew state, not only does not damage social stability but even strengthens and reinforces it. In this way, concealing the contradiction between the moral portrait of God and his political portrait serves the stability of society, which is the final aim of religion in the first kind of knowledge.

However, why does Spinoza conceal the contradiction in the concept of God in the second and third kinds of knowledge? Why does he avoid presenting his philosophy in the *Ethics* as a philosophy of circularity and contradiction, and opts rather to offer a philosophy of strict logical consistency, one best presented by a rigid Euclidean method? Any attempt to understand why Spinoza conceals the contradiction in the second and third kinds of knowledge must take into account his rebellion against the spirit of his era. For the young Spinoza, the zeitgeist was theological, and rebellion meant exchanging prejudice for reason. For the mature Spinoza, the zeitgeist – at least among his philosopher friends – was rationalist, and rebellion meant attributing a contradiction to reason in that it refers to existence in its entirety.

Yet Spinoza attributes contradiction not only to reason in that it refers to existence in its entirety, but also to prejudice. He does, however, distinguish, as we sought to demonstrate throughout this book, between the constructive contradiction that he attributes to the former and the destructive contradiction that he attributes to the latter. Yet, from a rhetorical point of view, if he had openly and explicitly declared that the concept of the God of reason, and not only that of prejudice, contains contradictions, all the great effort Spinoza invests in order to repeatedly uncover these contradictions would have been futile. Indeed, such an explicit declaration would have thwarted both his attempts to subdue the theologians in the extensive polemic he conducts against them throughout his writings, as well as his efforts to win over the rationalist philosophers who were more important to him, at least in the *Ethics*, than any other reader.

Had Spinoza explicitly affirmed the contradictions that pervade the concept of the God of reason, neither the theologians nor the philosophers would have been especially impressed by the distinction between this or that kind of contradiction. The theologians would have presented this declaration as the final proof of the precedence of revelation over reason, and they would have interpreted it as total admission on Spinoza's part that reason runs aground whenever it attempts to account for God.[1] Essentially, they would have claimed, if God contains contradictions, he also created a world and causes miracles. On the other hand, the rationalist philosophers would not have bothered to dive into the textual ocean of the *Ethics* if they knew that the central claim in the book is that reason, just like God *or* existence, is circular and ultimately self-contradicting. Indeed, from a rationalist perspective, this claim is, on its surface, absurd and invalid. And yet this is Spinoza's very first claim in the book, a claim camouflaged in the definition of the cause of itself. Just as Spinoza did not want the *Ethics* to serve as easy prey for his opponents, the theologians, he also did not wish to create, from the start, a chasm between himself and his friends, the philosophers. Therefore, Spinoza was forced to conceal the idea of the constructive contradiction.

Moreover, through concealing the contradiction, Spinoza succeeds in preventing mistaken equivalence between the unity of opposites he presents in his philosophy and the traditional mystical unity of opposites. Indeed, in total opposition to mystics, he does not maintain this equivalence in order to exempt himself from rational inquiry into God. The inverse is the case: Spinoza's insistence on the equivalence of opposites expresses his total loyalty to reason and his willingness to walk in its footsteps even when it leads him to the territory of contradiction. For Spinoza, the unity of opposites is the final conclusion of reason and not the departure point of prejudice. Therefore, it is philosophical and not mystical, and what it shares with the mystics is its name only. Spinoza, therefore, concealed the constructive contradiction "rather than provide the superstitious with material for raising new questions" (IV.39, Schol), to use his own words from another context.

In fact, Spinoza inherits from Maimonides, his main theological interlocutor, two basic ideas, which he ends up turning against him. First, Spinoza adopts the distinction between a nomothetic law system and a divine law system (*Guide for the Perplexed*, II: 40).[2] However, as opposed to Maimonides, Spinoza claims that the Torah of Moses (both Moses the prophet and Moses son of Maimon) is merely a nomothetic law system, while only his *Ethics* (*Torat-Hamidot* in Klatzkin's Hebrew translation) is divine. Second, Spinoza inherits from Maimonides the motif of contradiction, though he transforms it from an organizing principle of philosophical writing, as it is for Maimonides, to an organizing principle of a philosophical system as well as the essential characteristic of God, as it is for Spinoza.

Spinoza's decision to write the *Ethics* in a Euclidean model – which made the writing process no less exhausting (*prolixo*) (IV.18, Schol) and Sisyphean than the reading – was not only an attempt at concealing contradictions in order to prevent misunderstandings or distortions of his philosophical position. The Euclidean nature of Spinoza's grand project must also have been based on considerations internal to his system as it unfolds both in the second and in the third kind of knowledge. In the *Ethics* Spinoza seeks to understand experience through reason and he therefore enlists both the strongest and most basic experience and the most rational and systematic method of inquiry. Experience teaches us through intuition, without the need for the demonstration of deductive procedures, that existence contains contradiction because while existence is one, an infinite variety of things derive from it. Therefore, at the departure point of experience we have unity within difference. By applying the Euclidean method to experience Spinoza was interested in making certain, by the strictest rational means possible, that the contradiction experience located in existence is true. Only a comprehensive, fundamental, Euclidean inquiry, like that which Spinoza carries out in the *Ethics*, proves that if we approach existence as logically as possible, and if we maintain the most consistent instruments of thought, existence itself, as well as all that follows from it, reveals itself as involving contradictions. Removing contradiction from the concept of truth – we can claim in Spinoza's name against the philosophers who preceded him – is a grave error that leads either to a distortion of what is known (like in the different systems in the history of philosophy and theology before and after Spinoza), or to a paralysis of the one who knows (such as with the pre-Socratic philosophers).

The contradiction located by verified experience in existence appears again both in the second kind of knowledge from the viewpoint of reason (I, D1; I.16), and in the third kind of knowledge from the viewpoint of salvation (II.40, Schol 2; V.25, Dem). Not only is it the case that "God's infinite essence and his eternity are known to all," (II.47, Schol), but also that "we feel and know by experience [*sentimus experimurque*] that we are eternal" (V.23, Schol). The greatest secret of existence, of which we are part, is hidden in the most mundane experience, and whoever uncovers it from a logical perspective and lets it wash over him from an emotional perspective will be redeemed; but salvation is a dialectical identification of the most individual thing with the most general thing. Therefore, salvation is, principally, the immediate presence of the individual before God, and as such, it necessarily leads to social isolation. Consequently, the obligation to conceal the truth – even if it exists in every kind of knowledge – reaches its apex in the third kind of knowledge.

Here, it seems, we stand before an impressive intersection of Spinoza's philosophy and his biography, an intersection that appears only rarely in the history of philosophy. For in order to stand, unmediated, before God, Spinoza was prepared to bear great isolation in two complimentary contexts that take us back to his double rebellion against the spirit of his time.

First, Spinoza sought salvation beyond the confines of the great historical religions of his time and place. In order to do so, not only did he take upon himself, in a broad sense, the excommunication that the Jewish community imposed on him (as opposed to others who had been excommunicated, he never requested for the decision to be nullified), but in addition he chose not to convert to Christianity. The latter decision was certainly difficult, especially in light of the fact almost all of his colleagues, students, and correspondents were immersed in the Christian world, even if not in a simple and naïve way. Spinoza revealed that it was neither possible to accept the Jewish concept of God, which for him was totally transcendental, nor the Christian concept of God, which for him was totally immanent. Thus, taking part, even symbolically, in one of these two religions was understood by Spinoza as heresy against the God of reason. These two religions are false in that they account for God only partially. Only reason, which adjoins and unites these two contradictory conceptions of God, the transcendental and the immanent, can provide us with the complete concept.

Second, in order to stand unmediated before God, Spinoza was prepared not only to exile himself from the great historical religions, but also, and this was certainly exceedingly difficult, to alienate himself from his closest friends and colleagues. For he was not ready to uncover his great secret regarding the existence and meaning of the contradiction in the concept of God not only in the TTP and the *Ethics* that were originally intended for the public, but also in his letters and personal meetings with friends and colleagues.

Spinoza, as we saw throughout the different chapters of this book, maintained with remarkable zealousness complete silence regarding this sensitive issue not only with Blijenbergh, the strange grain merchant (Chapter 7), Hudde the politician and intellectual (Chapter 6), and Oldenburg the pedant scientist

(Introduction), but also with De Vries (Chapter 3), his student and friend who supported him and with whom Spinoza was especially close. Even if Spinoza had been prepared to hint at the path leading from the second kind of knowledge to the third, he would have been convinced that the ascent itself would require each person to make it on his own, since whoever is not capable of acting independently would not be capable of standing before God.

In the winter of 1676, a few months before his expected death due to worsening sickness, Spinoza had a series of meetings with Leibniz in The Hague.[3] The exact content of the meetings of the two philosophers is unknown, but from what Leibniz reported of them later on, we can be absolutely certain that Spinoza did not reveal his great secret even when death was already at his door and one of the greatest philosophers of Europe sat at his bedside. Indeed, the courtier-philosopher, just like Blijenbergh, the grain merchant and dilettante philosopher, left the series of meetings with Spinoza perplexed by his philosophy. As Leibniz wrote afterwards:

"He [Spinoza] has a strange metaphysics, full of paradoxes."[4]

Notes

1 The vicar Johannes Neercassel, who tried to stop the dissemination of the *Opera Posthuma* after he failed to prevent its publication, sadly reported to the Catholic authorities in Rome that the special attractive power of Spinoza's system was its rational and Euclidean treatment of religion and faith. See Klever, "Letter to and from Neercassel," pp. 337–338; Israel, *Radical Enlightenment*, pp. 289–294; Israel, "Spinoza as Expounder," p. 52.
2 See Menachem Lorberbaum, *Politics and the Limits of Law: Secularizing the Political in Medieval Jewish Thought*. Stanford: Stanford University Press, 2001, pp. 30–34.
3 See Nadler, *Spinoza*, pp. 340–342; Matthew Stewart, *The Courtier and the Heretic: Leibniz, Spinoza, and the Fate of God in the Modern World*. New York: W.W. Norton and Company, 2006, pp. 196–202.
4 "Il a une étrange Metaphysique, pleine de paradoxes," Gottfried Willhelm Leibniz, *Die Philosophischen Schriften von G.W. Leibniz*, C.I. Gerhardt (ed.), Berlin, 1875–1890 (reprinted by Hildesheim, 1965), Vol. 1, p. 118.

Index of names and subjects

Abravanel, Judah Leon 182n19
Adam 74, 156n3
Akkerman, Fokke 9n5, 10n5, 141n36
Al-Fakhar, Jehuda 10n6, 33, 158n21
Al-Farabi, Abu Nasr Muhammad 39n38
Allison, Henry E. 137n8, 137n11, 166n48, 186
Altmann, Alexander 181n13
Anaxagoras 15
ancient Hebrew state 6, 23–31, 36n15, 37n21, 39n39, 39n41, 187
Aristotle 100, 139n19, 148, 157n12, 157n14
attribute 87, 95n17, 130–1, 140n28, 140n32 (*see also I. D4*); indivisibility of 84–8; infinity of 46–7, 136n3, 174; of extension 84, 95n12, 121, 129, 140n30, 161, 182n18; of thought 60n16, 70, 88, 129–31, 140n30, 161, 169, 181n16; perfection of 65–75, 79n11
Aubrey, John 39n34

Bar-Elli, Gilead 93n1, 96n24
Baur, Erns 184n28
beatitude 74, 161
Bedjai, Marc 183n23
Ben-Shlomo, Yosef 35n12, 60n3, 114n33, 181n12, 182n19, 183n21
Bennett, Jonathan 10n9, 60n7, 93n1, 94n8, 111n1, 113n21, 136n7, 137n9, 137n11, 142, 185n36
Berger, Natalia 111n7
Bergson, Henri 61n11, 112n10
Biale, David 39n39, 41n58
Biderman, Shlomo 10n5, 181n13
Blijenbergh, Willem van 8, 9n3, 49n3, 61n17, 79n9, 79n11, 82n30, 95n16, 96n26, 143, 145–60, 183n24, 190, 191
Blumenstock, Konrad 107n3, 115n39

Boxel, Hugo 34n3, 61n17, 79n12, 80n13
Buber, Martin 142, 183n20

Caillois, Roland 107n2
Cartledge, Paul 80n12
Casearius 78n2
causa sui 52–3, 60n4, 60n8; *see also I. D1*
causes: efficient (*causa efficiens*) 8, 53, 64, 69, 100–2, 106–7, 109, 140n31, 166–7; external 8, 35n9, 60n5, 86, 102, 104, 110, 111n7, 115n38, 117n55, 143, 161, 171–9; final (*causa finalis*) 8, 69, 80n15, 81n21, 100–2, 106–7, 109, 116n51, 166–7, 171; internal 175–8
caution 4, 20, 28, 36n21, 38n31, 112n15, 177, 179
Christianity 36n21, 39n39, 79n9, 93, 149, 152, 157n15, 190
Cicero 38n30, 80n17
circularity 8, 45, 48, 119, 121–32, 137n11, 153, 161, 164–5, 170, 188
Cohen, Hermann 36n21, 43n69, 142n41
Colerus, Johan 78n2
common notions 88, 99, 186n38
conatus 8, 11n14, 61n11, 80n15, 81n22, 98–118, 119, 121, 125, 137n9, 137n10, 137n12, 139n22, 139n23, 141n39, 161–2, 166–8, 171
concealment 3–4, 9n2, 10n7, 20, 23, 30, 32–4, 47, 63, 73, 75–8, 87–8, 92–3, 95n16, 96n28, 96n29, 131–5, 145, 148–53, 154–5, 185n36, 187–91
contradiction: constructive 8, 9n2, 23–31, 32–4, 45, 60n7, 90, 92–3, 107, 110, 114n30, 120, 128, 134–5, 142n43, 176–80, 187–91; destructive 2, 6–8, 9n2, 24, 45, 75, 90–2, 110, 116n46, 134, 143, 175, 176–80, 181n17, 188
Cooper, Julie 40n48, 41n52, 42n60

Index of names and subjects 193

Cotta 80n17
Crescas, Hasdai 182n19
Crombie, Ian M. 137n11
Curley, Edwin 35n6, 40n44, 42n62, 42n64, 50n8, 60n4, 106, 113n21, 114n31, 114n36, 115n37, 137n8, 137n12, 138n18, 139, 141n35, 141n36, 156n7, 157n11, 157n13, 157n15, 160n36, 160n38, 182n17

Darwin, Charles 37n21
Della Rocca, Michael 40n44, 81n30, 107, 112n7, 113n21, 116n45
Democritus 79n12
Den Uyl, Douglas J. 35n8, 41n56
Descartes, René 1, 35n6, 85, 94n10, 94n11, 95n13, 115n37, 115n38, 136n7, 141n38, 157n15, 160n36, 182n19
dialectical thought 49n6, 90, 96n25, 156n9, 179, 181n9, 186n38, 190
Donagan, Alan 136n8, 137n11, 182n17
Dostoevsky, Fyodor 116n46
duration 42n62, 64, 113n20, 121–8, 131, 137n12, 138n15, 138n17, 139n18, 139n20, 139n22, 139n23, 140n27, 170, 181n17

education 29, 34, 41n54, 183n23
Elwes, R.H.M. 107n5, 114n32, 115n42
Epicurus 34n3, 70, 80n16, 80n17
eternity 8, 11n16, 49n6, 64, 86, 97n37, 102, 113n22, 119–42, 163–4, 168–70, 181n13, 181n14, 181n16, 181n17, 182n18, 184n31, 186n38, 190
Euclides/Eucilidean 2, 3, 4, 5, 7, 10n9, 36n20, 46, 48, 50n8, 75–7, 79n5, 84, 88, 91, 93, 99, 101, 106, 121, 130, 132, 134, 135, 141n34, 170, 177, 187, 188, 189, 191n1
excommunication 10n5, 36n21, 190
experience 42, 53–4, 65, 78n4, 84–5, 119, 120–1, 127, 167, 169–70, 179, 181n14, 184n25, 189–90
extension 73, 84, 95n12, 121, 129, 136n8, 140n30, 159n31, 161, 169, 181n9, 182n18

Feuer, Lewis S. 35n5, 37n23, 157n10
finiteness 7–8, 11n16, 51–5, 58, 61n12, 61n13, 62n21, 63, 66–8, 83–9, 102–7, 110, 114n36, 117n59, 118n62, 119, 123, 128–9, 138n15, 149, 161–2
Fraenkel, Carlos 39n38
Frankel, Steve 35n10

Frege, Gottlob 141n40
Freud, Sigmund 116n46
friendship 138n14, 146, 148, 157n12, 183n24
Frogel, Shai 50n7
Funkenstein, Amos 49n1

Gans, Chaim 35n7
Garber, Daniel 41n55
Geertz, Clifford 43n67
God 7, 45–8, 71, 75, 90, 103, 115n36, 136n3, 140n33, 141n39, 146, 167 (*see also I. D6*); as *sui generis* 8, 134, 178; as *unicam* 134–5, 141n38; *conatus* of 98–118, 168; *gloria* of 175–6; good and bad in 107–10, 145–6, 148, 156n9, 168; intellect of 57–8, 61n16, 61n17, 62n21, 75, 129–31, 140, 161, 169, 181n16, 182n18, 184n31 (*see also Letter 64*); intellectual love of (*amor dei intellectualis*) 8, 80n13, 128, 136n6, 140n30, 143, 148, 155–6, 161–86; traditional conception of 1–2, 15–16, 18–19, 43n67, 45–8, 55–6, 118n60
Goldstein, Rebecca 36n19
Golomb, Yaakov 116n46
good 8, 22, 27, 32, 37n25, 37n27, 50n7, 52, 68, 79n7, 92, 107–10, 140n27, 146, 148, 166–8, 171, 173, 183n21, 183n23
Gordon, Aharon Davi 185n35
Graham, Daniel 95n15
Guttmann, Julius 10n11

Halbertal, Mosh 36n14
HaLevi, Yehuda 59n1
Hampshire, Stuart 35n12, 49n5, 76, 80n19, 81n27, 81n29, 111n6, 137n11, 140n24, 181n12, 181n17, 185n36
Harvey, Zev 116n48, 116n52, 184n31
Hasidism 183n20
Hegel, Georg Wilhelm Friedrich 35n12
Heraclitus 95n16
Herder, Johann Gottfried 184n28
Hitler, Adolf 42n62
Hobbes, Thomas 36n14, 39n34, 39n38, 43n64
Hudde, Johannes 9n3, 70, 72–3, 81n25, 86–7, 123–4, 138n14, 190
Hughes, Gerard J. 95n14
human: body 108–9, 163, 170, 182n18, 183n20; mind 58, 74–5, 108, 136n7, 161, 163, 165, 169, 170, 178, 181n17, 182n18, 186n38
Hume, David 50n9

Ibn Tibbon, Shmuel 95n14
imagination 5, 36n12, 41n54, 48, 67–9, 71, 78, 80n12, 85–6, 101, 107–8, 116n47, 120–1, 146, 152, 160n34, 183n22
immanence 7, 55–8, 59, 62n22, 63, 65–6, 77, 106, 165–6, 177–80, 190
immortality 181n13
infiniteness 2, 7–8, 11n16, 45–7, 49n4, 51–5, 58, 61n12, 61n16, 62n21, 63–4, 66, 68, 70–5, 83–9, 90, 93n1, 94n8, 94n9, 102–7, 109–10, 117n59, 118n62, 119–20, 122–3, 125–6, 128–30, 133, 136n3, 136n4, 136n8, 137n9, 138n15, 138n18, 143, 161–72, 173–7, 179, 181n16, 182n18, 186n38, 189–90
Isaiah 156n9, 184n31
Israel, Jonathan I. 10n5, 10n6, 35n5, 35n6, 37n23, 40n42, 112n15, 114n32, 185n36, 191n1

Jacobi, Friedrich Heinrich 184n28
James, Susan 40n42
Jarrett, Charles E. 113n27
Jelles, Jarig 141n40
Jesus 6, 22, 28, 41n52
Jobani, Yuval 183n20
Judaism 10n6, 20, 36n21, 41n51, 42n64

Kabbalah 10n6
Kafka, Franz 116n46, 128, 140n26
Kasher, Asa 10n5, 181n13
Katz, Gideon 36n19, 37n24, 40n46, 41n53, 43n67, 157n11
Kaufmann, Yehezkel 142n41
Klatzkin, Jacob 107, 115n40, 189
Klever, W.N.A. 37n23, 78n2, 94n3, 96n30, 158n17, 181n12, 183n23, 191n1
Kneale, Martha 137n11, 139n19, 181n15, 181n17
knowledge: first kind 2, 4–7, 9n2, 18, 35n6, 45–6, 78, 187–8 (*see also* imagination); second kind 5, 7, 9n2, 45, 77, 80n13, 80n18, 88, 104, 111n1, 111n4, 136n6, 155, 163–5, 167–70, 179, 180n2, 181n13, 190–1; third kind 2, 4–5, 8–9, 45, 60n5, 80n13, 80n18, 81n28, 95n22, 104, 111n1, 117n56, 136n6, 143, 155, 161–86, 188–90
Koryé, Alexander 50n7

Laertius, Diogenes 80n16
Lalande, André 112n10
Law: civil 6, 21, 23, 26–34, 35n7, 43n64, 189; of contradiction 2, 78, 110, 134; of inertia 115n38; of morality 6, 21, 23, 25–6, 28–34, 147; of nature 16, 62n19, 74, 98, 104–5, 109, 117n57, 136n6, 138n15; of reason 78; religious 29, 33, 41n58, 49n1, 79n7, 189; self-destruction 116n46; self-preservation 116n46; those above the 147
Leibniz, Gottfried Wilhelm 95n16, 136n7, 140n24, 191, 191n3, 191n4
Levene, Nancy K. 113n24
Levi, Ze'ev 41n51, 42n64
Levinas, Emmanuel 1, 142n41
Levine, Evyatar 40n44, 43n64
Lloyd, Genevieve 41n54, 138n15
Lorberbaum, Menachem 10n6, 11n15, 37n24, 39n38, 43n65, 95n21, 191n2

Maimonides 3, 9n4, 10n7, 34n4, 36n14, 39n38, 50n7, 61n18, 95n14, 116n48, 116n52, 142n41, 184n31, 189
Margolin, Ron 183n20
Mason, Richard 10n9, 49n2, 95n17, 97n37, 137n11, 142n40
Meno 43n69, 137n11
Miran, Reuven 157n11
modes: definition of 8, 62n22, 103, 104, 137n13; finite 58, 61n12, 66–8, 117n59, 138n15, 162–3, 170; infinite 58, 61n12, 75, 88, 93n1, 117n59, 120, 122, 138n15, 138n18, 162–3, 170
morality 4–6, 11n13, 20–34, 37n25, 38n31, 42n59, 42n33, 42n64, 45, 79n9, 95n19, 102, 110, 116n48, 147, 152–3, 160–1, 168, 180n4, 184n31, 187–8
Morgan, Michael 39n38
Moses 24, 27, 30, 40n50, 41n58, 189
Motzkin, Aryeh Leo 43n64
Muffs, Yochanan 40n50
multitude 2, 4–5, 17–19, 25–6, 28, 34, 34n2, 35n11, 38n31, 38n32, 39n38, 40n46, 42n59, 42n61, 42n64, 66, 69, 147, 187
mysticism 97n37, 97, 189

Nadler, Steven 35n5, 37n23, 78n2, 96n30, 138n14, 157n10, 157n11, 157n13, 157n15, 181n13, 191n3
Naess, Arne 113n27
natura naturans 74, 89–90, 106, 109, 123, 129–30, 165–6, 167–8, 170, 179
natura naturata 74, 89–90, 105–6, 109–10, 123, 129–30, 165–8, 170, 179
nature 16–17, 35n8, 39n42, 46, 47, 48, 49n3, 51–4, 56, 58, 60n4, 60n9, 61n12,

Index of names and subjects 195

61n17, 62n19, 64, 66–7, 69–70, 72–4, 81n25, 83–90, 93n1, 94n2, 94n5, 97n34, 98, 99, 100–2, 104–9, 111n6, 114n36, 117n57, 119, 122, 123, 125–9, 135, 136n2, 136n5, 136n6, 138n15, 140n31, 156n4, 167, 169, 177, 181n10, 183n21, 186n37
Nauen, Franz 36n21
Neercassel, Johannes van 191n1
Nehamas, Alexander 43n69
Newton, Isaac 49n1, 115n37
Nietzsche, Friedrich 36n13, 36n20, 41n55, 50n7, 53, 60n8, 116n46

obedience: to God 6, 20–35; to the laws of morality 6, 20–35; to the political authority 6, 20–35, 38n30, 38n31, 42, 64
Oldenburg, Henry 9n3, 34n2, 35n5, 156n7, 158n19, 190
Otto, Rudolf 184n26

panpsychism 70, 80n18
parallelism 70, 74, 126, 129, 140n30, 180n9, 182n18
Parkinson, George H.R. 107, 115n37, 116n44
Parmenides 95n15
perfection 7–8, 47, 65–75, 77, 79n8, 79n9, 80n14, 81n21, 81n25, 81n27, 86, 93, 103–4, 113n28, 117n55, 127–8, 140n27, 146–50, 152–6, 158, 159n29, 159n30, 159n32, 160n36, 164–6, 171, 174–5, 178, 184n27, 186
philosopher 3–4, 15–16, 20–2, 24, 31, 33, 34n2, 34n3, 34n4, 35n10, 36n21, 38n32, 38n34, 39n38, 42n59, 42n60, 42n61, 42n63, 50n7, 59, 78n3, 79n9, 84–5, 91–2, 94n4, 95n16, 96n28, 137n11, 142n41, 145, 149–50, 152–3, 187–9, 191
Pines, Shlomo 9n4, 34n4, 36n14, 38n32, 50n7
Plato 3, 10n7, 15, 24, 34, 34n4, 39n38, 43n69, 50n7, 137n11, 139n19, 182n17, 185n36
Pollock, Frederick 181n17, 185n36
power 18, 20–35, 35n7, 37n26, 40n47, 42n64, 43, 68, 71–2, 74, 80n12, 86, 99–110, 112n9, 112n11, 114n30, 114n33, 114n36, 115n37, 117n57, 126, 138n14, 151, 168, 172, 177, 183n24, 184n25, 186n37
prophet/prophecy 6, 21–2, 27–8, 37n27, 40n49, 40n50, 41n51, 49n1, 158n20, 189
Protagoras 15

Quine, Willard Van Orman 96n27

Ravitzky, Aviezer 9n4
Rechnitzer, Hayyim 10n7
religio catholica 19
religion 1, 4–7, 11n13, 15–34, 35n6, 36n15, 36n16, 36n21, 38n32, 39n38, 41n52, 41n55, 42n64, 43n67, 45, 49n1, 50n9, 79n7, 142n51, 156n6, 157n15, 179, 185, 187–8, 190, 191n1
revelation 79n7, 113n24, 133, 149, 150, 152, 157n15, 158n22, 188
Rice, Lee C. 34n2, 182n19
Rieuwertsz, Jan 37n23
rituals 18
Rosen, Stanley 40n42
Rosenfeld, Shaul 10n9
Rosenthal, Michael A. 36n12, 40n44
Roth, Leon 157n13

salvation 8, 102, 131, 143, 156n6, 161–4, 166, 168, 171, 174, 180n2, 184n31, 190
Schlanger, Jacques 60n2
Schopenhauer, Arthur 112n10
Schuller, Georg 61n12, 61n16, 72, 81n24, 96n24
scripture/bible 10n6, 22, 39n38, 39n39, 40n50, 41n51, 47, 49n1, 50n8, 79n7, 147, 149, 151–2, 156n7, 158n21, 158n22, 175, 177
Scruton, Roger 60n8, 111n6, 113n21, 137n11, 157n11, 186n36
Seneca 32
Sheppard, Eugene 43n66
Shirley, Samuel 114n32
Siedler, Meir 36n21
Sigad, Ilana 157n12
Sigad, Ran 9n2, 36n20, 50n7, 50n8, 60n6, 60n8, 80n15, 97n35, 111n7, 112n13, 114n34, 117n56, 142n42, 180n1, 181n11, 186n36
singular things 62n20, 64, 89, 99–100, 102, 106, 125–6, 128, 141n37, 156n4, 163, 186n37
Smith, Steven B. 9n4, 34n3, 36n12, 40n44, 40n48, 41n55, 42n64
Socrates 15, 43n69, 137n11
Spinoza, Benedict de: *Compendium of Hebrew Grammar* 10n6; *Descartes' Principles of Philosophy* 115n38;

Spinoza, Benedict de *continued*
  Metaphysical Thoughts 35n11, 117n55, 145, 182n17; *Political Treatise* 35n8, 36n18; *Short Treatise on God, Man, and His Well-Being* 50n9, 60n3, 114n33, 160n36, 182n19, 183n21; *Theological-Political Treatise* 1–43, 49n1, 49n3, 57, 59, 61n17, 62n23, 75, 79n7, 91, 96n29, 96n32, 104, 105, 112n12, 114n 31, 114n33, 140n27, 147, 156n6, 156n8, 156n9, 158n21, 158n22, 159n26, 160n38, 167, 176–7, 183n21, 184n31, 187, 190; *Treatise on the Emendation of the Intellect* 46, 60n3, 81n27, 168, 170, 173, 181n12, 183n21
Stalin, Joseph 42n62
Steenbakkers, Piet 35n5
Stewart, Matthew 191n3
Strauss, Leo 3, 4, 9n2, 9n4, 10n7, 10n10, 33, 36n20, 42n61, 43n66, 49n1, 96n29, 112n12, 158n22
substance: as prior in nature to its affections 56–8; definition of 8, 62n22, 83, 87, 90, 103, 106, 114n32, 114n36, 137n13, 140n33, 167 (*see also I. D3*); Descartes' conception of 49n6; indivisibility of 84–8; *see also* God; *causa sui*; nature
superstition 1, 16–19, 34n4, 35n10, 35n11, 35n15, 57

Tactius 41n58
Talleyrand, Charles Maurice de 92
Taylor, C.C.W. 80n12
Terence 96n30, 183n23
Tessler, Aliza 114n30
theological political problem 15–16, 19–20, 23, 36n16, 40n49
theology/theologians 1–5, 26, 31, 33, 37n21, 39n39, 42n61, 46–7, 49n4, 52, 56, 58–9, 62n19, 66–7, 71, 79n7, 81n23, 93, 95n14, 95n18, 96n32, 97n37, 101, 107, 109, 116n51, 117n59, 118n60, 139n19, 140n27, 145–9, 151–2, 156n3, 156n9, 159n31, 169, 181n13, 186n36, 188, 189
time 7, 8, 11n16, 77, 83, 86, 119–42, 164, 168–70, 181n14, 181n17, 182n18
Tolstoy, Leo 81n26
Torquatus, Lucius Manlius 6, 22, 28, 37n30, 41n52
transcendence 7, 47, 55–8, 59, 62n22, 63, 65, 77, 87, 95n18, 113n29, 135, 165–6, 177–80, 190
trinity 93
Troyat, Henri 81n26
Turner, Victor 40n43

uno intuito 163, 165–7, 170

Van Bunge, Wiep 160n38
Van den Enden, Franciscus 96n30, 183n23
Velleius 80n17
virtus 19, 109
Vries, Simon Joosten de 9n3, 65, 78n2, 78n3, 113n29, 191

Walzer, Michael 30
White, W. Hale 107, 116n43
Wilson, Catherine 34n3
Wilson, Margaret D. 139n23
Witt, Johan de 15
Wolfson, Harry Austryn 49n4, 59n1, 60n4, 138n18, 139n19, 157n14, 182n19

Yovel, Yermiyahu 10n9, 10n11, 36n20, 42n64, 49n6, 60n7, 61n15, 79n5, 94n4, 96n25, 96n30, 107, 113n29, 115n37, 115n41, 116n46, 116n47, 138n15, 141n37, 181n14, 183n21, 183n23, 184n31, 185n33, 185n36

Index of references

Ethics

Part I

I.D1 48, 51–2, 63, 77, 112, 123, 128, 130–1, 177–8, 181n10, 190
I.D2 61n13
I.D3 62n22, 75, 83, 87, 90, 103, 106, 114n32, 115, 123, 137n13, 167
I.D4 87–8, 95n12, 112n9, 130–1, 140n28
I.D5 56, 62, 73, 75, 87, 103–4, 113n20, 121, 123, 125, 127, 137n13, 167
I.D6 46–7, 54, 66, 81n20, 88, 90, 94n2, 102, 117n55, 127–8, 131, 136n3, 141n39, 159n30, 167, 171, 174, 177–8
I.D6: Exp 73
I.D8 119, 121–2, 124, 131, 136n1, 137n11, 139n18, 170
I.D8: Exp 86, 121–2, 124, 138n17, 168
I.A1 179
I.A4 51, 53, 61n12, 64–6, 90, 106, 164, 167
I.A5 55, 94n11
I.A6 46, 87
I.1 51, 56, 87, 97n34, 117, 179
I.3 55
I.5 93n1, 56, 94n9
I.5: Dem 87, 58
I.6 95n12
I.7 94n2
I.7: Dem 120, 177
I.8: Schol 2 51–2, 54, 64, 66, 69, 87, 90, 93, 94, 106, 140, 141
I.9 90, 96n24
I.10 91, 92
I.10: Schol 72, 77, 89, 91, 92, 113, 140n25
I.10: Dem 85
I.11 72, 94, 112n8
I.11: Schol 46, 49, 66, 69, 73–4, 79, 174

I.13 84–5, 88
I.13: Schol 85, 88
I.13: Cor 84–5, 87, 94n6, 94n7, 95
I.13: Dem 87, 94n7, 94n9
I.14 60n7
I.14: Cor 64, 94n2, 103, 115n36, 134, 136, 166
I.15 102, 110, 174, 177
I.15: Schol 85, 95, 159n31
I.16 54, 61n12, 75, 77, 90–1, 96n25, 96n31, 109, 112, 130, 136n5, 140n32, 164, 190
I.16: Cor 69, 101–2, 167
I.16: Dem 91–2, 96n31
I.17 76, 109, 113n22
I.17: Cor 70, 109, 166, 181n10
I.17: Schol 57–8, 124, 140n32
I.18 66, 177, 179
I.19 73, 120, 122, 126
I.19: Dem 136n2
I.20 102, 112n15, 126, 136n2
I.20: Cor 2 174n1
I.21 54, 82n34, 37n59, 120, 122–4, 129, 131, 137n12, 138n15, 138n17, 138n18, 139, 181n16, 182, 17
I.21: Dem 123–4, 130–1, 138n15, 138n17, 140n32, 141n35
I.22 54, 37n59, 120, 138
I.23 54, 37n59, 120
I.23: Dem 136n4
I.24 63, 77, 79n5, 113n20, 124
I.24: Cor 49, 57, 64, 125, 139n22
I.25 57, 64–5, 69, 77, 112n15, 113n26, 124, 164–5
I.25: Schol 60n4, 64, 82n34, 90, 103, 109, 112n9, 130, 166
I.25: Cor 54, 61n13, 89, 96n23, 101, 112n9, 117n59, 163, 165
I.25: Dem 79n6, 139n21

I.26 159n30
I.27 159n30
I.28 51, 55, 138n15
I.28: *Schol* 81
I.29 87
I.29: *Schol* 74, 106, 112, 166
I.30 62n21
I.32: *Cor 2* 61n17
I.33: *Schol 1* 60n5, 61n10, 87, 99
I.33: *Schol 2* 51, 54, 56, 58, 67, 108–10, 117n59, 140n32, 177
I.34 109, 112n9, 126
I.35 126
I.36 51, 60n4, 61n12, 101–2, 113n26, 114n36, 167
Appendix to I 35n11, 48, 61n14, 62n19, 68, 71–2, 74–5, 77, 80n15, 81n21, 81n23, 99–101, 107, 110, 111n2, 113n16, 116n47, 116n51, 117n57, 180n2

Part II

Preface to II 161
II.D3 113n20, 121, 125, 127, 140n28
II.D5 139n22
II.D6 66, 81n20, 117n55, 127–8, 159n30, 171, 178
II.D7 55
II.A1 64, 169
II.1 66, 129–30
II.1: *Dem* 78n4, 129, 131
II.1: *Schol* 72
II.2 129
II.2: *Dem* 78, 129
II.3 129–31, 164
II.3: *Dem* 112n8, 129–31
II.4: *Dem* 130
II.6 181n9
II.7 126, 129, 140n30, 180n9, 182n18
II.7: *Schol* 104, 113n29, 181n9
II.8 120, 125–8, 132, 134–5, 141n37
II.8: *Cor* 82n34, 120, 125–8, 138n15, 141n37, 169
II.8: *Schol* 120, 125–8, 132–5
II.10: *Cor, Schol* 64
II.11: *Dem* 124
II.11: *Schol* 76
II.11: *Cor* 58, 75–6, 131
II.13 70, 95n19, 116n53, 121, 165, 169–70
II.13: *Schol* 73, 109, 159n30
II.13: *Cor, Schol* 70–1, 108, 113n28
II.13: *L7, Schol* 82n34, 89, 91, 110, 167
II.15: *Dem* 95n19
II.17: *Cor* 76
II.17: *Cor, Schol* 76
II.19: *Cor, Schol* 64
II.29: *Cor* 161
II.37 88, 186
II.38 99, 105, 162, 167
II.40: *Schol 1* 69, 88
II.40: *Schol 2* 5, 54, 69, 111n4, 162, 180n6, 190
II.41 5, 45
II.44: *Cor 1, Schol* 120, 121
II.44: *Cor 2* 120
II.44: *Cor 2, Dem* 124, 136n5, 140n23
II.45 64, 120, 125, 128n15
II.45: *Schol* 82n34, 125, 139n23, 182n7
II.47: *Schol* 190
II.49 74
II.49: *Schol* 115n36
II.49: *Cor, Schol* 120, 180n2, 180n3

Part III

Preface to Part III 80n18, 96n30, 98, 108
III.D2 70, 174
III.3 171, 174, 178
III.3: *Dem* 180n9
III.4 8, 102, 178
III.4: *Dem* 99
III.6 82n30, 98–100, 102–6, 115n38, 117n54, 141n39, 167
III.6: *Dem* 99, 100, 104, 112n9, 117n55
III.7 82, 99–102, 105, 113n26, 117n54, 117n57, 125, 162
III.7: *Dem* 99–102, 105, 107, 109, 112, 117n55, 162, 171
III.8 113, 125, 139n22
III.8: *Dem* 137
III.9 99, 105, 162, 167
III.9: *Schol* 11n14, 101, 111n2, 113n17, 167
III.11: *Schol* 74, 103, 110, 114
III.13 184n25
III.17: *Schol* 172
III.19 173
III.28 173
III.30: *Schol* 176
III.33 173
III.37 113n30
III.37: *Dem* 113n30
III.52: *Schol* 11n13
III.53: *Cor* 175
III.56: *Dem* 51, 53, 64, 66, 69, 87, 90, 101, 106, 165

III.59 172
III.59: Schol 35n9

General Definition of the Affects
II 8, 74, 81n27, 117n55, 171, 173–4, 178, 184n27
VI 8, 117n55, 171, 174, 177–9, 184n27
XXV 175
XXX 175–6
XLVIII 176
XLIV 175

Part IV

Preface to IV 47, 51, 64, 66, 68–9, 72, 74, 90, 101, 106, 113n16, 116n48, 128, 140n31
IV.D1 107
IV.D7 113n18, 167
IV.D8 107, 109, 117n57
IV.A1 102, 111, 168
IV.3 104, 110
IV.7 172
IV.14 172, 183n23
IV.18: Schol 161, 180n3, 189
IV.20: Schol 111n7
IV.21 180n2
IV.22 141n39
IV.26 117n54
IV.27 117n54
IV.35: Cor 156n4
IV.37: Schol 1 5, 11n13, 36n16
IV.37: Schol 2 42n59
IV.38 117n54
IV.39 95n19, 108
IV.39: Schol 189
IV.39: Dem 116n53, 117n54
IV.50: Schol 136
IV.50: Cor, Schol 161
IV.52 176, 178
IV.58 175
IV.60 95n19
IV.62: Dem 136n4

Part V

V.10: Schol 171, 184n25, 184n32
V.11 172
V.14 172
V.15 172, 175
V.15: Dem 171
V.16 172, 178
V.17 171, 173, 184n29
V.17: Cor 171, 173–4, 184n29
V.17: Dem 70, 173–4
V.19 173–4
V.20 173
V.20: Schol 35n10, 121, 170, 172, 178
V.20: Dem 173
V.21 141n37
V.22 163, 165, 181
V.22: Dem 163
V.23 169–70, 181n14, 181n17
V.23: Dem 121, 125, 127, 139, 169
V.23: Schol 82n30, 121, 168–9, 170, 190
V.24 62, 82, 89, 106, 114, 163–4, 165, 180n8
V.24: Dem 89, 164
V.25 163
V.25: Dem 82n30, 95n22, 162, 163, 165, 180, 190
V.26: Dem 95n22
V.27 163, 178, 179
V.27: Dem 74
V.28 162
V.29 124, 182n18
V.29: Dem 124
V.29: Schol 120, 121, 125
V.30 42n59, 131n1, 182
V.30: Dem 64, 86, 120, 122–3, 137n11, 138n15, 139, 163, 169
V.31 42n59, 82n30, 164, 178
V.31: Dem 163
V.31: Schol 74
V.32 82n30, 164, 178
V.32: Cor 163, 164, 184n30
V.33 136n6
V.34: Cor 136n6, 173
V.34: Cor, Schol 124, 139n18
V.35 8, 171, 173, 175, 177–8
V.35: Dem 184n30
V.36 82n30, 164, 178
V.36: Cor 171, 174–5
V.36: Cor, Schol 176, 180n5
V.36: Dem, Schol 161
V.38 172
V.38: Dem 181n13, 181n14
V.38: Schol 182n18
V.40 81n20
V.40: Dem 77
V.40: Schol 62n21
V.42: Dem 180n2
V.42: Schol 179

Letters

Letter 3 9n3, 158n19
Letter 6 138n14
Letter 8 78n2, 78n3
Letter 9 78n2, 94n5, 113n29
Letter 10 65, 78n3
Letter 13 42n61, 115n38
Letter 18 145, 153
Letter 19 61n17, 69, 74, 150–2, 157, 184n24
Letter 20 9n3, 79n9, 148–9, 151, 153, 158n16, 159n33
Letter 21 2, 45, 49n3, 67, 151–2, 154, 158n22, 158n23, 159n25
Letter 22 79n9, 151, 153, 156n2, 159n30
Letter 23 39n35, 79n11, 154, 156n1, 158n24, 160n35
Letter 24 154, 160n37
Letter 27 155, 156n1
Letter 30 34n2, 156n7
Letter 32 88
Letter 35 72–3, 86, 123–4, 138n15
Letter 36 73, 79n10, 86, 88
Letter 50 79n10, 141n40
Letter 54 61n17, 68, 79n12, 80n13
Letter 56 34n3, 80n12
Letter 63 81n24
Letter 64 61n16, 72, 88, 96n24, 121
Letter 68 35n5

For Product Safety Concerns and Information please contact our EU representative GPSR@taylorandfrancis.com
Taylor & Francis Verlag GmbH, Kaufingerstraße 24, 80331 München, Germany

www.ingramcontent.com/pod-product-compliance
Lightning Source LLC
Chambersburg PA
CBHW061826300426
44115CB00013B/2268